301067728

W9-BRT-473

DATE

McLEAN COUNTY UNIT #5
301-NCWHS

# PAUL MULDOON

# POEMS 1968-1998

FARRAR, STRAUS AND GIROUX NEW YORK

McLean County Unit #5
301 - NCWHS

FARRAR, STRAUS AND GIROUX
*19 Union Square West, New York 10003*

*Copyright © 2001 by Paul Muldoon*
*All rights reserved*
*Distributed in Canada by Douglas & McIntyre Ltd.*
*Printed in the United States of America*
*Published in the United Kingdom by Faber & Faber, Limited, London*
First edition, 2001

*Library of Congress Cataloging-in-Publication Data*
Muldoon, Paul.
    [Poems. Selections]
    Poems, 1968–1998 / Paul Muldoon.— 1st ed.
      p. cm.
    Includes index.
    ISBN 0-374-12543-0 (alk. paper)
    I. Title.

PR6063.U367 A6 2001
821'.914—dc21

                         00-045607

Designed by Gretchen Achilles

McLean County Unit #5
301 - NCWHS

FOR JEAN, DOROTHY, AND ASHER

# CONTENTS

**MULES** 1977

## WHY BROWNLEE LEFT 1980

# AUTHOR'S NOTE

This book comprises the complete texts of the eight main collections of poetry I have published over the last thirty years, from *New Weather* (1973) to *Hay* (1998). It does not include the uncollected work that appeared in magazines and in a number of small, interim publications: opera libretti written in verse, verse drama, poems for children, *Kerry Slides*, and *The Prince of the Quotidian*, a journalistic sequence which came out in 1994.

It is not, therefore, to be considered a "complete" or "collected" volume, but rather a making available of the volumes to which I refer, several of which aren't in print in the United Kingdom, Ireland, or the United States.

Other than to correct such factual errors as my having written "painfully" for "painstakingly," "bathyscope" for "bathysphere," "*Ranus ranus*" for "*Rana temporaria*," "jardonelle" for "jargonelle," and "aureoles" for "areolae," I have made scarcely any changes in the texts of the poems, since I'm fairly certain that, after a shortish time, the person through whom a poem was written is no more entitled to make revisions than any other reader.

P.M.

# NEW WEATHER 1973

# THE ELECTRIC ORCHARD

The early electric people had domesticated the wild ass.
They knew all about falling off.
Occasionally, they would have fallen out of the trees.
Climbing again, they had something to prove
To their neighbours. And they did have neighbours.
The electric people lived in villages
Out of their need of security and their constant hunger.
Together they would divert their energies

To neutral places. Anger to the banging door,
Passion to the kiss.
And electricity to earth. Having stolen his thunder
From an angry god, through the trees
They had learned to string his lightning.
The women gathered random sparks into their aprons,
A child discovered the swing
Among the electric poles. Taking everything as given,

The electric people were confident, hardly proud.
They kept fire in a bucket,
Boiled water and dry leaves in a kettle, watched the lid
By the blue steam lifted and lifted.
So that, where one of the electric people happened to fall,
It was accepted as an occupational hazard.
There was something necessary about the thing. The North Wall

Of the Eiger was notorious for blizzards,
If one fell there his neighbour might remark, Bloody fool.
All that would have been inappropriate,
Applied to the experienced climber of electric poles.
I have achieved this great height?
No electric person could have been that proud,
Thirty or forty feet. Perhaps not that,
If the fall happened to be broken by the roof of a shed.
The belt would burst, the call be made,

The ambulance arrive and carry the faller away
To hospital with a scream.
There and then the electric people might invent the railway,
Just watching the lid lifted by the steam.
Or decide that all laws should be based on that of gravity,
Just thinking of the faller fallen.
Even then they were running out of things to do and see.
Gradually, they introduced legislation

Whereby they nailed a plaque to every last electric pole.
They would prosecute any trespassers.
The high up, singing and live fruit liable to shock or kill
Were forbidden. Deciding that their neighbours
And their neighbours' innocent children ought to be stopped
For their own good, they threw a fence
Of barbed wire round the electric poles. None could describe
Electrocution, falling, the age of innocence.

## WIND AND TREE

In the way that the most of the wind
Happens where there are trees,

Most of the world is centred
About ourselves.

Often where the wind has gathered
The trees together and together,

One tree will take
Another in her arms and hold.

Their branches that are grinding
Madly together and together,

It is no real fire.
They are breaking each other.

Often I think I should be like
The single tree, going nowhere,

Since my own arm could not and would not
Break the other. Yet by my broken bones

I tell new weather.

## BLOWING EGGS

This is not the nest
That has been pulling itself together
In the hedge's intestine.
It is the cup of a boy's hands,

Whereby something is lost
More than the necessary heat gone forever
And death only after beginning.
There is more to this pale blue flint

In this careful fist
Than a bird's nest having been discovered
And a bird not sitting again.
This is the start of the underhand,

The way that he has crossed
These four or five delicate fields of clover
To hunker by this crooked railing.
This is the breathless and the intent

Puncturing of the waste
And isolate egg and this the clean delivery

Of little yolk and albumen.
These his wrists, surprised and stained.


## THRUSH

I guessed the letter
    Must be yours. I recognized
The cuttle ink,
    The serif on
The P. I read the postmark and the date,
    Impatience held
By a paperweight.
    I took your letter at eleven
To the garden
    With my tea.
And suddenly the yellow gum secreted
    Halfwayup
The damson bush
    Had grown a shell.
I let those scentless pages fall
    And took it
In my feckless hand. I turned it over
    On its back
To watch your mouth
    Withdraw. Making a lean white fist
Out of my freckled hand.


## THE GLAD EYE

Bored by Ascham and Zeno
In private conversation on the longbow,

I went out onto the lawn.
Taking the crooked bow of yellow cane,

I shot an arrow over
The house and wounded my brother.

He cried those huge dark tears
Till they had blackened half his hair.

Zeno could have had no real
Notion of the flying arrow being still,

Not blessed with the hindsight
Of photography and the suddenly frozen shot,

Yet that obstinate one
Eye inveigled me to a standing stone.

Evil eyes have always burned
Corn black and people have never churned

Again after their blink.
That eye was deeper than the Lake of the Young,

Outstared the sun in the sky.
Could look without commitment into another eye.


## HEDGES IN WINTER

Every year they have driven stake after stake after stake
Deeper into the cold heart of the hill.
Their arrowheads are more deadly than snowflakes,
Their spearheads sharper than icicles,

Yet stilled by snowflake, icicle.
They are already broken by their need of wintering,
These archers taller than any snowfall
Having to admit their broken shafts and broken strings,

Whittling the dead branches to the girls they like.
That they have hearts is visible,
The nests of birds, these obvious concentrations of black.
Yet where the soldiers will later put on mail,

The archers their soft green, nothing will tell
Of the heart of the mailed soldier seeing the spear he flung,
Of the green archer seeing his shaft kill.
Only his deliberate hand, a bird pretending a broken wing.


## MACHA

Macha, the Ice Age
Held you down,
Heavy as a man.
As he dragged

Himself away,
You sprang up
Big as half a county,
Curvaceous,

Drumlin country.
Now at war
With men,
Leading them against

Each other,
You had to prove
Your permanence.
You scored the ground

With a sharp brooch,
Mapped your first
Hillfort.
The day you fell,

At the hands of men,
You fell
Back over half a county.
Clutching a town

To your breasts.


## THE WAKING FATHER

My father and I are catching spricklies
Out of the Oona river.
They have us feeling righteous,
The way we have thrown them back.
Our benevolence is astounding.

When my father stood out in the shallows
It occurred to me that
The spricklies might have been piranhas,
The river a red carpet
Rolling out from where he had just stood,

Or I wonder now if he is dead or sleeping.
For if he is dead I would have his grave
Secret and safe,
I would turn the river out of its course,
Lay him in its bed, bring it round again.

No one would question
That he had treasures or his being a king,
Telling now of the real fish farther down.


## DANCERS AT THE MOY

This Italian square
And circling plain
Black once with mares
And their stallions,
The flat Blackwater
Turning its stones

Over hour after hour
As their hooves shone
And lifted together
Under the black rain,
One or other Greek war
Now coloured the town

Blacker than ever before
With hungry stallions
And their hungry mares
Like hammocks of skin,
The flat Blackwater
Unable to contain

Itself as horses poured
Over acres of grain
In a black and gold river.
No band of Athenians
Arrived at the Moy fair
To buy for their campaign,

Peace having been declared
And a treaty signed.
The black and gold river
Ended as a trickle of brown
Where those horses tore
At briars and whins,

Ate the flesh of each other
Like people in famine.
The flat Blackwater
Hobbled on its stones
With a wild stagger
And sag in its backbone,

The local people gathered
Up the white skeletons.
Horses buried for years
Under the foundations
Give their earthen floors
The ease of trampolines.

## IDENTITIES

When I reached the sea
I fell in with another who had just come
From the interior. Her family
Had figured in a past regime
But her father was now imprisoned.

She had travelled, only by night,
Escaping just as her own warrant
Arrived and stealing the police boat,
As far as this determined coast.

As it happened, we were staying at the same
Hotel, pink and goodish for the tourist
Quarter. She came that evening to my room
Asking me to go to the capital,
Offering me wristwatch and wallet,
To search out an old friend who would steal
Papers for herself and me. Then to be married,
We could leave from that very harbour.

I have been wandering since, back up the streams
That had once flowed simply one into the other,
One taking the other's name.

## CLONFEACLE

It happened not far away
In this meadowland
That Patrick lost a tooth.
I translate the placename

As we walk along
The river where he washed,
That translates stone to silt.
The river would preach

As well as Patrick did.
A tongue of water passing
Between teeth of stones.
Making itself clear,

Living by what it says,
Converting meadowland to marsh.
You turn towards me,
Coming round to my way

Of thinking, holding
Your tongue between your teeth.
I turn my back on the river
And Patrick, their sermons

Ending in the air.


## FEBRUARY

He heard that in Derryscollop there is a tree
For every day of the year,
And the extra tree is believed to grow
One year in every four.

He had never yet taken time to grieve
For this one without breasts
Or that one wearing her heart on her sleeve
Or another with her belly slashed.

He had never yet taken time to love
The blind pink fledgeling fallen out of the nest
Of one sleeping with open mouth
And her head at a list.

What was he watching and waiting for,
Walking Scollop every day?
For one intending to leave at the end of the year,
Who would break the laws of time and stay.

## KATE WHISKEY

I kept the whiskey in the caves
Well up in the hills. It was never safe
To have it about the houses,
Always crawling with excise and police.

The people could still get the stuff
As often as they liked, and easily enough,
For those were still the days
When making whiskey broke nobody's laws.

Selling it, though, was as grave
An offence as teaching those people to love,
Fathers and husbands and boys.

Water rushed through my caves with a noise
To tell me how I should always live.
I sold the water, the whiskey I would give.


## THINKING OF THE GOLDFISH

Replacing the lid of air
On its circle of water,
Thinking of the goldfish was

My classic final gesture.
Beating in its plastic bag,
It looked like a change of heart

I had bought for you to hold.
It was far too cold, so cold
There was nothing I could do

But leave it behind to die
At the top of the old house,
Its head in the clouds

Of its own breath. So I locked
The door, took your hand and word
And followed you. Only glad

Of the law that I would always
Own the light above my head,
If simply borrow from my side.

## VESPERS

It looks like there's
Nothing for it
But the bare floor.
You've given one blanket
Off the single bed

By way of reasonableness.
Couldn't we go to sleep
Together for once,
If only of necessity?
We could always keep

The sheet between us.
I'll do nothing you won't.
We'll both be colder
For being lost in thought,
Setting up difficulties

Where none ought to exist.
I'll put out the light,
And the night has fallen
Bodily and silent
Through the defunct window.

The frost has designs on it.


## THE CURE FOR WARTS

Had I been the seventh son of a seventh son
Living at the dead centre of a wood
Or at the dead end of a lane,
I might have cured by my touch alone
That pair of warts nippling your throat,

Who had no faith in a snail rubbed on your skin
And spiked on a thorn like a king's head,
In my spittle on shrunken stone,
In bathing yourself at the break of dawn
In dew or the black cock's or the bull's blood,

In other such secrets told by way of a sign
Of the existence of one or other god,
So I doubt if any woman's son
Could have cured by his touch alone
That pair of warts nibbling your throat.

## LEAVING AN ISLAND

The woman of the house
Is letting out the chickens.
Air trapped in the capsized

Boat where they coop
Is visible to the naked eye.
I see through you

In your crocheted dress.
Elevenses. Woman of the house,
This is just to say

We have left no clues.
Ferdinand, Miranda,
It was pure and simple.

Thank you, thank you.
For the dulse. For everything.
I read between your legs

And recognize that you who took
The world into your mouth
Have taught me ships in bottles,

The sea in shells.

# THE RADIO HORSE

I believed in those plains
Without grass or sky,
A levelled silence
Broken only by the credible woods.
Then the first soft thud
Of a horse by radio,

And already I could sense
This horse would carry
Not only the plans
Of that one's plot or counterplot
But your realer secrets.
Your intending to go

In your own hand or evidence
To prove you another spy
Infiltrating my lines.
If only you were as easily waylaid,
Predictable in your road,
As a horse by radio,

Its tittering in one distance
That clatters, thunders by,
Then thins and thins.
I believed in your riding all night
Lathered by your own sweat,
Your dressing as boys

Keeping in their shirts or jeans
Messages for my eyes only,
Whose latest are canc-
Elled to a word, that lost in codes,
Telling of their being delayed
By horses' thrown shoes.

# GOOD FRIDAY, 1971. DRIVING WESTWARD

It was good going along with the sun
Through Ballygawley, Omagh and Strabane.
I started out as it was getting light
And caught sight of hares all along the road
That looked to have been taking a last fling,
Doves making the most of their offerings
As if all might not be right with the day

Where I moved through morning towards the sea.
I was glad that I would not be alone.
Those children who travel badly as wine
Waved as they passed in their uppity cars
And now the first cows were leaving the byres,
The first lorry had delivered its load.
A whole country was fresh after the night

Though people were still fighting for the last
Dreams and changing their faces where I paused
To read the first edition of the truth.
I gave a lift to the girl out of love
And crossed the last great frontier at Lifford.
Marooned by an iffing and butting herd
Of sheep, Letterkenny had just then laid

Open its heart and we passed as new blood
Back into the grey flesh of Donegal.
The sky went out of its way for the hills
And life was changing down for the sharp bends
Where the road had put its thin brown arm round
A hill and held on tight out of pure fear.
Errigal stepped out suddenly in our

Path and the thin arm tightened round the waist
Of the mountain and for a time I lost
Control and she thought we hit something big
But I had seen nothing, perhaps a stick

Lying across the road. I glanced back once
And there was nothing but a heap of stones.
We had just dropped in from nowhere for lunch

In Gaoth Dobhair, I happy and she convinced
Of the death of more than lamb or herring.
She stood up there and then, face full of drink,
And announced that she and I were to blame
For something killed along the way we came.
Children were warned that it was rude to stare,
Left with their parents for a breath of air.


## SEANCHAS

Coming here, we were like that mountain whose base
We kept sidestepping. Thinking ourselves superior.
Having, we thought, our final attitude and bias.
Really, wanting a new slant. For the past hour
We heard the seanchai relearn
What he has always known,

Region of heroes, gentle maidens,
Giants that war and landgrab.
Each phrase opening like a fern.
Till some make fists of themselves, like the stones
In a landslide, a cadence
That comes in his way. He can adlib
No other route. If we play back the tape
He may take up where he left off.

Nothing. And no heroes people this landscape
Through which he sees us off.
The lifted wondering faces of his sheep
Stare back at us like nimble rain clouds, their bellies
Accumulate and are anonymous again. But having shape,
Separate and memorable.


## BEHOLD THE LAMB

You were first.
The ewe licked clean ochre and lake
But you would not move.
Weighted with stones yet
Dead your dead head floats.
Better dead than sheep,

The thin worm slurred in your gut,
The rot in your feet,
The red dog creeping at dawn.
Better than dipped in the hard white water,
Your stomach furred,
Your head hardboiled.

Better dead than dyed
In a bowl of pale whin petals.
Better than rolling down the hill,
Pale skull flaking.
First to break.
First for the scream of the clean bite.

Better dead with your delph head floating.

## HEDGEHOG

The snail moves like a
Hovercraft, held up by a
Rubber cushion of itself,
Sharing its secret

With the hedgehog. The hedgehog
Shares its secret with no one.
We say, Hedgehog, come out
Of yourself and we will love you.

We mean no harm. We want
Only to listen to what
You have to say. We want
Your answers to our questions.

The hedgehog gives nothing
Away, keeping itself to itself.
We wonder what a hedgehog
Has to hide, why it so distrusts.

We forget the god
Under this crown of thorns.
We forget that never again
Will a god trust in the world.


## LIVES OF THE SAINTS

Others have sought publicity
But the saints looked for higher things.
The people getting ready to fly
Off the roofs of public buildings
Had their eyes on the actual sky,
Never spreading their linen or bamboo wings

So briefly for a public death
Had they really been saints of the old school.
Those saints have the last laugh
At the reporters for the Chronicles
And the people taking photographs.
I think especially of Brendan setting sail

One day the sea was blueblack
As his body that overnight he had beaten,
Drifting along wherever God liked
And the people living by bread alone
Shouting after Good Luck, Good Luck.
All the Chronicles agreed. The boat was stone.

## EASTER ISLAND

Stonehenge, Newgrange
Were engineered

By men who whinged
In slow motion.

Thinking in terms
Of a stone's throw,

They crept with sickles
To steal a kiss

Under the mistletoe.
These islanders

Might winch for miles
To right abstractions

From the living rock.
No resurrection but

The Moving Stone
Compelled their homage.

## THE INDIANS ON ALCATRAZ

Through time their sharp features
Have softened and blurred,
As if they still inhabited
The middle distances,
As if these people have never
Stopped riding hard

In an opposite direction,
The people of the shattered lances
Who have seemed forever going back.
To have willed this reservation,
It is as if they are decided
To be islanders at heart,

As if this island
Has forever been the destination
Of all those dwindling bands.
After the newspaper and TV reports
I want to be glad that
Young Man Afraid of His Horses lives

As a brilliant guerrilla fighter,
The weight of his torque
Worn like the moon's last quarter,
Though only if he believes
As I believed of his fathers,
That they would not attack after dark.

## VAMPIRE

Seeing the birds in winter
Drinking the images of themselves
Reflected in a sheet of ice,
She thinks of that winter—
'Carefully appointed mirrors
Create the illusion of depth'—
When she covered her walls
From floor to ceiling with glass.

In January she would have
The 'carefully appointed mirrors'
Taken away. The thing ought
Not be bigger than the fact,
She would keep telling herself.
Or, already spending the daylight
Hours in bed, say, I am alive
Because I am alive.

For even then she believed herself
Native soil enough for herself,
Though already she would rise
Only as night was falling, quietly
Lifting the single milkbottle
That had stood on her step since morning,
The top repeatedly
Punctured by a thirsting bird.

## ELIZABETH

The birds begin as an isolated shower
Over the next county, their slow waltz
Swerving as if to avoid something
Every so often, getting thin

As it slants, making straight for
Us over your father's darkening fields,
Till their barely visible wings
Remember themselves, they are climbing again.
We wonder what could bring them this far

Inland, they belong to the sea.
You hold on hard like holding on to life,
Following the flock as it bends
And collapses like a breeze.
You want to know where from and why,
But birds would never keep still long enough
For me to be able to take a count.
We'll hold our ground and they'll pass.
But they're coming right overhead, you cry,

And storm inside and bang the door.
All I can hear is the flicking of bolts.
The one dull window is shutting
Its eye as if a wayward hurricane
With the name of a girl and the roar
Of devils were beginning its assaults.
But these are the birds of a child's painting,
Filling the page till nothing else is seen.
You are inside yet, pacing the floor,

Having been trapped in every way.
You hold yourself as your own captive.
My promised children are in your hands,
Hostaged by you in your father's old house.
I call you now for all the names of the day,
Lizzie and Liz and plain Beth.
You do not make the slightest sound.
When you decide that you have nothing to lose
And come out, there is nothing you can say.

We watch them hurtle, a recklessness of stars,
Into the acre that has not cooled

From my daylong ploughings and harrowings,
Their greys flecking the brown,
Till one, and then two, and now four
Sway back across your father's patchwork quilt,
Into your favourite elm. They will stay long
Enough to underline how soon they will be gone,
As you seem thinner than you were before.


## THE KISSING SEAT

The organized crime
Of the kissing seat,
How well it holds us.
We're caught and fixed

In its ornamental S.
Oughtn't we to be here
And now?
I watch the sunset,

You the moonrise,
It's two winds blowing
At one and the same.
We're both going where

We're looking. Elsewhere.
It's getting late now,
You've only a linen shift
Between you and harm.

Can't we agree at least
On which star's the Pole,
The word on that flower,
What atrophies the kidney

Of the private pool?


## GRASS WIDOW

And of course I cried
As I watched him go away.
    Europe must have cried
For Europe had no more say
When America left her.

    No other woman
Came between us. It seemed that
When I would lock the gleaming
    Door against his weight,
It was the water in which

    I showered that inter-
Vened. And the water that slopped
From the system he was meant
To have lagged. I overslept
    That winter morning,

    And had cause, I say,
For crying, when I walloped
Through the flooding house and saw
    Him go. As Europe
Watched America, I watched.

Now my dreams are filled
With reconciliations.
    Dreams I never willed,
Who have chosen the Ocean,
The Gulf Stream warming my heart.


## SKEFFINGTON'S DAUGHTER

*An Iron Maiden, brainchild of the Lieutenant*
*of the Tower under Henry the Eighth*

Not one to lose
Her head,
Her father had thought.
Now that her lover

Had left her pregnant,
He believed
That he understood
Her want.

Being his daughter,
She would have
Another chance.
No one would suffer,

It would be nothing
Like a death
In the family.
Leaving backstreet and foetus

Behind her,
She would again be taken
For that clever,
Careful virgin.

Not one to lose face.


## CUCKOO CORN

The seed that goes into the ground
After the first cuckoo
Is said to grow short and light
As the beard of a boy.

Though Spring was slow this year
And the seed late,
After that Summer the corn was long
And heavy as the hair of any girl.

They claimed that she had no errand
Near the thresher,
This girl whose hair floated as if underwater
In a wind that would have cleaned corn,

Who was strangled by the flapping belt.
But she had reason,
I being her lover, she being that man's daughter,
Knowing of cuckoo corn, of seed and season.

# THE UPRIVER INCIDENT

He thanked his parents for keeping still
And left them sleeping, deaf and blind
After their heavy meal,

Then stole away where the moon was full
And the dogs gave no sound.
He thanked the dogs for keeping still

And ran along the tops of the dark hills
That heaped like the sleeping anaconda
After its heavy meal,

To the bright square in the highest coil
That was the lady's window.
She thanked her parents for keeping still

And they ran together over a further hill
Like the lady's belly so hard and round
After its heavy meal,

Till they stood at the top of the waterfall,
Its deep pool where they drowned.
Let us thank waters for not keeping still
After their heavy meal.


# THE LOST TRIBE

Has it been only two years
Since the river went on fire?
Last year your father's heart wob-
Bled while he was dusting crops,

Too heavy for his light plane.
Was it three years ago, then,
The year I shot the wild duck
And we took her clutch of eggs,

Carefully, to our own bed?
They hatched out under our heat,
Their first passions being earth
And water, the sky that curved

Far over the huddling barns.
We taught the fields of kept corn
Good for both bread and porridge,
And as they were then of age,

The rightness of wearing clothes.
We hooked up their rubber shoes
For that sad day they waddled
Back into their rightful wild,

The heaven of riverbanks.
They had learned to speak our tongue,
Knew it was all for the best.
Was that not the year you lost

Another child, the oil slick
Again bloodied our own creek,
All innocents were set free,
Your father had learned to fly?

## THE FIELD HOSPITAL

Taking, giving back their lives
By the strength of our bare hands,
By the silence of our knives,
We answer to no grey South

Nor blue North, not self-defence,
The lie of just wars, neither
Cold nor hot blood's difference
In their discharging of guns,

But that hillside of fresh graves.
Would this girl brought to our tents
From whose flesh we have removed
Shot that George, on his day off,

Will use to weight fishing lines,
Who died screaming for ether,
Yet protest our innocence?
George lit the lanterns, in danced

Those gigantic yellow moths
That brushed right over her wounds,
Pinning themselves to our sleeves
Like medals given the brave.

## PARTY PIECE

The girl alone in the wood's
Corner had just then filled her
Glass with tomato and crushed
Ice. She wore a man's shrunk head
Slung over either shoulder,
A child's head hung at her waist.

He would have raped and killed her
Had this happened in the past,
Not yet telling wrong from right.
Since the world had grown older
He approached and introduced
Himself as something to eat,

Thinking still that wars were lost
Or won by hand to hand fights.
Though he had just then called her
Beautiful, they had just kissed,
She paused to bring back her dead
And his thin red line faltered.
That last war's end should have taught
The weakness of bright soldiers,
Those mushrooms at thigh and breast
Told of threat and counterthreat,
Yet they plunged helterskelter
Through a young wood and laid waste

A cornfield. Then this welter
Of steel and glass where they crashed
Through this heavy iron gate.
Their bodies are still smoulder-
Ing, they are like those old ghosts
Who skid past graveyards. Their heads,
Lifted clean off by the blast,
Lying here in the back seat
Like something dirty, hold our
Sadness in their eyes, who wished
For the explosion's heart, not
Pain's edge where we take shelter.

# THE YEAR OF THE SLOES, FOR ISHI

In the Moon
Of Frost in the Tepees,
There were two stars
That got free.
They yawned and stretched
To white hides,
One cutting a slit
In the wall of itself
And stepping out into the night.

In the Moon
Of the Dark Red Calf,
It had learned
To track itself
By following the dots
And dashes of its blood.
It knew the silence
Deeper
Than that of birds not singing.

In the Moon
Of the Snowblind,
The other fed the fire
At its heart
With the dream of a deer
Over its shoulder.
One water would wade through another,
Shivering,
Salmon of Knowledge leap the Fall.

In the Moon
Of the Red Grass Appearing,
He discovered her
Lying under a bush.
There were patches of yellowed
Snow and ice

Where the sun had not looked.
He helped her over the Black Hills
To the Ford of the Two Friends.

In the Moon
Of the Ponies Shedding,
He practised counting coups,
Knowing it harder
To live at the edge of the earth
Than its centre.
He caught the nondescript horse
And stepped
Down onto the prairies.

In the Moon
Of Making the Fat,
He killed his first bison.
Her quick knife ran under the skin
And offered the heart
To the sky.
They had been the horizon.
She saved what they could not eat
That first evening.

In the Moon
Of the Red Cherries,
She pledged that she would stay
So long as there would be
The Two-Legged
And the Four-Legged Ones,
Long as grass would grow and water
Flow, and the wind blow.
None of these things had forgotten.

In the Moon
Of the Black Cherries,
While he was looking for a place
To winter,

He discovered two wagons
Lying side by side
That tried to be a ring.
There were others in blue shirts
Felling trees for a square.

In the Moon
When the Calf Grows Hair,
There was a speck in the sky
Where he had left the tepee.
An eagle had started
Out of her side
And was waiting to return.
The fire was not cold,
The feet of six horses not circles.

In the Moon
Of the Season Changing,
He left the river
Swollen with rain.
He kicked sand over the fire.
He prepared his breast
By an ochre
That none would see his blood.
Any day now would be good to die.

In the Moon
Of the Leaves Falling,
I had just taken a bite out of the
Moon and pushed the plate
Of the world away.
Someone was asking for six troopers
Who had lain down
One after another
To drink a shrieking river.

In the Moon
Of the Trees Popping, two snails
Glittered over a dead Indian.
I realized that if his brothers
Could be persuaded to lie still,
One beside the other
Right across the Great Plains,
Then perhaps something of this original
Beauty would be retained.

MULES 1977

# LUNCH WITH PANCHO VILLA

I

'Is it really a revolution, though?'
I reached across the wicker table
With another $10,000 question.
My celebrated pamphleteer,
Co-author of such volumes
As *Blood on the Rose*,
*The Dream and the Drums*,
And *How It Happened Here*,
Would pour some untroubled Muscatel
And settle back in his cane chair.

'Look, son. Just look around you.
People are getting themselves killed
Left, right and centre
While you do what? Write rondeaux?
There's more to living in this country
Than stars and horses, pigs and trees,
Not that you'd guess it from your poems.
Do you never listen to the news?
You want to get down to something true,
Something a little nearer home.'

I called again later that afternoon,
A quiet suburban street.
'You want to stand back a little
When the world's at your feet.'
I'd have liked to have heard some more
Of his famous revolution.
I rang the bell, and knocked hard
On what I remembered as his front door,
That opened then, as such doors do,
Directly on to a back yard.

Not any back yard, I'm bound to say,
And not a thousand miles away
From here. No one's taken in, I'm sure,
By such a mild invention.
But where (I wonder myself) do I stand,
In relation to a table and chair,
The quince tree I forgot to mention,
That suburban street, the door, the yard—
All made up as I went along
As things that people live among.

And such a person as lived there!
My celebrated pamphleteer!
Of course, I gave it all away
With those preposterous titles.
*The Bloody Rose? The Dream and the Drums?*
The three-day wonder of the flowering plum!
Or was I desperately wishing
To have been their other co-author,
Or, at least, to own a first edition
Of *The Boot Boys and Other Battles?*

'When are you going to tell the truth?'
For there's no such book, so far as I know,
As *How it Happened Here,*
Though there may be. There may.
What should I say to this callow youth
Who learned to write last winter—
One of those correspondence courses—
And who's coming to lunch today?
He'll be rambling on, no doubt,
About pigs and trees, stars and horses.

## THE CENTAURS

I can think of William of Orange,
Prince of gasworks-wall and gable-end.
A plodding, snow-white charger
On the green, grassy slopes of the Boyne,
The milk-cart swimming against the current

Of our own backstreet. Hernan Cortes
Is mustering his cavalcade on the pavement,
Lifting his shield like the lid of a garbage-can.
His eyes are fixed on a river of Aztec silver,
He whinnies and paws the earth

For our amazement. And Saul of Tarsus,
The stone he picked up once has grown into a hoof.
He slings the saddle-bags over his haunches,
Lengthening his reins, loosening his girth,
To thunder down the long road to Damascus.


## THE BIG HOUSE

I was only the girl under the stairs
But I was the first to notice something was wrong.
I was always first up and about, of course.
Those hens would never lay two days running
In the same place. I would rise early
And try round the haggard for fresh nests.
The mistress let me keep the egg-money.

And that particular night there were guests,
Mrs de Groot from the bridge set
And a young man who wrote stories for children,
So I wanted everything to be just right
When they trooped down to breakfast that morning.

I slept at the very top of that rambling house,
A tiny room with only a sky-light window.
I had brushed my hair and straightened my dress
And was just stepping into the corridor
When it struck me. That old boarded-up door
Was flung open. A pile of rubble and half-bricks
Was strewn across the landing floor.

I went on down. I was stooping among the hay-stacks
When there came a clatter of hooves in the yard.
The squire's sure-footed little piebald mare
Had found her own way home, as always.
He swayed some. Then fell headlong on the cobbles.

There was not so much as the smell of whiskey on him.
People still hold he had died of fright,
That the house was haunted by an elder brother
Who was murdered for his birthright.
People will always put two and two together.

What I remember most of that particular morning
Was how calmly everyone took the thing.
The mistress insisted that life would go on quietly
As it always had done. Breakfast was served
At nine exactly. I can still hear Mrs de Groot
Telling how she had once bid seven hearts.
The young man's stories were for grown-ups, really.


## EPONA

I have no heart, she cries. I am driving her madder,
Out of her depth, almost, in the tall grass
Of Parsons' triangular meadow.
Because I straddle some old jackass

Whose every hoof curves like the blade
Of a scythe. It staggers over
Towards a whitethorn hedge, meaning to rid
Itself of me. Just in time, I slither

Off the sagging, flabbergasted back.
To calm a jackass, they say, you take its ear like a snaffle
Between your teeth. I bite her ear and shoo her back
Into the middle of my life.


## CASS AND ME

Do you remember me, Cass,
The brim of his hat over my face,
My father's slicker trailing the ground
When I was a child? Once you came round

And I climbed on your shoulders.
Once you were stronger, taller, older.
We leaned out across the yard
As a giant would across the world.

The sow fled west with her farrow,
The hound made a rainbow under the barrow.
The cock crowed out of time,

So large we loomed.
Which of us, I wonder, had grown,
Whose were those wide eyes at my groin?

That winter of my third-form year,
While the other boys played penny poker
Or listened to the latest Hendrix,
Or simply taunted Joe and Cyril,

I fell in with the school caretaker.
He was like me, from the country,
We seemed to speak the same language.
He knew the names of all the trees,

He knew them by their wizened leaves.
Books, too. He had gathered hundreds.
He loved their very smells, their shapes.
There was this book that I might like

That he would give me as a present.
*How to Play Championship Tennis.*
We would meet the next morning at break
In his little workshop.

The book lay squarely on the table.
I reached for it. But as I stooped
He leaned across and grabbed my pecker.
I ran out by the unkempt lawn

Through a fine, insinuating drizzle.
The net had long been taken down
Yet here were Joe and Cyril, knocking up;
Their fluent lobs, their deft volleys,

As if they had found some other level.

## CHEESECAKE

The mother was going through
An old chest of drawers
When she found the plain brown envelope
Among his childhood things.
The name she had given her son
Was never this name in such ugly type.
When she opened the envelope
There was a sheaf
Of photographs in cellophane.
Should he not somehow
Have been the one confused,
Did she not even now hold the proof?
When, all of a sudden, there,
And there once more,
Among those bodies her own body posed.

## NED SKINNER

Was 'a barbaric yawp',
If you took Aunt Sarah at her word.
He would step over the mountain
Of a summer afternoon
To dress a litter of pigs
On my uncle's farm.

Aunt Sarah would keep me in,
Taking me on her lap
Till it was over.
Ned Skinner wiped his knife
And rinsed his hands
In the barrel at the door-step.

He winked, and gripped my arm.
'It doesn't hurt, not so's you'd notice,
And God never slams one door
But another's lying open.
Them same pigs can see the wind.'
My uncle had given him five shillings.

Ned Skinner came back
While my uncle was in the fields.
'Sarah,' he was calling, 'Sarah.
You weren't so shy in our young day.
You remember yon time in Archer's loft?'
His face blazed at the scullery window.
'Remember? When the hay was won.'

Aunt Sarah had the door on the snib.
'That's no kind of talk
To be coming over. Now go you home.'
Silence. Then a wheeze.
We heard the whiskey-jug
Tinkle, his boots diminish in the yard.
Aunt Sarah put on a fresh apron.


## MA

Old photographs would have her bookish, sitting
Under a willow. I take that to be a croquet
Lawn. She reads aloud, no doubt from Rupert Brooke.
The month is always May or June.

Or with the stranger on the motor-bike.
Not my father, no. This one's all crew-cut
And polished brass buttons.
An American soldier, perhaps.
                              And the full moon

Swaying over Keenaghan, the orchards and the cannery,
Thins to a last yellow-hammer, and goes.
The neighbours gather, all Keenaghan and Collegelands,
There is story-telling. Old miners at Coalisland
Going into the ground. Swinging, for fear of the gas,
The soft flame of a canary.


## K E E N

I never dreamt you would die
Till your horse came back to me
With long reins trailing,
Your blood on its brow
And your polished saddle

Empty. I started up quickly.
One leap from the settle,
The next to the lintel,
A final fling as far as the stirrup.
I went off at full gallop.

I would find you stretched
By that low whin bush
Without pope or bishop,
Without priest or monk
To preside or pray over you,

But some withered old woman
Who had wrapped you in her mantle.
Your blood was flowing still,
I knew of no way to staunch it.
I cupped my hands and drank it.
     —*after the Irish of Eibhlín Ní Chonaill*

## VAQUERO

He has blown in from the badlands
Where, steadily coming to grief

Through hunger and thirst
And his belly too big for his eyes,

He must have lashed himself
Upright in the ornamental saddle

On this dilapidated, riddled
Jennet. He has been dead a week now,

His face blue-green, mulatto.
And the halo of buzzards

That was once a rippling, swirling lasso
No wider now than his hat-band.


## OUR LADY OF ARDBOE

I

Just there, in a corner of the whin-field,
Just where the thistles bloom.
She stood there as in Bethlehem
One night in nineteen fifty-three or four.

The girl leaning over the half-door
Saw the cattle kneel, and herself knelt.

## II

I suppose that a farmer's youngest daughter
Might, as well as the next, unravel
The winding road to Christ's navel.

Who's to know what's knowable?
Milk from the Virgin Mother's breast,
A feather off the Holy Ghost?
The fairy thorn? The holy well?

Our simple wish for there being more to life
Than a job, a car, a house, a wife—
The fixity of running water.

For I like to think, as I step these acres,
That a holy well is no more shallow
Nor plummetless than the pools of Shiloh,
The fairy thorn no less true than the Cross.


## III

Mother of our Creator, Mother of our Saviour,
Mother most amiable, Mother most admirable.
Virgin most prudent, Virgin most venerable,
Mother inviolate, Mother undefiled.

And I walk waist-deep among purples and golds
With one arm as long as the other.

## BIG LIZ

After the sleekness of moleskin trews
I seem at last to have got to grips
With this old collier.
He hunkers over his pint of bitter

In his best suit and starched collar.
Somehow, this half-hearted stripper
Sheds new light on herself and him.
She opens up before us like a seam,

Stepping back through the hoops
Of flannel petticoats, the grain of trees,
To the inevitability of earth.

And though our cheers might raise the roof
He hunkers still, his hard eye level
With the diamond in her navel.


## THE DUCKING STOOL

While they were squatting stark naked
On those hollowed, chalky flags
She had taken no oaths
Nor pow-wowed with twelve devils
Nor worn the collar of a Pater Noster
Front to back or back to front,

Neither whispered the Horseman's Word
Nor kissed the buttocks
Of anything like a yearling goat.
This was nothing if not mild.
He got up all of a sudden and left her
At the bottom of a garden.

A child

Sitting out her Sabbaths
The rickety, only child on the see-saw.
Was no one coming back to play,
Might a life not hang in the balance?
No abler then to prove her blamelessness

Than were Maeve and Bronagh,
Rowena and Morag, such sisters
As drowned on that long arm of the law,
Nor ready for such logic.
She was summoned now by her grandfather
For another game of hide-and-seek

Through the ancient, three-storey rectory
He knew like the back of his hand.
She would crouch in some narrow wardrobe
Among stinking, mildewed foxes
While his steps faltered at the door,
Which, opening, might throw light on her.

## THE GIRLS IN THE POOLROOM

The girls in the poolroom
Were out on their own limbs.

How could I help
But make men of them?

There was Emily
Who was lovely and tall and slim.

I used to meet her in the pub
And sometimes she came home.

She raved about Albert Camus
And the twenty-third psalm.

I asked her once, 'Are you asleep?'
She said, 'I am. I am.'


## BOON

'And what's the snow that melts the soonest?'
Mercy was thirteen, maybe fourteen.
'And how would you catch a yellow bittern?'
She was half-way down the mountainside

Before I'd realised. 'I would be right glad
If you knew next Sunday.' Her parting shot
Left me more intent than Lancelot
Upon the Grail. Or whoever it was. Sir Galahad.

'A yellow bittern?' I'd consulted Will Hunter,
Who carried a box of matches
And had gone by himself to the pictures.
He wrinkled his nose. 'I know green linnets

You take with just a pinch of salt
On their tails. That's according to most people.
A yellow bittern. They might be special.'
'And the snow that's first to melt?'

I'd got that wrong. He was almost certain.
'The snow that scarcely ever lies
Falls on a lady's breasts and thighs.'
That week stretched longer than the Creation!

We climbed the hills to the highest hill-farm
Without a word of snow or bittern

And viewed the extravagant wilderness
Of the brawling townlands round the Moy,

The cries from the football-field grown so dim
We might be listening on the wireless.
When I'd all but forgotten that she'd forgotten
Mercy would take me in her arms.

## THE WOOD

*For John and Madeline*

They tell me how they bought
An hour of silence
From a juke-box in New York
Or San Francisco once,

That now they intend
To go back to their home place
For a bit of peace,

A house overlooking a lake
And a wood for kindling.

'But you can't fell trees
That have stood for as long
As anyone remembers?'

'The wood we have in mind will stand
While it has lost its timber.'

McLean County Unit #5
301 - NCWHS

# AT MASTER McGRATH'S GRAVE

### I

He had a long white streak
On his deep chest,
A small white patch
Over one of his shoulders,
And two white claws
On each of his forepaws.

Over his lean back
He was all ticked with white,
As if a shower of hail
Had fallen and never melted.

### II

Should he not still smoulder,
Our shooting star,
That claimed the Waterloo Cup
In eighteen sixty-nine?

I'm standing at the edge
Of Lord Lurgan's demesne
Where the Master is stretched
Under his plinth,
A bucket of quicklime
Scattered all along his length.

### III

The overhanging elm-trees
And the knee-high grass
Are freshly tinged
By this last sun-shower.

I'm not beside myself with grief,
Not even so taken by McGrath,

It's just the way these elm-trees
Do more and more impinge,
The knee-high grass
Has brought me to my knees.


## BLEMISH

Were it indeed an accident of birth
That she looks on the gentle earth
And the seemingly gentle sky
Through one brown and one blue eye.


## THE BEARDED WOMAN, BY RIBERA

I've seen one in a fairground,
Swigging a quart of whiskey,
But nothing like this lady
Who squats in the foreground
To suckle the baby,
With what must be her husband
Almost out of the picture.

Might this be the Holy Family
Gone wrong?

Her face belongs to my grand-da
Except that her beard
Is so luxuriantly black.
One pap, her right, is bared

And borrowed by her child,
Who could not be less childlike.
He's ninety, too, if he's a day.

I'm taken completely
By this so unlikely Madonna.

Yet my eye is drawn once again,
Almost against its wishes,
To the figure in the shadows,
Willowy and clean-shaven,
As if he has simply wandered in
Between mending that fuse
And washing the breakfast dishes.


## THE MERMAN

He was ploughing his single furrow
Through the green, heavy sward
Of water. I was sowing winter wheat
At the shoreline, when our farms met.

Not a furrow, quite, I argued.
Nothing would come of his long acre
But breaker growing out of breaker,
The wind-scythe, the rain-harrow.

Had he no wish to own such land
As he might plough round in a day?
What of friendship, love? Such qualities?

He remembered these same fields of corn or hay
When swathes ran high along the ground,
Hearing the cries of one in difficulties.

## PARIS

A table for two will scarcely seat
The pair of us! All the people we have been
Are here as guests, strategically deployed
As to who will go best with whom.
A convent girl, a crashing bore, the couple

Who aren't quite all they seem.
A last shrimp curls and winces on your plate
Like an embryo. 'Is that a little overdone?'
And these country faces at the window
That were once our own. They study the menu,

Smile faintly, and are gone.
Chicken Marengo! It's a far cry from the Moy.
'There's no such person as Saint Christopher,
Father Talbot gave it out at Mass.
Same as there's no such place as Limbo.'

The world's less simple for being travelled,
Though. In each fresh, neutral place
Where our differences might have been settled
There were men sitting down to talk of peace
Who began with the shape of the table.


## THE NARROW ROAD TO THE DEEP NORTH

A Japanese soldier
Has just stumbled out of the forest.
The war has been over
These thirty years, and he has lost

All but his ceremonial sword.
We offer him an American cigarette.

He takes it without a word.
For all this comes too late. Too late

To break the sword across his knee,
To be right or wrong.
He means to go back to his old farm

And till the land. Though never to deny
The stone its sling,
The blade of grass its one good arm.


## THE MIXED MARRIAGE

My father was a servant-boy.
When he left school at eight or nine
He took up billhook and loy
To win the ground he would never own.

My mother was the school-mistress,
The world of Castor and Pollux.
There were twins in her own class.
She could never tell which was which.

She had read one volume of Proust,
He knew the cure for farcy.
I flitted between a hole in the hedge
And a room in the Latin Quarter.

When she had cleared the supper-table
She opened *The Acts of the Apostles*,
*Aesop's Fables*, *Gulliver's Travels*.
Then my mother went on upstairs

And my father further dimmed the light
To get back to hunting with ferrets

Or the factions of the faction-fights,
The Ribbon Boys, the Caravats.


## DE SECRETIS MULIERUM

They're nothing, really, all the girls I've known
With legs up their oxters,
Their hair all blossom and their long bones
Laden with fruit,
Nothing to Harry Conway's daughter.

Don't get me wrong—it's not as if she's awkward.
If you can picture a dappled orchard
That's scarcely been touched by frost,
And where all those other tits and bums
Are deep in conversation. What weight they've lost!
What windfalls strew the pathways!

Well, she's the one, if you can make her out,
Whose head is full—no, not of pears, not plums—
But pomegranates, pawpaws.


## LARGESSE

A body would think
The world was its meat and drink.

It fits like a dream!
What's the fish-pond to the fish,
Avocado and avocado-dish,
But things shaped by their names?

For only by embroidery
Will a star take root in the sky,
A flower have a pillow for ground.
How many angels stand on a pinhead?

Twelve o'clock. We climb to bed.
A trout leaps in the far pond,
The sound of one hand clapping.

And the avocado-stone is mapping
Its future through the wreck
Of dinner-table and dining-room.

Numberless cherubim and seraphim.
Alleluia on my prick!

## CIDER

Though we lie by their sides we may never know
The lengths to which our roads might go,
Or so we like to think. They end as we end—
Dead in their beds, going round the bend,

In mid-sentence at quays.
I have lain by your side for long enough,
Our sheets are littered with those yellow moths
That wanted only their names in lights.

I want you to bring me down to the estuary.
At low tide we might wade out to an island, Hy
Brasil, the Land of Youth.

I'm through with drinking for another night,
Lead me down to the estuary. While I'm in two minds,
Now that the glass had taken my other hand.

## THE RUCKSACK

That morning Lars fell
He dragged the rest
Down with him.

My base-camp flickers,
True if small,
Where I buried them.

My eyes have failed,
My beard is blue with rime.
I hack another step

From the perpendicular.
Should I give up, turn back?
When, that one step

Ahead, on the crest,
Stands my little Sherpa,
Wild and weatherbeaten,

Lending me a hand.
He wears my own old rucksack
From the first expedition.


## AT MARTHA'S DELI

So Will had finally broken off with Faith!
There she stood, gnawing a shish-kebab.
It seemed they no longer soaked in one bath-tub
And made that kind of little wave.

Now she came over, wiping her hands in her dress
And asking if I might not be her friend.

I led her down through the bracken
And listened again to what the doctors told her

Of how she might live only a year,
To where earlier on I had come upon the vixen
That must have thought this her finest kill.

The taste of blood on a greased knife
Whereby she would happily drink herself to death.
She kissed me hard. I might have been her own Will.


## THE COUNTRY CLUB

'But what would interest you about the brook,
It's always cold in summer, warm in winter.'
'Warm in December, cold in June, you say?'
Doc Pinkerton was a great one for chapter and verse.

'I don't suppose the water's changed at all.
You and I know enough to know it's warm
Compared with cold, and cold compared with warm,
But all the fun's in how you say a thing.'

'Well, it shouldn't seem true when it's not.'
He took out his watch. 'I'd best be getting home.'

Just after three. The bar was shutting down.
Ella Stafford was high as a kite.
She was wearing one of those little black dresses
And a kiss-curl something like Veronica Lake's.

She was right side of thirty, husband out of town,
It seemed I might have fallen on my feet.

Neither of them was so far gone, as it turned out.
She slept the whole way to their villa
On the Heights. She kissed me wetly on the chin
And staggered in through the bougainvillaea.

I fetched a pot of coffee from an all-night café
And drove up to watch the new day breaking.

Cicadas were clipping the lawns and ornamental bushes.
I was coming back down onto the highway
When I met Lee Pinkerton's Chevrolet.
We drew up close. He rolled down his window.

'There's been some trouble over Stafford's way.
Took a shot at his wife.' He gave me a knowing look.
'She'd been seeing a lot of some other fella,
Or so it seems. I can't make head nor tail of it.'

## BANG

For that moment we had been the others
These things happen to—
A tree would give its neighbour the elbow
And both look the other way,
The birds were whistling
At the ordinariness of it all.
Our slow coming to in a renovated clearing,
The farfetched beginning to reassemble.
Which of us had that leg belonged to?

It brought me back years to that Carnival
In the next parish—the football pitch, the striped marquee
And the dark's unrestricted parking—
The priest who built them on his hands and knees
Beside some girl who had lost an ear-ring,

She moaning the name of the one who scored the goal
Earlier that evening.

## DUFFY'S CIRCUS

Once Duffy's Circus had shaken out its tent
In the big field near the Moy
God may as well have left Ireland
And gone up a tree. My father had said so.

There was no such thing as the five-legged calf,
The God of Creation
Was the God of Love.
My father chose to share such Nuts of Wisdom.

Yet across the Alps of each other the elephants
Trooped. Nor did it matter
When Wild Bill's Rain Dance
Fell flat. Some clown emptied a bucket of stars

Over the swankiest part of the crowd.
I had lost my father in the rush and slipped
Out the back. Now I heard
For the first time that long-drawn-out cry.

It came from somewhere beyond the corral.
A dwarf on stilts. Another dwarf.
I sidled past some trucks. From under a freighter
I watched a man sawing a woman in half.

## MULES

Should they not have the best of both worlds?

Her feet of clay gave the lie
To the star burned in our mare's brow.
Would Parsons' jackass not rest more assured
That cross wrenched from his shoulders?

We had loosed them into one field.
I watched Sam Parsons and my quick father
Tense for the punch below their belts,
For what was neither one thing or the other.

It was as though they had shuddered
To think, of their gaunt, sexless foal
Dropped tonight in the cowshed.

We might yet claim that it sprang from earth
Were it not for the afterbirth
Trailed like some fine, silk parachute,
That we would know from what heights it fell.


## ARMAGEDDON, ARMAGEDDON

I

At last, someone had heard tell of Larry Durrell.
We leaned round headland after headland
When there it was, his Snow-White Villa.
Wasn't it dazzling?
                    Well, it was rather white.
The orange and lemon groves, the olives,
Are wicked for this purity of light.
In a while now we will go ashore, to Mouse Island.

The light is failing. Our mouths are numb with aniseed,
Her little breasts are sour as Jeanne Duval's.
And darknesses weigh down further the burgeoning trees
Where she kneels in her skimpy dress
To gather armful after armful.
Nuzzling the deep blues, the purples. Spitting the stars.


## II

When Oisin came back to Ireland
After three hundred years
On one of those enchanted islands
Somewhere in the Western Seas,

He thought nothing of dismounting
From his enchanted steed
To be one again with the mountains,
The bogs and the little fields.

There and then he began to stoop,
His hair, and all his teeth, fell out,
A mildewed belt, a rusted buckle.
The clays were heavy, black or yellow,
Those were the colours of his boots.
And I know something of how he felt.


## III

Not to worry. From where I lived
We might watch Long Bullets being played,
Follow the course of a pair of whippets,
Try to keep in time with a Lambeg Drum.

There'd be Derryscollop, and Cloveneden,
The parish where W. R. Rodgers held sway.
And where the first Orange Lodge was founded,
An orchard full of No Surrenders.

We could always go closer if you wanted,
To where Macha had challenged the charioteer
And Swift the Houyhnhnm,
The open field where her twins were whelped.
Then, the scene of the Armagh Rail Disaster.
Why not brave the Planetarium?


IV

You had been sleeping, O my lover,
A good half-hour, it seemed,
And I woke you only to discover
How you might have dreamed,
How you might have dreamed.

Might some glistening inspector
By his one dull incisor
And simple rule-of-thumb
Already have beavered through
To our last-carriage-but-one?

Did he hint something of blockades,
Of trees felled across the lines,
And then hand back our tickets
Ratified by their constellations?

## V

Now that I had some idea of our whereabouts
We could slow a little and not be afraid.
Who was that? Only the bull behind the hedge,
It was showing us the whites of its eyes.

Why should those women be carrying water
If all the wells were poisoned, as they said,
And the fish littering the river?
Had the sheep been divided from the goats,
Were Twin and Twin at each other's throats?

I knew these fields. How long were they fallow?
Those had been Archer's sixty yellow acres,
These Hunter's forty green and grey.
Had Hunter and Archer got it into their heads
That they would take the stars in their strides?

## VI

My brother had mislaid his voice
Since it happened. His eyes had grown simple,
His hand alone would describe
Our father's return from the betting-shop
To be torn between his own two ponies,
Their going their different ways.

He had guarded our mother bent-double
Over the kitchen sink, her face in the basin.
She had broken another of her best dishes,
We would bury her when we were able.

Some violence had been done to Grace,
She had left for our next-of-kin.
My brother gave us half of his last mangold
And the warning of bayonets fixed in the bushes.

## VII

A summer night in Keenaghan
So dark my light had lingered near its lamp
For fear of it. Nor was I less afraid.
At the Mustard Seed Mission all was darkness.

I had gone out with the kettle
To a little stream that lay down in itself
And breathed through a hollow reed
When yon black beetle lighted on my thumb
And tickled along my palm
Like a blood-blister with a mind of its own.

My hand might well have been some flat stone
The way it made for the underside.
I had to turn my wrist against its wont
To have it walk in the paths of uprightness.

# WHY BROWNLEE LEFT 1980

# WHIM

She was sitting with a pint and a small one
That afternoon in the Europa Hotel,
Poring over one of those old legends—
*Cu Chulainn and the Birds of Appetite*—
When he happened along, and took a pew.

'Pardon me, for I couldn't help but notice
You've got the O'Grady translation.'
'What of it? What's it to you?'
'Standish O'Grady? Very old-fashioned.
*Cu Chulainn and the Birds of Appetite?*
More like *How Cu Chulainn Got His End.*'
He smiled. She was smiling too.
'If you want the flavour of the original
You should be looking to Kuno Meyer.
As it happens, I've got the very edition
That includes this particular tale.
You could have it on loan, if you like,
If you'd like to call back to my place, now.'

Not that they made it as far as his place.
They would saunter through the Botanic Gardens
Where they held hands, and kissed,
And by and by one thing led to another.
To cut not a very long story short,
Once he got stuck into her he got stuck
Full stop.
            They lay there quietly until dusk
When an attendant found them out.
He called an ambulance, and gently but firmly
They were manhandled onto a stretcher
Like the last of an endangered species.

## OCTOBER 1950

Whatever it is, it all comes down to this:
My father's cock
Between my mother's thighs.
Might he have forgotten to wind the clock?

Cookers and eaters, Fuck the Pope,
Wow and flutter, a one-legged howl,
My sly quadroon, the way home from the pub—
Anything wild or wonderful—

Whatever it is, it goes back to this night,
To a chance remark
In a room at the top of the stairs;
To an open field, as like as not,
Under the little stars.
Whatever it is, it leaves me in the dark.

## THE GEOGRAPHY LESSON

You should have seen them, small and wild
Against a map of the known world,

The back row of the class of '61.
Internal exiles at thirteen or fourteen.

Most couldn't read, though Mungo Park
Could write his name. He'd made his mark

As surely as some old explorer
Would christen a mountain, or a river.

To chart his progress, bench by embellished bench,
Till he petered out next to Lefty Lynch

Who kept ladybirds in a match-box,
Some with two, others with seven spots.

Who knew it all. Where to listen for the cuckoo
When she touched down from Africa.

Why bananas were harvested while green
But would hanker after where they'd grown,

Their sighing from the depths of a ship
Or from under the counter in Lightbody's shop,

How all that greenness turned to gold
Through unremembering darkness, an unsteady hold.


## THE WEEPIES

Most Saturday afternoons
At the local Hippodrome
Saw the Pathe-News rooster,
Then the recurring dream

Of a lonesome drifter
Through uninterrupted range.
Will Hunter, so gifted
He could peel an orange

In a single, fluent gesture,
Was the leader of our gang.
The curtain rose this afternoon
On a lion, not a gong.

When the crippled girl
Who wanted to be a dancer
Met the married man
Who was dying of cancer,

Our hankies unfurled
Like flags of surrender.
I believe something fell asunder
In even Will Hunter's hands.


## BRAN

While he looks into the eyes of women
Who have let themselves go,
While they sigh and they moan
For pure joy,

He weeps for the boy on that small farm
Who takes an oatmeal Labrador
In his arms,
Who knows all there is of rapture.


## CUBA

My eldest sister arrived home that morning
In her white muslin evening dress.
'Who the hell do you think you are,
Running out to dances in next to nothing?
As though we hadn't enough bother
With the world at war, if not at an end.'
My father was pounding the breakfast-table.

'Those Yankees were touch and go as it was—
If you'd heard Patton in Armagh—
But this Kennedy's nearly an Irishman
So he's not much better than ourselves.
And him with only to say the word.
If you've got anything on your mind
Maybe you should make your peace with God.'

I could hear May from beyond the curtain.
'Bless me, Father, for I have sinned.
I told a lie once, I was disobedient once.
And, Father, a boy touched me once.'
'Tell me, child. Was this touch immodest?
Did he touch your breast, for example?'
'He brushed against me, Father. Very gently.'


## THE BISHOP

The night before he was to be ordained
He packed a shirt and a safety razor
And started out for the middle of nowhere,
Back to the back of beyond,

Where all was forgiven and forgotten,
Or forgotten for a time. He would court
A childhood sweetheart.
He came into his uncle's fortune.

The years went by. He bought another farm of land.
His neighbours might give him a day
In the potatoes or barley.
He helped them with their tax demands.

There were children, who married
In their turn. His favourite grand-daughter

Would look out, one morning in January,
To find him in his armchair, in the yard.

It had snowed all night. There was a drift
As far as his chin, like an alb.
'Come in, my child. Come in, and bolt
The door behind you, for there's an awful draught.'

## THE BOUNDARY COMMISSION

*You remember that village where the border ran*
*Down the middle of the street,*
*With the butcher and baker in different states?*
Today he remarked how a shower of rain

Had stopped so cleanly across Golightly's lane
It might have been a wall of glass
That had toppled over. He stood there, for ages,
To wonder which side, if any, he should be on.

## EARLY WARNING

My father brought out his donkey-jacket,
Tipped a bucket
Of blue-stone into the knapsack sprayer,
A wing and a prayer
Against apple-scab disease,
And mizzled the lone crab-apple tree
In our back garden,
That was bowed down more by children
Than by any crop.

We would swing there on a fraying rope,
Lay siege to the tree-house,
Draw up our treaties
In its modest lee.

We would depend on more than we could see.

Our Protestant neighbour, Billy Wetherall,
Though he knew by the wireless
Of apple-scab in the air,
Would sling his hammock
Between two sturdy Grenadiers
And work through the latest *Marvel* comic.

## LULL

I've heard it argued in some quarters
That in Armagh they mow the hay
With only a week to go to Christmas,
That no one's in a hurry

To save it, or their own sweet selves.
Tomorrow is another day,
As your man said on the Mount of Olives.
The same is held of County Derry.

Here and there up and down the country
There are still houses where the fire
Hasn't gone out in a century.

I know that eternal interim;
I think I know what they're waiting for
In Tyrone, Fermanagh, Down and Antrim.

# I REMEMBER SIR ALFRED

The gardens of Buckingham Palace
Were strewn once with Irish loam
So those English moles that knew their place
Would have no sense of home.

Watching Irish navvies drinking pints
This evening in Camden Town
I remember Sir Alfred McAlpine—
The shortest distance between two points
Is a straight line.

The spirit of Sir Alfred McAlpine
Paces the meadow, and fixes his theodolite
On something beyond the horizon,
Love, or fidelity.

Charles Stewart Parnell, the I.R.A.,
Redheaded women, the way back to the digs,
The Irish squire
Who trained his spy-glass
On a distant spire
And imagined himself to be attending Mass.

Now Sir Alfred has dislodged a hare
That goes by leaps and bounds
Across the grazing,
Here and there,
This way and that, by singleminded swervings.

# IRELAND

The Volkswagen parked in the gap,
But gently ticking over.

You wonder if it's lovers
And not men hurrying back
Across two fields and a river.



## ANSEO

When the Master was calling the roll
At the primary school in Collegelands,
You were meant to call back *Anseo*
And raise your hand
As your name occurred.
*Anseo*, meaning here, here and now,
All present and correct,
Was the first word of Irish I spoke.
The last name on the ledger
Belonged to Joseph Mary Plunkett Ward
And was followed, as often as not,
By silence, knowing looks,
A nod and a wink, the Master's droll
'And where's our little Ward-of-court?'

I remember the first time he came back
The Master had sent him out
Along the hedges
To weigh up for himself and cut
A stick with which he would be beaten.
After a while, nothing was spoken;
He would arrive as a matter of course
With an ash-plant, a salley-rod.
Or, finally, the hazel-wand
He had whittled down to a whip-lash,
Its twist of red and yellow lacquers
Sanded and polished,
And altogether so delicately wrought
That he had engraved his initials on it.

I last met Joseph Mary Plunkett Ward
In a pub just over the Irish border.
He was living in the open,
In a secret camp
On the other side of the mountain.
He was fighting for Ireland,
Making things happen.
And he told me, Joe Ward,
Of how he had risen through the ranks
To Quartermaster, Commandant:
How every morning at parade
His volunteers would call back *Anseo*
And raise their hands
As their names occurred.

## WHY BROWNLEE LEFT

Why Brownlee left, and where he went,
Is a mystery even now.
For if a man should have been content
It was him; two acres of barley,
One of potatoes, four bullocks,
A milker, a slated farmhouse.
He was last seen going out to plough
On a March morning, bright and early.

By noon Brownlee was famous;
They had found all abandoned, with
The last rig unbroken, his pair of black
Horses, like man and wife,
Shifting their weight from foot to
Foot, and gazing into the future.

## IMMRAMA

I, too, have trailed my father's spirit
From the mud-walled cabin behind the mountain
Where he was born and bred,
TB and scarlatina,
The farm where he was first hired out,
To Wigan, to Crewe junction,
A building-site from which he disappeared
And took passage, almost, for Argentina.

The mountain is coming down with hazel,
The building-site a slum,
While he has gone no further than Brazil.

That's him on the verandah, drinking rum
With a man who might be a Nazi,
His children asleep under their mosquito-nets.

## PROMISES, PROMISES

I am stretched out under the lean-to
Of an old tobacco-shed
On a farm in North Carolina.
A cardinal sings from the dogwood
For the love of marijuana.
His song goes over my head.
There is such splendour in the grass
I might be the picture of happiness.
Yet I am utterly bereft
Of the low hills, the open-ended sky,
The wave upon wave of pasture
Rolling in, and just as surely
Falling short of my bare feet.
Whatever is passing is passing me by.

I am with Raleigh, near the Atlantic,
Where we have built a stockade
Around our little colony.
Give him his scallop-shell of quiet,
His staff of faith to walk upon,
His scrip of joy, immortal diet—
We are some eighty souls
On whom Raleigh will hoist his sails.
He will return, years afterwards,
To wonder where and why
We might have altogether disappeared,
Only to glimpse us here and there
As one fair strand in her braid,
The blue in an Indian girl's dead eye.

I am stretched out under the lean-to
Of an old tobacco-shed
On a farm in North Carolina,
When someone or other, warm, naked,
Stirs within my own skeleton
And stands on tip-toe to look out
Over the horizon,
Through the zones, across the ocean.
The cardinal sings from a redbud
For the love of one slender and shy,
The flight after flight of stairs
To her room in Bayswater,
The damson freckle on her throat
That I kissed when we kissed Goodbye.

## TRUCE

It begins with one or two soldiers
And one or two following

With hampers over their shoulders.
They might be off wildfowling

As they would another Christmas Day,
So gingerly they pick their steps.
No one seems sure of what to do.
All stop when one stops.

A fire gets lit. Some spread
Their greatcoats on the frozen ground.
Polish vodka, fruit and bread
Are broken out and passed round.

The air of an old German song,
The rules of Patience, are the secrets
They'll share before long.
They draw on their last cigarettes

As Friday-night lovers, when it's over,
Might get up from their mattresses
To congratulate each other
And exchange names and addresses.


## HISTORY

Where and when exactly did we first have sex?
Do you remember? Was it Fitzroy Avenue,
Or Cromwell Road, or Notting Hill?
Your place or mine? Marseilles or Aix?
Or as long ago as that Thursday evening
When you and I climbed through the bay window
On the ground floor of Aquinas Hall
And into the room where MacNeice wrote 'Snow',
Or the room where they say he wrote 'Snow'.

## PALM SUNDAY

To tell the range of the English longbows
At Agincourt, or Crécy,
We need look no further than the yews
That, even in Irish graveyards,
Are bent on Fitzwilliams, and de Courcys.
These are the date-palms of the North.

They grow where nothing really should.
No matter how many are gathered
They never make a wood.
The coffin-board that yearns to be a tree
Goes on to bear no small, sweet gourds
As might be trampled by another Christ.

Today's the day for all such entrances.
I was wondering if you'd bring me through
To a world where everything stands
For itself, and carries
Just as much weight as me on you.
My scrawny door-mat. My deep red carpet.

## THE AVENUE

Now that we've come to the end
I've been trying to piece it together,
Not that distance makes anything clearer.
It began in the half-light
While we walked through the dawn chorus
After a party that lasted all night,
With the blackbird, the wood-pigeon,
The song-thrush taking a bludgeon
To a snail, our taking each other's hand
As if the whole world lay before us.

## SOMETHING OF A DEPARTURE

Would you be an angel
And let me rest,
This one last time,
Near that plum-coloured beauty spot
Just below your right buttock?

Elizabeth, Elizabeth,
Had words not escaped us both
I would have liked to hear you sing
*Farewell to Tarwathie*
Or *Ramble Away*.

Your thigh, your breast,
Your wrist, the ankle
That might yet sprout a wing—
You're altogether as slim
As the chance of our meeting again.

So put your best foot forward
And steady, steady on.
Show me the plum-coloured beauty spot
Just below your right buttock,
And take it like a man.


## HOLY THURSDAY

They're kindly here, to let us linger so late,
Long after the shutters are up.
A waiter glides from the kitchen with a plate
Of stew, or some thick soup,

And settles himself at the next table but one.
We know, you and I, that it's over,

That something or other has come between
Us, whatever we are, or were.

The waiter swabs his plate with bread
And drains what's left of his wine,
Then rearranges, one by one,
The knife, the fork, the spoon, the napkin,
The table itself, the chair he's simply borrowed,
And smiles, and bows to his own absence.


## MAKING THE MOVE

When Ulysses braved the wine-dark sea
He left his bow with Penelope,

Who would bend for no one but himself.
I edge along the book-shelf,

Past bad Lord Byron, Raymond Chandler,
*Howard Hughes; The Hidden Years,*

Past Blaise Pascal, who, bound in hide,
Divined the void to his left side:

Such books as one may think one owns
Unloose themselves like stones

And clatter down into this wider gulf
Between myself and my good wife;

A primus stove, a sleeping-bag,
The bow I bought through a catalogue

When I was thirteen or fourteen
That would bend, and break, for anyone,

Its boyish length of maple upon maple
Unseasoned and unsupple.

Were I embarking on that wine-dark sea
I would bring my bow along with me.


## THE PRINCESS AND THE PEA

This is no dream
By Dulac out of the Brothers Grimm,
A child's disquiet,
Her impish mouth,
The quilt upon embroidered quilt
Of satin and shot silk,
Her lying there, extravagant, aloof,
Like cream on milk.

This is the dream of her older sister,
Who is stretched on the open grave
Of all the men she has known.
Far down, something niggles. The stir
Of someone still alive.
Then a cry, far down. It is your own.


## GRIEF

If I think at all of the broken-down hearse
In the yard off the Moy square,
I think of a high-stepping black horse
Stopped in mid-stride
Half-way up, say, Charlemont Street;
The immediate family looking on in horror.

He jolts to his knees on the kidney-stones
Where a frenzy of maggots
Make short work of so much blood and guts.
The hearse hasn't even been uncoupled.
His luminous, blue-pink skeleton
Simply disintegrates.

Till there's nothing left of our black horse
But the plume of his ornamental harness,
A tendril, a frond
Wavering among the cobbles;
The immediate family, and the family friends,
Leafing through their Bibles.

## COME INTO MY PARLOUR

When someone died, for miles around,
You were sure to find Coulter
In the graveyard at Collegelands
With his spade and navvy's shovel.
Once a plane broke up in mid-air
And he collected the bits and pieces,
A pocket-watch, a monocle,
As if all should come as second nature
To one who has strayed no farther
Than a ripple from its stone.

What Coulter took as his text
Was this bumpy half-acre of common.
Few graves were named or numbered
For most were family plots.
If the family had itself lost track
He knew exactly which was which
And what was what,

Where among the heights and hollows
Were the Quinns, and the O'Briens.

'I've been at the burying
Of so many of the Souper McAuleys
I declare they must be stacked
As high as dinner-plates.
Mind you, this ground's so wet
They're away again like snow off a ditch.
Them, and the best of good timber
Are come into the kingdom.'

And I saw over his tilting shoulder
The grave of my mother,
My father's grave, and his father's;
The slightly different level
Of the next field, and the next;
Each small, one-sided collision
Where a neighbour had met his future.
Here an O'Hara, there a Quinn,
The wreckage of bath-tubs and bedsteads,
Of couches and mangles,
That was scattered for miles around.

## THE ONE DESIRE

The palm-house in Belfast's Botanic Gardens
Was built before Kew
In the spirit that means to outdo
The modern by the more modern,

That iron be beaten, and glass
Bent to our will,
That heaven be brought closer still
And we converse with the angels.

The palm-house has now run to seed;
Rusting girders, a missing pane
Through which some delicate tree
Led by kindly light
Would seem at last to have broken through.
We have excelled ourselves again.


## IMMRAM

I was fairly and squarely behind the eight
That morning in Foster's pool-hall
When it came to me out of the blue
In the shape of a sixteen-ounce billiard cue
That lent what he said some little weight.
'Your old man was an ass-hole.
That makes an ass-hole out of you.'
My grandfather hailed from New York State.
My grandmother was part Cree.
This must be some new strain in my pedigree.

The billiard-player had been big, and black,
Dressed to kill, or inflict a wound,
And had hung around the pin-table
As long as it took to smoke a panatella.
I was clinging to an ice-pack
On which the *Titanic* might have foundered
When I was suddenly bedazzled
By a little silver knick-knack
That must have fallen from his hat-band.
I am telling this exactly as it happened.

I suppose that I should have called the cops
Or called it a day and gone home
And done myself, and you, a favour.

But I wanted to know more about my father.
So I drove west to Paradise
Where I was greeted by the distant hum
Of *Shall We Gather at the River?*
The perfect introduction to the kind of place
Where people go to end their lives.
It might have been *Bringing In the Sheaves.*

My mother had just been fed by force,
A pint of lukewarm water through a rubber hose.
I hadn't seen her in six months or a year,
Not since my father had disappeared.
Now she'd taken an overdose
Of alcohol and barbiturates,
And this, I learned, was her third.
I was told then by a male nurse
That if I came back at the end of the week
She might be able to bring herself to speak.

Which brought me round to the Atlantic Club.
The Atlantic Club was an old grain-silo
That gave onto the wharf.
Not the kind of place you took your wife
Unless she had it in mind to strip
Or you had a mind to put her up for sale.
I knew how my father had come here by himself
And maybe thrown a little crap
And watched his check double, and treble,
With highball hard on the heels of highball.

She was wearing what looked like a dead fox
Over a low-cut sequinned gown,
And went by the name of Susan, or Suzanne.
A girl who would never pass out of fashion
So long as there's an 'if' in California.
I stood her one or two pink gins
And the talk might have come round to passion

Had it not been for a pair of thugs
Who suggested that we both take a wander,
She upstairs, I into the wild blue yonder.

They came bearing down on me out of nowhere.
A Buick and a Chevrolet.
They were heading towards a grand slam.
Salami on rye. I was the salami.
So much for my faith in human nature.
The age of chivalry how are you?
But I side-stepped them, neatly as Salome,
So they came up against one another
In a moment of intense heat and light,
Like a couple of turtles on their wedding-night.

Both were dead. Of that I was almost certain.
When I looked into their eyes
I sensed the import of their recent visions,
How you must get all of wisdom
As you pass through a wind-shield.
One's frizzled hair was dyed
A peroxide blond, his sinewy arms emblazoned
With tattoos, his vest marked *Urgent*.
All this was taking on a shape
That might be clearer after a night's sleep.

When the only thing I had ever held in common
With anyone else in the world
Was the ramshackle house on Central Boulevard
That I shared with my child-bride
Until she dropped out to join a commune,
You can imagine how little I was troubled
To kiss Goodbye to its weathered clapboard.
When I nudged the rocker on the porch
It rocked as though it might never rest.
It seemed that I would forever be driving west.

I was in luck. She'd woken from her slumbers
And was sitting out among flowering shrubs.
All might have been peace and harmony
In that land of milk and honey
But for the fact that our days are numbered,
But for Foster's, the Atlantic Club,
And now, that my father owed Redpath money.
Redpath. She told me how his empire
Ran a little more than half-way to hell
But began on the top floor of the Park Hotel.

Steel and glass were held in creative tension
That afternoon in the Park.
I strode through the cavernous lobby
And found myself behind a nervous couple
Who registered as Mr and Mrs Alfred Tennyson.
The unsmiling, balding desk-clerk
Looked like a man who would sell an alibi
To King Kong on the Empire State Building,
So I thought better of passing the time of day.
I took the elevator all the way.

You remember how, in a half-remembered dream,
You found yourself in a long corridor,
How behind the first door there was nothing,
Nothing behind the second,
Then how you swayed from room to empty room
Until, beyond that last half-open door
You heard a telephone . . . and you were wakened
By a woman's voice asking you to come
To the Atlantic Club, between six and seven,
And when you came, to come alone.

I was met, not by the face behind the voice,
But by yet another aide-de-camp
Who would have passed for a Barbary pirate
With a line in small-talk like a parrot
And who ferried me past an outer office

To a not ungracious inner sanctum.
I did a breast-stroke through the carpet,
Went under once, only to surface
Alongside the raft of a banquet-table—
A whole roast pig, its mouth fixed on an apple.

Beyond the wall-length, two-way mirror
There was still more to feast your eyes upon
As Susan, or Susannah, danced
Before what looked like an invited audience,
A select band of admirers
To whom she would lay herself open.
I was staring into the middle distance
Where two men and a dog were mowing her meadow
When I was hit by a hypodermic syringe.
And I entered a world equally rich and strange.

There was one who can only have been asleep
Among row upon row of sheeted cadavers
In what might have been the Morgue
Of all the cities of America,
Who beckoned me towards her slab
And silently drew back the covers
On the vermilion omega
Where she had been repeatedly stabbed,
Whom I would carry over the threshold of pain
That she might come and come and come again.

I came to, under a steaming pile of trash
In the narrow alley-way
Behind that old Deep Water Baptist mission
Near the corner of Sixteenth and Ocean—
A blue-eyed boy, the Word made flesh
Amid no hosannahs nor hallelujahs
But the strains of Blind Lemon Jefferson
That leaked from the church
Through a hole in a tiny stained-glass window,
In what was now a torrent, now had dwindled.

And honking to Blind Lemon's blues guitar
Was a solitary black cat
Who would have turned the heads of Harlem.
He was no louder than a fire-alarm,
A full-length coat of alligator,
An ermine stole, his wide-brimmed hat
Festooned with family heirlooms.
I watch him trickle a fine white powder
Into his palm, so not a grain would spill,
Then snort it through a rolled-up dollar bill.

This was angel dust, dust from an angel's wing
Where it glanced off the land of cocaine,
Be that Bolivia, Peru.
Or snow from the slopes of the Andes, so pure
It would never melt in spring.
But you know how over every Caliban
There's Ariel, and behind him, Prospero;
Everyone taking a cut, dividing and conquering
With lactose and dextrose,
Everyone getting right up everyone else's nose.

I would tip-toe round by the side of the church
For a better view. Some fresh cement.
I trod as lightly there
As a mere mortal at Grauman's Chinese Theatre.
An oxy-acetylene torch.
There were two false-bottomed
Station-waggons. I watched Mr See-You-Later
Unload a dozen polythene packs
From one to the other. *The Urgent Shipping Company.*
It behoved me to talk to the local P.D.

'My father, God rest him, he held this theory
That the Irish, the American Irish,
Were really the thirteenth tribe,
The Israelites of Europe.
All along, my father believed in fairies

But he might as well have been Jewish.'
His laugh was a slight hiccup.
I guessed that Lieutenant Brendan O'Leary's
Grandmother's pee was green,
And that was why she had to leave old Skibbereen.

Now, what was all this about the Atlantic cabaret,
*Urgent*, the top floor of the Park?
When had I taken it into my head
That somebody somewhere wanted to see me dead?
Who? No, Redpath was strictly on the level.
So why, rather than drag in the Narcs.,
Why didn't he and I drive over to Ocean Boulevard
At Eighteenth Street, or wherever?
Would I mind stepping outside while he made a call
To such-and-such a luminary at City Hall?

We counted thirty-odd of those brown-eyed girls
Who ought to be in pictures,
Bronzed, bleached, bare-breasted,
Bare-assed to a man,
All sitting, cross-legged, in a circle
At the feet of this life-guard out of Big Sur
Who made an exhibition
Of his dorsals and his pectorals
While one by one his disciples took up the chant
*The Lord is my surf-board. I shall not want.*

He went on to explain to O'Leary and myself
How only that morning he had acquired the lease
On the old Baptist mission,
Though his was a wholly new religion.
He called it *The Way of the One Wave*.
This one wave was sky-high, like a wall of glass,
And had come to him in a vision.
You could ride it forever, effortlessly.
The Lieutenant was squatting before his new guru.
I would inform the Missing Persons Bureau.

His name? I already told you his name.
Forty-nine. Fifty come July.
Five ten or eleven. One hundred and eighty pounds.
He could be almost anyone.
And only now was it brought home to me
How rarely I looked in his eyes,
Which were hazel. His hair was mahogany brown.
There was a scar on his left forearm
From that time he got himself caught in the works
Of a saw-mill near Ithaca, New York.

I was just about getting things into perspective
When a mile-long white Cadillac
Came sweeping out of the distant past
Like a wayward Bay mist,
A transport of joy. There was that chauffeur
From the 1931 Sears Roebuck catalogue,
Susannah, as you guessed,
And this refugee from F. Scott Fitzgerald
Who looked as if he might indeed own the world.
His name was James Earl Caulfield III.

This was how it was. My father had been a mule.
He had flown down to Rio
Time and time again. But he courted disaster.
He tried to smuggle a wooden statue
Through the airport at Lima.
The Christ of the Andes. The statue was hollow.
He stumbled. It went and shattered.
And he had to stand idly by
As a cool fifty or sixty thousand dollars worth
Was trampled back into the good earth.

He would flee, to La Paz, then to Buenos Aires,
From alias to alias.
I imagined him sitting outside a hacienda
Somewhere in the Argentine.
He would peer for hours

Into the vastness of the pampas.
Or he might be pointing out the constellations
Of the Southern hemisphere
To the open-mouthed child at his elbow.
He sleeps with a loaded pistol under his pillow.

The mile-long white Cadillac had now wrapped
Itself round the Park Hotel.
We were spirited to the nineteenth floor
Where Caulfield located a secret door.
We climbed two perilous flights of steps
To the exclusive penthouse suite.
A moment later I was ushered
Into a chamber sealed with black drapes.
As I grew accustomed to the gloom
I realized there was someone else in the room.

He was huddled on an old orthopaedic mattress,
The makings of a skeleton,
Naked but for a pair of draw-string shorts.
His hair was waistlength, as was his beard.
He was covered in bedsores.
He raised one talon.
'I forgive you,' he croaked. 'And I forget.
On your way out, you tell that bastard
To bring me a dish of ice-cream.
I want Baskin-Robbins banana-nut ice-cream.'

I shimmied about the cavernous lobby.
Mr and Mrs Alfred Tennyson
Were ahead of me through the revolving door.
She tipped the bell-hop five dollars.
There was a steady stream of people
That flowed in one direction,
Faster and deeper,
That I would go along with, happily,
As I made my way back, like any other pilgrim,
To Main Street, to Foster's pool-room.

QUOOF 1983

# GATHERING MUSHROOMS

The rain comes flapping through the yard
like a tablecloth that she hand-embroidered.
My mother has left it on the line.
It is sodden with rain.
The mushroom shed is windowless, wide,
its high-stacked wooden trays
hosed down with formaldehyde.
And my father has opened the Gates of Troy
to that first load of horse manure.
Barley straw. Gypsum. Dried blood. Ammonia.
Wagon after wagon
blusters in, a self-renewing gold-black dragon
we push to the back of the mind.
We have taken our pitchforks to the wind.

All brought back to me that September evening
fifteen years on. The pair of us
tripping through Barnett's fair demesne
like girls in long dresses
after a hail-storm.
We might have been thinking of the fire-bomb
that sent Malone House sky-high
and its priceless collection of linen
sky-high.
We might have wept with Elizabeth McCrum.
We were thinking only of psilocybin.
You sang of the maid you met on the dewy grass—
*And she stooped so low gave me to know*
*it was mushrooms she was gathering O.*

He'll be wearing that same old donkey-jacket
and the sawn-off waders.
He carries a knife, two punnets, a bucket.
He reaches far into his own shadow.
We'll have taken him unawares
and stand behind him, slightly to one side.

He is one of those ancient warriors
before the rising tide.
He'll glance back from under his peaked cap
without breaking rhythm:
his coaxing a mushroom—a flat or a cup—
the nick against his right thumb;
the bucket then, the punnet to left or right,
and so on and so forth till kingdom come.

We followed the overgrown tow-path by the Lagan.
The sunset would deepen through cinnamon
to aubergine,
the wood-pigeon's concerto for oboe and strings,
allegro, blowing your mind.
And you were suddenly out of my ken, hurtling
towards the ever-receding ground,
into the maw
of a shimmering green-gold dragon.
You discovered yourself in some outbuilding
with your long-lost companion, me,
though my head had grown into the head of a horse
that shook its dirty-fair mane
and spoke this verse:

*Come back to us. However cold and raw, your feet*
*were always meant*
*to negotiate terms with bare cement.*
*Beyond this concrete wall is a wall of concrete*
*and barbed wire. Your only hope*
*is to come back. If sing you must, let your song*
*tell of treading your own dung,*
*let straw and dung give a spring to your step.*
*If we never live to see the day we leap*
*into our true domain,*
*lie down with us now and wrap*
*yourself in the soiled grey blanket of Irish rain*
*that will, one day, bleach itself white.*
*Lie down with us and wait.*

## TRANCE

My mother opens the scullery door
on Christmas Eve, 1954,
to empty the dregs
of the tea-pot on the snowy flags.
A wind out of Siberia
carries such voices as will carry
through to the kitchen—

Someone mutters a flame from lichen
and eats the red-and-white Fly Agaric
while the others hunker in the dark,
taking it in turn
to drink his mind-expanding urine.
One by one their reindeer
nuzzle in.

My mother slams the door
on her star-cluster of dregs
and packs me off to bed.
At 2 a.m. I will clamber downstairs
to glimpse the red-and-white
up the chimney, my new rocking-horse
as yet unsteady on its legs.

## THE RIGHT ARM

I was three-ish
when I plunged my arm into the sweet-jar
for the last bit of clove-rock.

We kept a shop in Eglish
that sold bread, milk, butter, cheese,
bacon and eggs,

Andrews Liver Salts,
and, until now, clove-rock.

I would give my right arm to have known then
how Eglish was itself wedged between
*ecclesia* and *église*.

The Eglish sky was its own stained-glass vault
and my right arm was sleeved in glass
that has yet to shatter.



## THE MIRROR

*In memory of my father*


I

He was no longer my father
but I was still his son;
I would get to grips with that cold paradox,
the remote figure in his Sunday best
who was buried the next day.

A great day for tears, snifters of sherry,
whiskey, beef sandwiches, tea.
An old mate of his was recounting
their day excursion
to Youghal in the Thirties,
how he was his first partner
on the Cork/Skibbereen route
in the late Forties.
There was a splay of Mass cards
on the sitting-room mantelpiece
which formed a crescent round a glass vase,
his retirement present from C.I.E.

## II

I didn't realize till two days later
it was the mirror took his breath away.

The monstrous old Victorian mirror
with the ornate gilt frame
we had found in the three-storey house
when we moved in from the country.

I was afraid that it would sneak
down from the wall and swallow me up
in one gulp in the middle of the night.

While he was decorating the bedroom
he had taken down the mirror
without asking for help;
soon he turned the colour of terracotta
and his heart broke that night.

## III

There was nothing for it
but to set about finishing the job,
papering over the cracks,
painting the high window,
stripping the door, like the door of a crypt.
When I took hold of the mirror
I had a fright. I imagined him breathing through it.
I heard him say in a reassuring whisper:
*I'll give you a hand, here.*

And we lifted the mirror back in position
above the fireplace,
my father holding it steady
while I drove home
the two nails.

*—from the Irish of Michael Davitt*

# THE HANDS

To the chopping-block, on which the farmer Sebastian split
logs against the Asturian cold,
the Guardia Civil would shove him and spit:
Now clench the fist with which you made so bold.

Four of them held him under.
He writhed and whimpered, in a state of shock.
The axe would fall, and sunder
the hands that had quarried rock.

With bloody stumps he loped across the land.
They laughed as they shot after him. And when he blared
one came over to stop his mouth with loam.

He lay dead in the field. But his far-fetched hands
would stir at night, and the villagers heard
the fists come blattering on their windows, looking for home.

*—after the German of Erich Arendt*


# THE SIGHTSEERS

My father and mother, my brother and sister
and I, with uncle Pat, our dour best-loved uncle,
had set out that Sunday afternoon in July
in his broken-down Ford

not to visit some graveyard—one died of shingles,
one of fever, another's knees turned to jelly—
but the brand-new roundabout at Ballygawley,
the first in mid-Ulster.

Uncle Pat was telling us how the B-Specials
had stopped him one night somewhere near Ballygawley
and smashed his bicycle

and made him sing the Sash and curse the Pope of Rome.
They held a pistol so hard against his forehead
there was still the mark of an O when he got home.


## MY FATHER AND I AND BILLY TWO RIVERS

Our favoured wrestler, the Mohawk Indian.

We would sit in the local barber shop—
'Could he not afford a decent haircut?'—
to watch him suffer the slings and arrows
of a giant Negro who fought dirty.

The Negro's breath-taking crotch-hold and slam
left all of us out for a count of ten.

The barber knew the whole thing was a sham.

Next week would see Billy back on his feet
for one of his withering Tomahawk Chops
to a Britisher's craw,

                    dusting him out
of the ring and into the wide-mouthed crowd
like a bale of tea at the Boston Tea Party.

## QUOOF

How often have I carried our family word
for the hot water bottle
to a strange bed,
as my father would juggle a red-hot half-brick
in an old sock
to his childhood settle.
I have taken it into so many lovely heads
or laid it between us like a sword.

A hotel room in New York City
with a girl who spoke hardly any English,
my hand on her breast
like the smouldering one-off spoor of the yeti
or some other shy beast
that has yet to enter the language.

## BIG FOOT

Comes, if he comes at all, among sumach
and birches, stops half-
way across the clearing . . . Wood-smoke,
the cabin where you mourn your wife,

where, darkening the tiny window,
is the fur coat
you promised her when she was twenty
or twenty-one, you forget.

## BEAVER

Let yourself in by the leaf-yellow door.
Go right up the stairs.

Along the way you may stumble upon
one girl in a dress

of flour-bag white, the turkey-red
of another's apron.

Give it no more thought
than you would a tree felled across a stream

in the Ozarks or the Adirondacks.
Step over her as you would across

a beaver dam.
And try to follow that stream back

to the top of the stairs,
to your new room with its leaf-yellow floor.


## MARY FARL POWERS: *PINK SPOTTED TORSO*

### I

She turns from the sink
potato in hand. A Kerr's Pink,
its water-dark
port-wine birthmark
that will answer her knife
with a hieroglyph.

The open book of Minnesota
falls open at Main Street, an almost total
sky, sweet nothings in the Soda
Fountain, joy-
rides among the tidal
wheat-fields, midnight swims with the Baumgartner boy.

You saw through that flooded granite quarry
to the wreckage of an Oldsmobile,
saw, never more clearly,
him unmanacle
himself from buckled steel, from the weight of symbol,
only to be fettered by an ankle.

## EDWARD KIENHOLZ: *THE STATE HOSPITAL*

Where a naked man, asleep, is strapped
to the lower bunk of a bed.
The bed-pan is so tantalizingly out of reach
we may assume he has trouble
with his bowels.
He will have been beaten by an orderly,
a bar of soap wrapped
in a towel.

His head, when we come to examine the head
we would never allow ourselves to touch,
is a fish bowl
in which two black fish, or mauve,
take it in turns to make eyes and mouths
or grapple with one bright idea.

Yet the neon-lit, plastic dream-bubble
he borrowed from a comic strip—
and which you and I might stretch
to include Hope, Idaho—
here takes in only the upper bunk of the bed
where a naked man, asleep, is strapped.


## GLANDERS

When you happened to sprain your wrist or ankle
you made your way to the local shaman,
if 'shaman' is the word for Larry Toal,
who was so at ease with himself, so tranquil,

a cloud of smoke would graze on his thatch
like the cow in the cautionary tale,
while a tether of smoke curled down his chimney
and the end of the tether was attached

to Larry's ankle or to Larry's wrist.
He would conjure up a poultice of soot and spit
and flannel-talk, how he had a soft spot

for the mud of Flanders,
how he came within that of the cure for glanders
from a Suffolkman who suddenly went west.

## THE SALMON OF KNOWLEDGE

Out of the world of blood and snatters,
the inch-to-the-mile

world of the eel,
the yardstick of lymph,

the unquenchable oomph
of her whip, her thigh-length boot

on the other foot,
her hackled gulp of semen—

out of this world is the first salmon
of the year, his ass-hole

clean as a whistle.
Here lies one who reached for the sky.

There is a bay-leaf over his eye
and his name is writ in water.


## FROM STRENGTH TO STRENGTH

A Charolais, the new cow-calf
will plunge out of her own shadow
as if from the bath.

Her bath towel
is a rich brocade.
She pummels herself. A talcum-rime.

She wants to meet the full-length
mirror head-on.
She is palmed off by the meadow,

me, my aluminium bucket.
She takes her milk like medicine.
Though she may lift her fraying tail

to skitter-dung,
she goes from strength to strength,
a grasping, veal-pale tongue.

## CHERISH THE LADIES

In this, my last poem about my father,
there may be time enough
for him to fill their drinking-trough
and run his eye over

his three mooley heifers.
Such a well-worn path,
I know, from here to the galvanized bath.
I know, too, you would rather

*I saw behind the hedge to where the pride*
*of the herd, though not an Irish*
*bull, would cherish*
*the ladies with his electric cattle-prod.*

As it is, in my last poem about my father
he opens the stand-pipe
and the water scurries along the hose
till it's curled

in the bath. One heifer
may look up
and make a mental note, then put her nose
back to the salt-lick of the world.

## YGGDRASILL

From below, the waist-thick pine
seemed to arch
its back. It is a birch,
perhaps. At any rate, I could discern
a slight curvature of the spine.

They were gathered in knots
to watch me go.
A pony fouled the hard-packed snow
with her glib cairn,
someone opened a can of apricots.

As I climb
my nose is pressed to the bark.
The mark
of a cigarette burn
from your last night with him.

A snapshot of you and your sister
walking straight
through 1958,
*The Works of Laurence Sterne*
your only aid to posture.

The air is aerosol-
blue and chill. I have notched
up your pitch-
pine scent and the maidenhair fern's
spry arousal.

And it would be just swell and dandy
to answer
them with my tonsure,
to return
with the black page from *Tristram Shandy.*

Yet the lichened
tree trunk will taper
to a point where one scrap of paper
is spiked, and my people yearn
for a legend:

*It may not be today*
*or tomorrow, but sooner or later*
*the Russians will water*
*their horses on the shores of Lough Erne*
*and Lough Neagh.*


## MINK

A mink escaped from a mink-farm
in South Armagh
is led to the grave of Robert Nairac
by the fur-lined hood of his anorak.

## THE FROG

Comes to mind as another small upheaval
amongst the rubble.
His eye matches exactly the bubble
in my spirit-level.
I set aside hammer and chisel
and take him on the trowel.

The entire population of Ireland
springs from a pair left to stand
overnight in a pond
in the gardens of Trinity College,
two bottles of wine left there to chill
after the Act of Union.

There is, surely, in this story
a moral. A moral for our times.
What if I put him to my head
and squeezed it out of him,
like the juice of freshly squeezed limes,
or a lemon sorbet?

## A TRIFLE

I had been meaning to work through lunch
the day before yesterday.
Our office block is the tallest in Belfast;
when the Tannoy sounds

another bomb alert
we take four or five minutes to run down
the thirty-odd flights of steps
to street level.

I had been trying to get past
a woman who held, at arm's length, a tray,
and on the tray the remains of her dessert—

a plate of blue-pink trifle
or jelly sponge,
with a dollop of whipped cream on top.

## FROM LAST POEMS

### IV

Not that I care who's sleeping with whom
now she's had her womb
removed, now it lies in its own glar
like the last beetroot in the pickle jar.

### VII

I would have it, were I bold,
without relish, my own lightly broiled
heart on the side.

### IX

I would be happy in the knowledge
that as I laboured up the no-through-road
towards your cottage
you ran to meet me. Your long white shift,
its spray of honesty and thrift.

XIV

Ours would be a worldly wisdom, heaven-sent;
the wisdom before the event.


## SKY-WOMAN

When she hoiked it off
in the August dark

her blouse was man-made,
nylon or rayon.

I still see her under-
arm rash of sparks.

She has straddled me
since, like Orion.

More and more, I make
do with her umlaut

as, more and more, she
turns her back on me

to fumble with
the true Orion's belt.

## KISSING AND TELLING

Or she would turn up *The Songs of Leonard Cohen*
on the rickety old gramophone.

And you knew by the way she unbound her tresses
and stepped from her William Morris dresses

you might just as well be anyone.

Goat's-milk cheeses, Navajo rugs,
her reading aloud from *A Dictionary of Drugs*—

she made wine of almost everything.

How many of those she found out on the street
and fetched back to her attic room—

*to promise nothing, to take nothing for granted*—

how many would hold by the axiom
she would intone as though it were her mantra?

I could name names. I could be indiscreet.


## THE UNICORN DEFENDS HIMSELF

I

Somewhere in or around the turn
of the sixteenth century,
we come upon the fourth
in a series of Flemish tapestries
on the hunt of the unicorn.

Kicking out with his tattered hind
hooves, he tilts
at a hunting-hound
with his barley-sugar stick of horn;
the unicorn defends himself.


II

Once you swallowed a radar-blip
of peyote
you were out of your tree,
you hadn't a baldy
where you were or who you were with.

Only that you had fallen asleep
on the water bed
in a loft on the Lower East Side,
and woke between two bodies, true,
one wire-haired and one smooth.


III

The focal point is not, in truth,
his *coup de ventre*
to the milt-
sleek hunting-hound,
by which our eye is led astray.

Everything centres
on that spear tip poised to squander
the cleft
of his 'innocent behind'.
At Houston Street and Lafayette

the unicorn defends himself.

## BLEWITS

They will be all fingers and thumbs
as they offer you a light
or try to catch the bartender's eye
for two fresh whiskey sours.

They will seem shy
as they help you with your wrap,
though their palms are spread
across your breasts. They hail a cab.

And later, in the wee, small hours,
you will lie on the bed
of your own entrails,

to be fist-fucked all night
by blewits, or by chanterelles,
until the morning that never comes.

## THE DESTROYING ANGEL

Will perch on your left epaulette
like a cockatoo
in her off-white ruff,
or the floozie traipsing through
the pavilion bar
in her mother's high-heeled shoes.
It is the eve of battle
and they—for now they are two—
they pout and preen themselves
and witter on about Nabokov.

Yes, lepidoptery.
So much more to him than *Lolita*.

So much. So very much.
They much prefer *A Russian Beauty*.
At last, one cockatoo flaps away
into the snow-dark sky
and one stays behind to smooch
in your left ear.
Another gin and Angostura bitters
and you are part of her dream

kitchen's ceramic hob,
the bathtub's
ever-deepening shades of avocado,
the various whatnots,
the row upon row of whodunits . . .

The disembodied tinkle of a horse
outside your tent.
Otherwise all is calm.
The destroying angel wants to drink
to your campaign.
A gin and tonic, this time.
You will unbutton your tunic
and raise a glass. She raises hers.
Try as you may,
you cannot make them chink or chime.


## AISLING

I was making my way home late one night
this summer, when I staggered
into a snow drift.

Her eyes spoke of a sloe-year,
her mouth a year of haws.

Was she Aurora, or the goddess Flora,
Artemidora, or Venus bright,
or Anorexia, who left
a lemon stain on my flannel sheet?

It's all much of a muchness.

In Belfast's Royal Victoria Hospital
a kidney machine
supports the latest hunger-striker
to have called off his fast, a saline
drip into his bag of brine.

A lick and a promise. Cuckoo spittle.
I hand my sample to Doctor Maw.
She gives me back a confident *All Clear.*


## THE MORE A MAN HAS THE MORE A MAN WANTS

At four in the morning he wakes
to the yawn of brakes,
the snore of a diesel engine.
Gone. All she left
is a froth of bra and panties.
The scum of the Seine
and the Farset.
Gallogly squats in his own pelt.
A sodium street light
has brought a new dimension
to their black taxi.
By the time they force an entry
he'll have skedaddled
among hen runs and pigeon lofts.

The charter flight from Florida
touched down at Aldergrove
minutes earlier,
at 3.54 a.m.
Its excess baggage takes the form
of Mangas Jones, Esquire,
who is, as it turns out, Apache.
He carries only hand luggage.
'Anything to declare?'
He opens the powder-blue attaché-
case. 'A pebble of quartz.'
'You're an Apache?' 'Mescalero.'
He follows the corridor's
arroyo till the signs read *Hertz*.

He is going to put his foot down
on a patch of waste ground
along the Stranmillis embankment
when he gets wind
of their impromptu fire.
The air above the once-sweet stream
is aquarium-
drained.
And six, maybe seven, skinheads
have formed a quorum
round a burnt-out heavy-duty tyre.
So intent on sniffing glue
they may not notice Gallogly,
or, if they do, are so far gone.

Three miles west as the crow flies
an all-night carry-out
provides the cover
for an illegal drinking club.
While the bar man unpacks a crate
of Coca-Cola,
one cool customer
takes on all comers in a video game.

He grasps what his two acolytes
have failed to seize.
Don't they know what kind of take-away
this is, the glipes?
Vietmanese. Viet-ma-friggin'-*knees*.
He drops his payload of napalm.

Gallogly is wearing a candy-stripe
king-size sheet,
a little something he picked up
off a clothes line.
He is driving a milk van
he borrowed from the Belfast Co-op
while the milkman's back
was turned.
He had given the milkman a playful
rabbit punch.
When he stepped on the gas
he flooded the street
with broken glass.
He is trying to keep a low profile.

The unmarked police car draws level
with his last address.
A sergeant and eight constables
pile out of a tender
and hammer up the stairs.
The street bristles with static.
Their sniffer dog, a Labrador bitch,
bursts into the attic
like David Balfour in *Kidnapped*.
A constable on his first dawn swoop
leans on a shovel.
He has turned over a
new leaf in her ladyship's herb patch.
They'll take it back for analysis.

All a bit much after the night shift
to meet a milkman
who's double-parked his van
closing your front door after him.
He's sporting your
Donegal tweed suit and your
Sunday shoes and politely raises your
hat as he goes by.
You stand there with your mouth open
as he climbs into the still-warm
driving seat of your Cortina
and screeches off towards the motorway,
leaving you uncertain
of your still-warm wife's damp tuft.

Someone on their way to early Mass
will find her hog-tied
to the chapel gates—
O Child of Prague—
big-eyed, anorexic.
The lesson for today
is pinned to her bomber jacket.
It seems to read *Keep off the Grass*.
Her lovely head has been chopped
and changed.
For Beatrice, whose fathers
knew Louis Quinze,
to have come to this, her perruque
of tar and feathers.

He is pushing the maroon Cortina
through the sedge
on the banks of the Callan.
It took him a mere forty minutes
to skite up the M1.
He followed the exit sign
for Loughgall and hared
among the top-heavy apple orchards.

This stretch of the Armagh/Tyrone
border was planted by Warwickshiremen
who planted in turn
their familiar quick-set damson hedges.
The Cortina goes to the bottom.
Gallogly swallows a plummy-plum-plum.

'I'll warrant them's the very pair
o' boys I seen abroad
in McParland's bottom, though where
in under God—
*for thou art so possessed with murd'rous hate—*
where they come from God only knows.'
'They were mad for a bite o' mate,
I s'pose.'
'I doubt so. I come across a brave dale
o' half-chawed damsels. Wanst wun disappeared
I follied the wun as yelly as Indy male.'
'Ye weren't afeared?'
'I follied him.' 'God save us.'
'An' he driv away in a van belongin' t'*Avis*.'

The grass sprightly as Astroturf
in the September frost
and a mist
here where the ground is low.
He seizes his own wrist
as if, as if
Blind Pew again seized Jim
at the sign of the 'Admiral Benbow'.
As if Jim Hawkins led Blind Pew
to Billy Bones
and they were all one and the same,
he stares in disbelief
at an aspirin-white spot he pressed
into his own palm.

Gallogly's thorn-proof tweed jacket
is now several sizes too big.
He has flopped
down in a hay shed
to ram a wad of hay into the toe
of each of his ill-fitting
brogues, when he gets the drift
of ham and eggs.
Now he's led by his own wet nose
to the hacienda-style
farmhouse, a baggy-kneed animated
bear drawn out of the woods
by an apple pie
left to cool on a windowsill.

She was standing at the picture window
with a glass of water
and a Valium
when she caught your man
in the reflection of her face.
He came
shaping past the milking parlour
as if he owned the place.
Such is the integrity
of their quarrel
that she immediately took down
the legally held shotgun
and let him have both barrels.
She had wanted only to clear the air.

Half a mile away across the valley
her husband's U.D.R. patrol
is mounting a check-point.
He pricks up his ears
at the crack
of her prematurely arthritic hip-
joint,
and commandeers one of the jeeps.

There now, only a powder burn
as if her mascara had run.
The bloody puddle
in the yard, and the shilly-shally
of blood like a command wire
petering out behind a milk churn.

A hole in the heart, an ovarian
cyst.
Coming up the Bann
in a bubble.
Disappearing up his own bum.
Or, running on the spot
with all the minor aplomb
of a trick-cyclist.
So thin, side-on, you could spit
through him.
His six foot of pump water
bent double
in agony or laughter.
Keeping down-wind of everything.

*White Annetts. Gillyflowers. Angel Bites.*
When he names the forgotten names
of apples
he has them all off pat.
His eye like the eye of a travelling rat
lights on the studied negligence
of these scraws of turf.
A tarpaulin. A waterlogged pit.
He will take stock of the Kalashnikov's
filed-down serial number,
seven sticks of unstable
commercial gelignite
that have already begun to weep.
*Red Strokes. Sugar Sweet. Widows Whelps.*

Buy him a drink and he'll regale you
with how he came in for a cure
one morning after the night before
to the *Las Vegas* Lounge and Cabaret.
He was crossing the bar's
eternity of parquet floor
when his eagle eye
saw something move on the horizon.
If it wasn't an Indian.
A Sioux. An ugly Sioux.
He means, of course, an Oglala
Sioux busily tracing the family tree
of an Ulsterman who had some hand
in the massacre at Wounded Knee.

He will answer the hedge-sparrow's
*Littlebitofbreadandnocheese*
with a whole bunch
of freshly picked watercress,
a bulb of garlic,
sorrel,
with many-faceted blackberries.
Gallogly is out to lunch.
When his cock rattles its sabre
he takes it in his dab
hand, plants one chaste kiss
on its forelock,
and then, with a birl and a skirl,
tosses it off like a caber.

The U.D.R. corporal had come off duty
to be with his wife
while the others set about
a follow-up search.
When he tramped out just before twelve
to exercise the greyhound
he was hit by a single high-velocity
shot.

You could, if you like, put your fist
in the exit wound
in his chest.
He slumps
in the spume of his own arterial blood
like an overturned paraffin lamp.

Gallogly lies down in the sheugh
to munch
through a Beauty of
Bath. He repeats himself, *Bath*,
under his garlic-breath.
*Sheugh*, he says. *Sheugh*.
He is finding that first 'sh'
increasingly difficult to manage.
*Sh*-leeps. A milkmaid sinks
her bare foot
to the ankle
in a simmering dung hill
and fills the slot
with beastlings for him to drink.

In Ovid's conspicuously tongue-in-cheek
account of an eyeball
to eyeball
between the goddess Leto
and a shower of Lycian reed cutters
who refuse her a cup of cloudy
water
from their churned-up lake,
*Live then forever in that lake of yours*,
she cries, and has them
bubble
and squeak
and plonk themselves down as bullfrogs
in their icy jissom.

A country man kneels on his cap
beside his neighbour's fresh
grave-mud
as Gallogly kneels to lap
the primrose-yellow
custard.
The knees of his hand-me-down duds
are gingerish.
A pernickety seven-
year-old girl-child
parades in her mother's trousseau
and mumbles a primrose
Kleenex tissue
to make sure her lipstick's even.

Gallogly has only to part the veil
of its stomach wall
to get right under the skin,
the spluttering heart
and collapsed lung,
of the horse in *Guernica*.
He flees the Museum of Modern Art
with its bit between his teeth.
When he began to cough
blood, Hamsun rode the Minneapolis/
New York night train
on top of the dining-car.
One long, inward howl.
A porter-drinker without a thrapple.

A weekend trip to the mountains
north of Boston
with Alice, Alice A.
and her paprika hair,
the ignition key
to her family's Winnebago camper,
her quim
biting the leg off her.

In the oyster bar
of Grand Central Station
she gobbles a dozen Chesapeakes—
'Oh, I'm not particular as to size'—
and, with a flourish of Tabasco,
turns to gobble him.

A brewery lorry on a routine delivery
is taking a slow,
dangerous bend.
The driver's blethering
his code name
over the Citizens Band
when someone ambles
in front of him. Go, Johnny, go, go, go.
He's been dry-gulched
by a sixteen-year-old numb
with Mogadon,
whose face is masked by the seamless
black stocking filched
from his mum.

When who should walk in but Beatrice,
large as life, or larger,
sipping her one glass of lager
and singing her one song.
If he had it to do all over again
he would let her shave his head
in memory of '98
and her own, the French, Revolution.
The son of the King of the Moy
met this child on the Roxborough
estate. *Noblesse*, she said. *Noblesse
oblige*. And her tiny nipples
were bruise-bluish, wild raspberries.
The song she sang was 'The Croppy Boy'.

Her *grand'mère* was once asked to tea
by Gertrude Stein,
and her *grand'mère* and Gertrude
and Alice B., *chère* Alice B.
with her hook-nose,
the three of them sat in the nude
round the petits fours
and repeated *Eros is Eros is Eros*.
If he had it to do all over again
he would still be taken in
by her Alice B. Toklas
Nameless Cookies
and those new words she had him learn:
hash, hashish, *lo perfido assassin*.

Once the local councillor straps
himself into the safety belt
of his Citroën
and skids up the ramp
from the municipal car park
he upsets the delicate balance
of a mercury-tilt
boobytrap.
Once they collect his smithereens
he doesn't quite add up.
They're shy of a foot, and a calf
which stems
from his left shoe like a severely
pruned-back shrub.

Ten years before. The smooth-as-a-
front-lawn at Queen's
where she squats
before a psilocybin god.
The indomitable gentle-bush
that had Lanyon or Lynn
revise their elegant ground plan
for the university quad.

With calmness, with care,
with breast milk, with dew.
There's no cure now.
There's nothing left to do.
The mushrooms speak through her.
Hush-hush.

'Oh, I'm not particular as to size,'
Alice hastily replied
and broke off a bit of the edge
with each hand
and set to work very carefully,
nibbling
first at one
and then the other.
On the Staten Island ferry
two men are dickering
over the price
of a shipment of Armalites,
as Henry Thoreau was wont to quibble
with Ralph Waldo Emerson.

That last night in the Algonquin
he met with a flurry
of sprites,
the assorted shades
of Wolfe Tone, Napper Tandy,
a sanguine
Michael Cusack
brandishing his blackthorn.
Then Thomas Meagher
darts up from the Missouri
on a ray
of the morning star
to fiercely ask
what has become of Irish hurling.

*Everyone has heard the story of*
*a strong and beautiful bug*
*which came out of the dry leaf*
*of an old table of apple-tree wood*
*that stood*
*in a farmer's kitchen in Massachusetts*
*and which was heard gnawing out*
*for several weeks—*
When the phone trills
he is careful not to lose his page—
*Who knows what beautiful and winged life*
*whose egg*
*has been buried for ages*
*may unexpectedly come forth?* 'Tell-tale.'

Gallogly carries a hunting bow
equipped
with a bow sight
and a quiver
of hunting arrows
belonging to her brother.
Alice has gone a little way off
to do her job.
A timber wolf,
a caribou,
or merely a trick of the light?
As, listlessly,
he lobs
an arrow into the undergrowth.

Had you followed the river Callan's
Pelorus Jack
through the worst drought
in living memory
to the rains of early Autumn
when it scrubs its swollen,
scab-encrusted back
under a bridge, the bridge you look down from,

you would be unlikely to pay much heed
to yet another old banger
no one could be bothered to tax,
or a beat-up fridge
well-stocked with gelignite,
or some five hundred yards of Cortex.

He lopes after the dribs of blood
through the pine forest
till they stop dead
in the ruins of a longhouse
or hogan.
Somehow, he finds his way
back to their tent.
Not so much as a whiff of her musk.
The girl behind the Aer Lingus
check-in desk
at Logan
is wearing the same scent
and an embroidered capital letter *A*
on her breast.

*Was she Aurora, or the goddess Flora,*
*Artemidora, or Venus bright,*
*or Helen fair beyond compare*
*that Priam stole from the Grecian sight?*
*Quite modestly she answered me*
*and she gave her head one fetch up*
*and she said I am gathering musheroons*
*to make my mammy ketchup.*
The dunt and dunder
of a culvert-bomb
wakes him
as it might have woke Leander.
*And she said I am gathering musheroons*
*to make my mammy ketchup O.*

Predictable as the gift of the gab
or a drop of the craythur
he noses round the six foot deep
crater.
Oblivious to their Landrover's
olive-drab
and the Burgundy berets
of a snatch-squad of Paratroopers.
Gallogly, or Gollogly,
otherwise known as Golightly,
otherwise known as Ingoldsby,
otherwise known as English,
gives forth one low cry of anguish
and agrees to come quietly.

They have bundled him into the cell
for a strip-
search.
He perches
on the balls of his toes, my my,
with his legs spread
till both his instep arches
fall.
He holds himself at arm's
length from the brilliantly Snowcem-ed
wall, a game bird
hung by its pinion tips
till it drops, in the fullness of time,
from the mast its colours are nailed to.

They have left him to cool his heels
after the obligatory
bath,
the mug shots, fingerprints
et cetera.
He plumps the thin bolster
and hints
at the slop bucket.

Six o'clock.
From the A Wing of Armagh jail
he can make out
the Angelus bell
of St Patrick's cathedral
and a chorus of 'For God and Ulster'.

The brewery lorry's stood at a list
by the *Las Vegas*
throughout the afternoon,
its off-side rear tyres down.
As yet, no one has looked agog
at the smuts and rusts
of a girlie mag
in disarray on the passenger seat.
An almost invisible, taut
fishing line
runs from the Playmate's navel
to a pivotal
beer keg.
As yet, no one has risen to the bait.

*I saw no mountains, no enormous spaces,*
*no magical growth and metamorphosis*
*of buildings, nothing remotely like*
*a drama or a parable*
in which he dons these lime-green
dungarees,
green Wellingtons,
a green helmet of aspect terrible.
*The other world to which mescalin*
*admitted me was not the world of visions;*
*it existed out there, in what I could see*
*with my eyes open.*
He straps a chemical pack on his back
and goes in search of some Gawain.

Gallogly pads along the block
to raise his visor
at the first peep-hole.
He shamelessly
takes in her lean piglet's
back, the back
and boyish hams
of a girl at stool.
At last. A tiny goat's-pill.
A stub of crayon
with which she has squiggled
a shamrock, yes,
but a shamrock after the school
of Pollock, Jackson Pollock.

*I stopped and stared at her face to face*
*and on the spot a name came to me,*
*a name with a smooth, nervous sound:*
*Ylayali.*
*When she was very close*
*I drew myself up straight*
*and said in an impressive voice,*
*'Miss, you are losing your book.'*
And Beatrice, for it is she, she squints
through the spy-hole
to pass him an orange,
an Outspan orange some visitor has spiked
with a syringe-ful
of vodka.

*The more a man has the more a man wants,*
*the same I don't think true.*
*For I never met a man with one black eye*
*who ever wanted two.*
In the Las Vegas Lounge and Cabaret
the resident group—
pot bellies, Aran knits—
have you eating out of their hands.

*Never throw a brick at a drowning man*
*when you're near to a grocer's store.*
*Just throw him a cake of Sunlight soap,*
*let him wash himself ashore.*
You will act the galoot, and gallivant,
and call for another encore.

Gallogly, Gallogly, O Gallogly
juggles
his name like an orange
between his outsize baseball glove
paws,
and ogles
a moon that's just out of range
beyond the perimeter wall.
He works a gobbet of Brylcreem
into his quiff
and delves
through sand and gravel,
shrugging it off
his velveteen shoulders and arms.

*Just*
*throw*
*him*
*a*
*cake*
*of*
*Sunlight*
*soap,*
*let*
*him*
*wash*
*him-*
*self*
*ashore.*

Into a picture by Edward Hopper
of a gas station
in the Midwest
where Hopper takes as his theme
light, the spooky
glow of an illuminated sign
reading Esso or Mobil
or what-have-you—
into such a desolate oval
ride two youths on a motorbike.
A hand gun. Balaclavas.
The pump attendant's grown so used
to hold-ups he calls after them:
*Beannacht Dé ar an obair.*

The pump attendant's not to know
he's being watched by a gallowglass
hot-foot from a woodcut
by Derricke,
who skips across the forecourt
and kicks the black
plastic bucket
they left as a memento.
Nor is the gallowglass any the wiser.
The bucket's packed with fertilizer
and a heady brew
of sugar and Paraquat's
relentlessly gnawing its way through
the floppy knot of a Durex.

It was this self-same pump attendant
who dragged the head and torso
clear
and mouthed an Act of Contrition
in the frazzled ear
and overheard
those already-famous last words
*Moose . . . Indian.*

'Next of all wus the han'.' 'Be Japers.'
'The sodgers cordonned-off the area
wi' what-ye-may-call-it tape.'
'Lunimous.' 'They foun' this hairy
han' wi' a drowneded man's grip
on a lunimous stone no bigger than a . . .'

'Huh.'

MEETING THE BRITISH 1987

I spent last night in the nursery of a house in Pennsylvania. When I put out the light I made my way, barefoot, through the aftermath of Brandywine Creek. The constellations of the northern hemisphere were picked out in luminous paint on the ceiling. I lay under a comforting, phosphorescent Plough, thinking about where the Plough stopped being the Plough and became the Big Dipper. About the astronomer I met in Philadelphia who had found a star with a radio telescope. The star is now named after her, whatever her name happens to be. As all these stars grew dim, it seemed like a good time to rerun my own dream-visions. They had flashed up just as I got into bed on three successive nights in 1972. The first was a close-up of a face, Cox's face, falling. I heard next morning how he had come home drunk and taken a nose-dive down the stairs. Next, my uncle Pat's face, falling in slo-mo like the first, but bloody. It turned out he had slipped off a ladder on a building-site. His forehead needed seven stitches. Lastly, a freeze-frame trickle of water or glycerine on a sheet of smoked glass or perspex. I see it in shaving-mirrors. Dry Martinis. Women's tears. On windshields. As planes take off or land. I remembered how I was meant to fly to Toronto this morning, to visit my younger brother. He used to be a research assistant at the University of Guelph, where he wrote a thesis on nitrogen-fixing in soya beans, or symbiosis, or some such mystery. He now works for the Corn Producers' Association of Ontario. On my last trip we went to a disco in the Park Plaza, where I helped a girl in a bin-liner dress to find her contact-lens.

—Did you know that Spinoza was a lens-grinder?

—Are you for real?

Joe was somewhere in the background, sniggering, flicking cosmic dandruff from his shoulders.

—A lens, I went on, is really a lentil. A pulse.

Her back was an imponderable green furrow in the ultraviolet strobe.

—Did *you* know that Yonge Street's the longest street in the world?

—I can't say that I did.

—Well, it starts a thousand miles to the north, and it ends right here.

## THE CONEY

Although I have never learned to mow
I suddenly found myself half-way through
last year's pea-sticks
and cauliflower-stalks
in our half-acre of garden.
My father had always left the whetstone
safely wrapped
in his old tweed cap
and balanced on one particular plank
beside the septic tank.

This past winter he had been too ill
to work. The scythe would dull
so much more quickly in my hands
than his, and was so often honed
that while the blade
grew less and less a blade
the whetstone had entirely disappeared
and a lop-eared
coney was now curled inside the cap.
He whistled to me through the gap

in his front teeth;
'I was wondering, chief,
if you happen to know the name
of the cauliflowers in your cold-frame
that you still hope to dibble
in this unenviable
bit of ground?'
'They would be *All the Year Round*.'
'I guessed as much'; with that he swaggered
along the diving-board

and jumped. The moment he hit the water
he lost his tattered
bathing-togs

to the swimming-pool's pack of dogs.
'Come in'; this flayed
coney would parade
and pirouette like honey on a spoon:
'Come on in, Paddy Muldoon.'
And although I have never learned to swim
I would willingly have followed him.


## MY GRANDFATHER'S WAKE

If the houses in Wyeth's Christina's dream
and Malick's *Days of Heaven*
are triremes, yes,
triremes riding the 'sea of grain',
then each has a little barge
in tow—a freshly-dug grave.

I was trying to remember, Nancy,
how many New England graveyards you own,
all silver birch
and neat white picket-fences.

If only that you might make room
for a nine-banded armadillo
found wandering in Meath
sometime in the 1860s;
a man-ox, a fish with three gold teeth
described by Giraldus Cambrensis.

Our cow chained in the byre
was a galley-slave from *Ben Hur*
to the old-fashioned child of seven
they had sent in search of a bucket of steam.

## GOLD

*For Gerard Quinn*

You loomed like Merlin
over the class
of 1962,

your soutane-
pocket like the scar
of an appendectomy.

———

Just a year earlier
old Frost
had swung the lead

while hailing Kennedy—
*A golden age*
*of poetry and power.*

———

Twenty years on you reach
into the breast
of a wind-cheater

for your blue pencil:
'All cancelled;
*Nothing gold can stay.'*

———

Not the dead weight
of a grouse
flaunted from an open car.

Not Soutine's
*Hare on a Green Shutter.*
Not Marilyn.

## PROFUMO

My mother had slapped a month-long news embargo
on his very name. The inhalation
of my first, damp
menthol fag behind the Junior Common Room.

The violet-scented Thirteenth Birthday card
to which I would affix a stamp
with the Queen's head upside down, swalk,
and post to Frances Hagan.

The spontaneously-combustible *News of the World*
under my mother's cushion
as she shifted from ham to snobbish ham;

'Haven't I told you, time and time again,
that you and she are chalk
and cheese? Away and read Masefield's "Cargoes." '

## CHINOOK

I was micro-tagging Chinook salmon
on the Qu'Appelle
river.

I surged through the melt-water
in my crocus
waders.

I would give each brash,
cherubic
face its number.

*Melt*-water? These were sultry
autumn
fish hang-gliding downstream.

Chinook. Their very name
a semantic
quibble.

The autumn, then, of *Solidarity*,
your last in Cracow.
Your father

rising between borsch
and carp,
relinquishing the table to Pompeii.


## THE MIST-NET

Though he checked the mist-net
every day for a month

he caught only two tiny birds;
one Pernod-sip,

one tremulous crème-de-menthe;
their tiny sobs

were his mother's dying words:
*You mustn't. You mustn't.*

## THE MARRIAGE OF
## STRONGBOW AND AOIFE

I might as well be another guest
at the wedding-feast
of Strongbow and Aoife MacMurrough
as watch you, Mary,

try to get to grips
with a spider-crab's
crossbow and cuirass.
A creative pause before the second course

of Ireland's whole ox on a spit;
the invisible waitress
brings us each a Calvados and water-ice.

It's as if someone had slipped
a double-edged knife between my ribs
and hit the spot exactly.

## BROCK

Small wonder
he's not been sighted all winter;
this old brock's
been to Normandy and back

through the tunnels and trenches
of his subconscious.
His father fell victim
to mustard-gas at the Somme;

one of his sons lost a paw
to a gin-trap at Lisbellaw:

another drills
on the Antrim hills'

still-molten lava
in a moth-eaten Balaclava.
An elaborate
system of foxholes and duckboards

leads to the terminal moraine
of an ex-linen baron's
croquet-lawn
where he's part-time groundsman.

I would find it somewhat *infra dig*
to dismiss him simply as a pig
or heed Gerald of Wales'
tall tales

of badgers keeping badger-slaves.
For when he shuffles
across the esker
I glimpse my grandfather's whiskers

stained with tobacco-pollen.
When he piddles against a bullaun
I know he carries bovine TB
but what I *see*

is my father in his Sunday suit's
bespoke lime and lignite,
patrolling his now-diminished estate
and taking stock of this and that.

## THE WISHBONE

Maureen in England, Joseph in Guelph,
my mother in her grave.

———

At three o'clock in the afternoon
we watch the Queen's
message to the Commonwealth
with the sound turned off.

———

He seems to favour *Camelot*
over *To Have and Have Not*.

———

Yet we agree, my father and myself,
that here is more than enough
for two: a frozen chicken,
spuds, sprouts, *Paxo sage* and onion.

———

The wishbone like a rowelled spur
on the fibula of Sir—or Sir—


## THE LASS OF AUGHRIM

On a tributary of the Amazon
an Indian boy
steps out of the forest
and strikes up on a flute.

Imagine my delight
when we cut the outboard motor
and I recognize the strains
of *The Lass of Aughrim*.

'He hopes,' Jesus explains,
'to charm
fish from the water

on what was the tibia
of a priest
from a long-abandoned Mission.'

## MEETING THE BRITISH

We met the British in the dead of winter.
The sky was lavender

and the snow lavender-blue.
I could hear, far below,

the sound of two streams coming together
(both were frozen over)

and, no less strange,
myself calling out in French

across that forest-
clearing. Neither General Jeffrey Amherst

nor Colonel Henry Bouquet
could stomach our willow-tobacco.

As for the unusual
scent when the Colonel shook out his hand-

kerchief: *C'est la lavande,*
*une fleur mauve comme le ciel.*

They gave us six fishhooks
and two blankets embroidered with smallpox.

## CROSSING THE LINE

A windswept gallery. With its telephones
down and the jiggery-pokery
of *Quantel*
dissolving in the monitors.

———

Two rival commanders
are dining by candle-
light on medallions of young peccary.

———

Like synchronized dolphins,
their flunkeys
hand each a napkin
torn from the script of a seven-part series
based on the *Mabinogion.*

———

Where Pryderi's gifts of hounds and horses
turn out to have been fungus.

# BECHBRETHA

At a garden-party in Hillsborough, County Down,
ten or more summers ago
a swarm of bees
rolled all its thingamy
into one ball
and lodged in the fork of a tree.
There was mayhem.
A few of us had the presence of mind
to grab another canapé
and hold on to our glasses of wine.
Mostly, though,
there was a mad dash for Government House.
Once inside, I found myself
smack up against Merlyn Rees
who was hugging his breasts
like a startled nymph.
I'm not sure what possessed me
to suggest he ask Enoch Powell
over from Loughbrickland.
I suppose that when I think of bees
I think of a row of hives
running up the side of an orchard
in Loughbrickland,
and then I think of Enoch Powell.
Believe it or not, Merlyn took me at my word
and dispatched an equerry
to make the call.
I was stifling a chuckle
at the notion of Enoch Agricola
(and half-remembering how those hives are fake)
when the equerry slunk back
and whispered something in Merlyn's ear.
They both left the room.
Now that I had the floor to myself
I launched into a small meditation
on Loughbrickland.

I described the 'brick' in Loughbrickland
as 'a stumbling block'
and referred to Bricriu Poison-Tongue
of *Bricriu's Feast*.
Then I touched on another local king,
Congal the One-Eyed,
who was blinded by a bee-sting.
This led me neatly to the *Bechbretha*,
the Brehon judgements
on every conceivable form
of bee-dispute,
bee-trespass and bee-compensation.
My maiden speech was going swimmingly
and I was getting to my point
when a cheer went up
and everyone crowded to the windows.
A man in hat and veil
(whom I still take to have been Enoch Powell)
had brushed the swarm into a box
and covered it with the Union Jack.
Try as I might to win them back
with the fact that 90 per cent of British bees
were wiped out by disease
between 1909 and 1917
I'd lost them . . .
Merlyn had chosen this moment to reappear
through a secret door
in the book-lined wall
(which raised a nervous laugh
among the Castle Catholics)
and, not to be outdone,
called for order as he reached
into his mulberry cummerbund.
'This,' he said, 'is the very handkerchief
that Melmoth the Wanderer
left at the top of the cliff.'

## CHRISTO'S

Two workmen were carrying a sheet of asbestos
down the Main Street of Dingle;
it must have been nailed, at a slight angle,
to the same-sized gap between Brandon

and whichever's the next mountain.
Nine o'clock. We watched the village dogs
take turns to spritz the hotel's refuse-sacks.
I remembered Tralee's unbiodegradable flags

from the time of the hunger-strikes.
We drove all day past mounds of sugar-beet,
hay-stacks, silage-pits, building-sites,
a thatched cottage even—

all of them draped in black polythene
and weighted against the north-east wind
by concrete blocks, old tyres; bags of sand
at a makeshift army post

across the border. By the time we got to Belfast
the whole of Ireland would be under wraps
like, as I said, 'one of your man's landscapes'.
'Your man's? You don't mean Christo's?'


## THE EARTHQUAKE

The jacket of her chalk-stripe suit
over a straight-backed chair,

her tie's navy-blue
rope-burn.

A cymbal-hiss
from her eight-year-old's drum-kit?

A goose saying *Boo*
to some great event?

———

One delicately-tufted lynx's ear,
the fibre-optics

of her hair;
slowly last night comes back to him.

———

That hacienda's frump
of pampas-grass,

a pair of cryptic
eagles guarding its front door.

———

Her arm goes out to check for rain—
a shoulder-bruise

as from a rifle-butt—
and finds *Radio Eireann*.

———

Ireland has moved; they haven't.

## THE FOX

Such an alarm
as was raised last night
by the geese
on John Mackle's goose-farm.

I got up and opened
the venetian blind.
You lay
three fields away

in Collegelands
graveyard, in ground
so wet you weren't so much
buried there as drowned.

That was a month ago.
I see your face
above its bib
pumped full of formaldehyde.

You seem engrossed,
as if I'd come on you
painstakingly writing your name
with a carpenter's pencil

on the lid
of a mushroom-box.
You're saying, *Go back to bed.
It's only yon dog-fox.*

# THE SOAP-PIG

I must have been dozing in the tub
when the telephone
rang and a small white grub
crawled along the line
and into my head:
Michael Heffernan was dead.

All I could think of
was his Christmas present
from what must have been 1975.
It squatted there on the wash-stand,
an amber, pig-shaped
bar of soap.

He had breezed into Belfast
in a three-quarter-length coney-fur
to take up the post
of Drama Producer
with the still-reputable Beeb,
where I had somehow wangled a job.

Together we learned from Denys
Hawthorne and Allan McClelland
to float, like Saint Gennys,
on our own hands
through airwaves mostly jammed by cub-
reporters and poisoned pups.

He liked to listen at full tilt
to bootleg tapes
of Ian Paisley's assaults
on Papes,
regretful only that they weren't in quad.
His favourite word was *quidditas*.

I could just see the Jesuitical,
kitsch-camp slip-
knot in the tail
of even that bar of soap.
For this was Heffernan
saying, 'You stink to high heaven.'

Which I well knew. Many's an Arts Club
night with Barfield and Mason
ended with me throwing up
at the basin.
Anne-Marie looked on, her unspoken
'That's to wash, not boke in.'

This, or any, form of self-regard
cut no ice
with Michael, who'd undergone heart-
surgery at least twice
while I knew him. On a trip
once to the Wexford slobs

he and I had shared
a hotel room. When he slipped
off his shirt
there were two unfashionably-broad lap-
els where the surgeons had sawn
through the xylophone

on which he liked to play
Chopin or *Chop-
sticks* until he was blue
in the face; be-bop, doo-wop:
they'd given him a tiny, plastic valve
that would, it seemed, no more dissolve

than the soap-pig I carried
on successive flits
from Marlborough Park (and Anne-Marie)

to the Malone Avenue flat
(*Chez Moy*, it was later dubbed)
to the rented house in Dub (as in *Dub-*

lin) Lane,
until, at last, in Landseer Street
Mary unpeeled its cellophane
and it landed on its feet
among porcelain, glass and heliotrope
pigs from all parts of the globe.

When we went on holiday to France
our house-sitter was troub-
led by an unearthly fragrance
at one particular step
on the landing. It was no pooka,
of course, but the camomile soap-pig

that Mary, in a fit of pique,
would later fling into the back yard.
As I unpicked
the anthracite-shards
from its body, I glimpsed the scrab-
nosed, condemned slab

of our sow that dropped
dead from a chill in 1966,
its uneven litter individually wrapped
in a banana box
with polystyrene and wood-shavings;
this time Mary was leaving,

taking with her the gold
and silver pigs, the ivory.
For Michael Heffernan, the common cold
was an uncommon worry
that might as easily have stopped
him in his tracks. He'd long since escaped

Belfast for London's dog-eat-dog
back-stab
and leap-frog.
More than once he collap-
sed at his desk. But Margaret
would steady him through the Secretariat

towards their favourite restaurant
where, given my natural funk
I think of as restraint,
I might have avoided that Irish drunk
whose slow jibes
Michael parried, but whose quick jab

left him forever at a loss for words.
For how he would delib-
erate on whether two six-foot boards
sealed with ship's
varnish and two tea-chests
(another move) on which all this rests

is a table; or this merely a token
of some ur-chair,
or—being broken—
a chair at all: the mind's a razor
on the body's strop.
And the soap-pig? It's a bar of soap,

now the soap-sliver
in a flowered dish
that I work each morning into a lather
with my father's wobbling-brush,
then reconcile to its pool of glop
on my mother's wash-stand's marble top.

## THE TOE-TAG

They became you, that pair of kid gloves
so small
they folded into the halves
of a walnut-shell.

———

A Rolls-Royce Silver Shadow
idling in the drive,
a Silver Ghost
in the meadow,
their seats upholst-
ered with the hides of stillborn calves.

———

A jigger of blood on your swish organza.

———

The intricate, salt-stiff
family motif
in a month-drowned Aranman's *geansaí*
becomes you. Your ecstasy
at having found
among the orangery's body-bags
of peat one pot of sand
and one untimely, indigo-flowering cactus
like a big toe with its tag.

## GONE

Since one of our functions is to forget
the smell of an apple-cannery,
talcumed catkins,
the forked

twig astounding itself as a catapult,
the subcutaneous
freckle on a cue-ball,
the story of O. Henry,

what should we make of that couple
we never quite became,
both turning up one lunch-hour

in an auction-room
to bid, unwittingly, against each other
for the set of ten Venetian goblets?

## PAUL KLEE: *THEY'RE BITING*

The lake supports some kind of bathysphere,
an Arab dhow

and a fishing-boat
complete with languorous net.

Two caricature anglers
have fallen hook, line and sinker

for the goitred,
spiny fish-caricatures

with which the lake is stocked.
At any moment all this should connect.

When you sent me a postcard of *They're Biting*
there was a plane sky-writing

*I LOVE YOU* over Hyde Park.
Then I noticed the exclamation-mark

at the painting's heart.
It was as if I'd already been given the word

by a waist-thick conger
mouthing *No* from the fishmonger's

otherwise-drab window
into which I might glance to check my hair.

## SOMETHING ELSE

When your lobster was lifted out of the tank
to be weighed
I thought of woad,
of madders, of fugitive, indigo inks,

of how Nerval
was given to promenade
a lobster on a gossamer thread,
how, when a decent interval

had passed
(*son front rouge encor du baiser de la reine*)
and his hopes of Adrienne

proved false,
he hanged himself from a lamp-post
with a length of chain, which made me think

of something else, then something else again.

## SUSHI

'Why do we waste so much time in arguing?'
We were sitting at the sushi-bar
drinking *Kirin* beer
and watching the Master chef
fastidiously shave
salmon, tuna and yellowtail
while a slightly more volatile
apprentice
fanned the rice,
every grain of which was magnetized
in one direction—east.
Then came translucent strips
of octopus,
squid and conger,
pickled ginger
and pale-green horseradish . . .
'It's as if you've some kind of death-wish.
You won't even talk . . .'
On the sidewalk
a woman in a leotard
with a real leopard
in tow.
For an instant I saw beyond the roe
of sea-urchins,
the erogenous
zones of shad and sea-bream;
I saw, when the steam
cleared, how this apprentice
had scrimshandered a rose's
exquisite petals
not from some precious metal
or wood or stone
('I might just as well be eating alone.')
but the tail-end of a carrot:
how when he submitted this work of art
to the Master—

*Is it not the height of arrogance*
*to propose that God's no more arcane*
*than the smack of oregano,*
*orgone,*
*the inner organs*
*of beasts and fowls, the mines of Arigna,*
*the poems of Louis Aragon?—*
it might have been alabaster
or jade
the Master so gravely weighed
from hand to hand
with the look of a man unlikely to confound
Duns Scotus, say, with Scotus Eriugena.

## 7, MIDDAGH STREET

**WYSTAN**

Quinquereme of Nineveh from distant Ophir;
a blizzard off the Newfoundland coast
had, as we slept, metamorphosed

the *Champlain's* decks
to a wedding cake,
on whose uppermost tier stood Christopher

and I like a diminutive bride and groom.
A heavy-skirted Liberty would lunge
with her ice-cream
at two small, anxious

boys, and Erika so grimly wave
from the quarantine-launch
she might as truly have been my wife
as, later that day, Barcelona was Franco's.

There was a time when I thought it mattered
what happened in Madrid

or Seville
and, in a sense, I haven't changed
my mind; the forces of Good and Evil
were indeed ranged

against each other, though not unambiguously.
I went there on the off-chance
they'd let me try
my hand at driving an ambulance;

there turned out to be some bureau-
cratic hitch.
When I set out for the front on a black burro
it promptly threw me in the ditch.

I lay there for a year, disillusioned, dirty,
until a firing-party

of Chinese soldiers
came by, leading dishevelled ponies.
They arranged a few sedimentary boulders
over the body of a Japanese

spy they'd shot
but weren't inclined to bury,
so that one of his feet stuck out.
When a brindled pariah

began to gnaw
on it, I recognized the markings of the pup
whose abscessed paw
my father had lanced on our limestone doorstep.

———

Those crucial years he tended
the British wounded

in Egypt, Gallipoli
and France, I learned to play

Isolde to my mother's Tristan.
Are they now tempted to rechristen

their youngest son
who turned his back on Albion

a Quisling?
Would their *chaise-longue*

philosophers have me somehow inflate
myself and float

above their factories and pylons
like a flat-footed barrage-balloon?

———

For though I would gladly return to Eden
as that ambulance-driver
or air-raid warden
I will never again ford the river
to parley with the mugwumps
and fob them off with monocles and mumps;
I will not go back as *Auden*.

———

And were Yeats living at this hour
it should be in some ruined tower

not malachited Ballylee
where he paid out to those below

one gilt-edged scroll from his pencil
as though he were part-Rapunzel

and partly Delphic oracle.
As for his crass, rhetorical

posturing, 'Did that play of mine
send out certain men (*certain* men?)

the English shot . . .?'
the answer is 'Certainly not'.

If Yeats had saved his pencil-lead
would certain men have stayed in bed?

For history's a twisted root
with art its small, translucent fruit

and never the other way round.
The roots by which we were once bound

are severed here, in any case,
and we are all now dispossessed;

prince, poet, construction worker,
salesman, soda fountain jerker—

all equally isolated.
Each loads flour, sugar and salted

beef into a covered wagon
and strikes out for his Oregon,

each straining for the ghostly axe
of a huge, blond-haired lumberjack.

———

'If you want me look for me under your boot-soles';
when I visited him in a New Hampshire hospital
where he had almost gone for a Burton
with peritonitis
Louis propped himself up on an ottoman
and read aloud the ode to Whitman
from *Poeta en Nueva York*.
The impossible Eleanor Clark
had smuggled in a pail of oysters and clams
and a fifth column
of Armagnac.
Carson McCullers extemporized a blues harmonica
on urinous pipkins and pannikins
that would have flummoxed Benjamin Franklin.
I left them, so, to the reign
of the ear of corn
and the journey-work of the grass-leaf
and found my way next morning to Bread Loaf
and the diamond-shaped clearing in the forest
where I learned to play softball with Robert Frost.

———

For I have leapt with Kierkegaard
out of the realm of Brunel and Arkwright

with its mills, canals and railway-bridges
into this great void
where Chester and I exchanged love-pledges
and vowed
our marriage-vows. As he lay asleep
last night the bronze of his exposed left leg
made me want nothing so much as to weep.
I thought of the terrier, of plague,

of Aschenbach at the Lido.
Here was my historical
Mr W. H., my 'onlie begetter' and fair lady;
*for nothing this wide universe I call . . .*


### GYPSY

*Save thou, my rose; in it thou art my all.*
In Mother's dream my sister, June,
was dressed in her usual cal-
ico but whistling an unfamiliar tune
when a needlecord
*dea ex machina*
came hoofing it across the boards—
a Texan moo-cow
with a red flannel tongue,
a Madamish leer
and a way with the song
it insinuated into Mother's ear;
'You've only to put me in the act
to be sure of the Orpheum contract.'

She did. We followed that corduroy cow
through Michigan, Kansas,
Idaho.
But the vaudeville audiences
were dwindling. Mack Sennett's
Bathing Beauties
had seen to that. Shakespeare's Sonnets,
*Das Kapital*, Boethius,
Dainty June and her Newsboy Songsters—
all would succumb to Prohibition,
G-men, gangsters,
bathtub gin.
June went legit. In Minneapolis
I spirit-gummed pink gauze on my nipples.

And suddenly I was waiting in the wings
for the big production-routine
to end. I was wearing a swanky
gaberdine
over my costume of sherbet-green tulle.
I watched two girl-Pawnees
in little else but pony-tails
ride two paint ponies
on a carousel. They loosed mock arrows
into the crowd, then hung
on for dear life when the first five rows
were showered with horse-dung.
I've rarely felt so close to nature
as in Billy Minsky's Burlesque Theatre.

This was Brooklyn, 1931. I was an under-age
sixteen. Abbott and Costello
were sent out front while the stage
was hosed down and the ponies hustled
back to the *Ben Hur* stables.
By the time I came on
the customers were standing on the tables,
snapping like caymans
and booing even the fancy cyclorama
depicting the Garden of Eden.
Gradually the clamour
faded as I shed
all but three of my green taffeta fig-leaves
and stood naked as Eve.

'I loved the act. Maybe you'd wanna buy
Sam?' asked Nudina, over a drink.
Nudina danced with a boa
constrictor that lived under the sink
in the women's room. 'He's a dear.'
'So *this* is a speakeasy,'
Mother whispered. We'd ordered beer
and pizza.

'Don't look now,' said Nudina, 'but Waxey's
just come in.' 'Waxey?' 'A friend of mine
from Jersey. Runs applejack
through special pipelines
in the sewers. Never even been subpoenaed.
But let's get back to discussing the serpent.'

I've no time for any of that unladylike stuff.
An off-the-shoulder shoulder-strap,
the removal of one glove—
it's knowing exactly when to stop
that matters,
what to hold back, some sweet disorder . . .
The same goes for the world of letters.
When I met George Davis in Detroit
he managed the Seven Arts
bookstore. I was on the Orpheum circuit.
Never, he says, give all thy heart;
there's more enterprise in walking not quite
naked. Now he has me confined to quarters
while we try to solve *The G-String Murders*.

We were looking over my scrapbook entries
from *The New Yorker*,
*Fortune, Town and Country*,
when I came on this from the *Daily Worker*:
'Striptease is a capitalistic cancer,
a product of the profit system.'
Perhaps we cannot tell the dancer
from the dance. Though I've grown accustomed
to returning the stare
of a life-size cut-out of Gypsy Rose Lee
from the World's Fair
or *The Ziegfeld Follies*
I keep that papier-mâché cow's head packed
just in case vaudeville does come back.

## BEN

Come back, Peter. Come back, Ben Britten.
The monstrous baritone

of a flushed, ungainly
Cyril Connolly

swaggers across the ocean
from the crow's-nest of *Horizon*

to chide Pimpernell and Parsnip
with deserting Europe's 'sinking ship';

Auden and Isherwood
have no sense of the greater good

but 'an eye on the main chance'.
Harold Nicolson's latest intelligence

has them in league with Goebbels.
And the Dean of St Paul's?—

'Since you left us, the stink is less.'
Then a question in the House.

The Minister, in his reply, takes Wystan
for the tennis-star H. W. Austin

which, given his line in tennis shoes
(though not the soup-stained ties

and refusal ever to change his smalls),
seems just. Perhaps the Dean of St Paul's

himself did time
with Uncle Wizz in an airless room

(a collaboration on *John* Bunyan?)
and has some grounds for his opinion.

In this, as in so many things,
it won't be over till the fat lady sings.


**CHESTER**

The fat lady sings to *Der Rosenkavalier*
*Die Zeit, die ist ein sonderbar Ding*;
in time Octavian will leave her
for Sophie, Sophie

leave Ochs:
Feldmarschalls trade their Marschallins
for those time-honoured trophies—
cunts, or fresh, young cocks.

Among the miscellaneous
Jack Tars
I met last week in a Sands Street bar

I came on one whose uncircumcised dong's
sand-vein was a seam of beryl, abstruse
as this lobster's.


**SALVADOR**

This lobster's not a lobster but the telephone
that rang for Neville Chamberlain.

It droops from a bare branch
above a plate, on which the remains of lunch

include a snapshot of Hitler
and some boiled beans left over

from *Soft Construction: A Premonition
of Civil War*. When Breton

hauled me before his kangaroo-court
I quoted the Manifesto; we must disregard

moral and aesthetic considerations
for the integrity of our dream-visions.

What if I dreamed of Hitler as a masochist
who raises his fist

only to be beaten?
I might have dreamed of fucking André Breton

he so pooh-poohed my *Enigma of William Tell*.
There I have Lenin kneel

with one massive elongated buttock
and the elongated peak

of his cap supported by two forked sticks.
This time there's a raw beef-steak

on the son's head. My father croons a lullaby.
Is it that to refer, however obliquely,

is to refer? In October 1934,
I left Barcelona by the back door

with a portfolio of work
for my first one-man show in New York.

A starry night. The howling of dogs.
The Anarchist taxi-driver carried two flags,

Spanish and Catalan. Which side was I on?
Not one, or both, or none.

I who had knelt with Lenin in Breton's court
and sworn allegiance to the proletariat

had seen the chasm
between myself and surrealism

begin as a hair-crack on a tile.
In *Soft Construction* I painted a giant troll

tearing itself apart limb
by outlandish limb.

Among the broken statues of Valladolid
there's one whose foot's still welded

to the granite plinth
from which, like us, it draws its strength.

From that, and from those few boiled beans.
We cannot gormandize upon

the flesh of Cain and Abel
without some melancholic vegetable

bringing us back to earth, to the boudoir
in the abattoir.

Our civil wars, the crumbling of empires,
the starry nights without number

safely under our belts,
have only slightly modified the tilt

of the acanthus leaf,
its spiky puce-and-alabaster an end in itself.

# CARSON

In itself, this old, three-storey brownstone
is unremarkable, and yet so vivid was the reverie
in which it appeared to George one night
that when he drove
next morning to Brooklyn Heights
he found it true. I had just left Reeves
and needed a place to stay. As must Wynstan,

dear Wynnie-Pooh, who's given to caution
the rest of us every
time we sit down, be it to jerky
or this afternoon's Thanksgiving dinner, every
blessed time, 'We'll have crawfish, turkey,
salad and savoury,
and no political discussion'—

a form of grace
that would surely have raised an eyebrow
at even the Last Supper,
never mind a household where no time ago
when the Richard Wrights moved in the super
moved out, unwilling, it seemed, to draw and hew
and tend the furnace for fellow Negroes.

Nothing is too much bother
for Eva, our cook, a former Cotton Club chorine
whom Gypsy found, who can so glamourize
pork-belly, grits and greens
I imagine myself back in Columbus,
Georgia, imagine, indeed, a paddle-steamer careen
and clarion up the East River

from the Chattahoochee, its cargo of blue dimity,
oil lamps and the things
of childhood washed
overboard; my Christmas stocking

limps from the stern like an oriole's nest:
when an orange in the toe spreads its black wing
the stocking, too, is empty.

The magnolia tree at my window's a bonsai
in the glass globe
I jiggle like a cocktail-
waiter from the Keynote Club,
so that Chester's Kwakiutl
false-face and glib,
Jane and Paul Bowles, the chimpanzee

and its trainer, Gypsy
and hers, are briefly caught up in an eddy
of snow; pennies
from heaven, Wynstan's *odi*
*atque amo* of Seconal and bennies:
then my cloudy
globe unclouds to reveal the tipsy

MacNeice a monarch
lying in state on a Steinway baby grand
between the rotting
carcasses of two pack-mules from *Un Chien Andalou*
while a strait-laced Benjamin Britain
picks out a rondo
in some elusive minor key.

If only I might as readily dismiss
the chord a fire-siren struck
in all of us this afternoon (we chased the engines
two or three blocks
till we tired) or the ingenuous
slow-slow-quick
I felt again for Reeves—the Dismas

on my right side—or Erika Mann's
piercing my left

as we stood in Cranberry Street; flute-music,
panting of hinds, her spindrift
gaze; peacocks, sandalwood, the musky
otto of her cleft:
two girls, I thought, two girls in silk kimonos.


LOUIS

Both beautiful, one a gazebo.
When Hart Crane fell
from the *Orizaba*
it was into the *trou normand* of the well

at Carrickfergus Castle.
All very Ovidian,
as the ghostly
*Healfdene*

once remarked of both sorts of kipper
we were forced to eat
at supper

every night in Reykjavik;
one tasted of toe-nails, one of the thick
skin on the soles of the feet.

———

He now affects an ulster lined with coypu
and sashays like an albino rabbit
down the same Fifth Avenue
where Avida Dollars
once squired an ocelot
on a solid
gold chain snaffled from Bonwit Teller's.
It seems that Scott Fitzgerald wrote *Ivanhoe*
or the *Rubáiyát*
and Chester Kallman = Agape.

_____

Wystan likes to tell how he lost his faith
in human nature

in a movie-theatre
at 85th

and York, where the neighbourhood Huns
had taken a break from baking buns

to egg
on Hitler to his *Sieg*

*im Poland*; the heavy bear that went to bed
with Delmore Schwartz was bad

and the rye in Yorkville's *Schwartzbrot*
shot through with ergot.

Since when he's set himself up as a stylite
waiting for hostilities

to cease, a Dutch master
intent only on painting an oyster

or lemon
(all those afternoons in the Ashmolean)

or the slur of light in a red goblet
while Montagues and Capulets

run riot, as they did five years ago
in the Short Strand and Sandy Row.

Then my father preached 'Forget the past'
and episcopized

into the wind
and again refused to sign the Covenant;

though the seam of gold a Unitedman strikes
in Wicklow in 1796

which Parnell will later pan and assay
to make a ring for Kitty O'Shea

was well and truly played
out, no bishop could ever quite contemplate

a life merely nasty, British and short.
Delmore was ushered

from that same movie-theatre
with 'Everything you do matters';

the displacement of soap-suds in a basin
may have some repercussion

for a distant ship:
only last night I tried to butt the uneven

pages of a *Belfast Newsletter* from 1937
into some sort of shape . . .

―――

*Imagine a great white highway*
*a quarter of a mile broad*
*extending the length of Ireland*
*from the Giant's Causeway*
*to Mizen Head*
*and you can grasp the magnitude*
*of our annual output of linen.*

―――

Among the blue flowers of the flax a linnet
sang out 'Lundy'

at the implications of that bleach-
green. 'It was merely a figure of speech.'

'Call it what you like.
The grey skies of an Irish Republic

are as nothing compared to this blue dome.'
He tailed off over the flax-dam

to return with a charm of goldfinches
who assailed me with their 'Not an inch'

and their 'No', and yet again, 'No'.
As they asperged me with kerosene

I recognized the voice of Sir Edward Carson;
'Bid me strike a match and blow.'

———

In dreams begin responsibilities;
it was on account of just such an allegory
that Lorca
was riddled with bullets

and lay mouth-down
in the fickle shadow of his own blood.
As the drunken soldiers of the *Gypsy Ballads*
started back for town

they heard him calling through the mist,
'When I die leave the balcony shutters open.'
For poetry *can* make things happen—
not only can, but *must*—

and the very painting of that oyster
is in itself a political gesture.

As O'Daly well knows. It was in the olive-grove
where Lorca's buried
that he envisaged *Two Pieces of Bread*
*Expressing the Idea of Love*

with its miniature duellists and chess-pawn
expressing also his idea of Spain.
(If only he were here
today to make his meaning absolutely clear.)

So that, for me, brandy and smoked
quail and a crumpled baguette
conjure O'Daly, then themselves, then Beckett's
'¡Uptherepublic!',

then Beatrice and Benedick
in the back seat of Eleanor's mother's Pontiac.

———

After drinking all night in a Sands Street shebeen
where a sailor played a melodeon
made from a merman's spine
I left by the back door of Muldoon's

(it might have been the Rotterdam)
on a Monday morning, falling in with
the thousands of shipyardmen who tramped
towards the front gates of Harland and Wolff.

The one-eyed foreman had strayed out of Homer;
'MacNeice? That's a Fenian name.'
As if to say, 'None of your sort, none of you

will as much as go for a rubber hammer
never mind chalk a rivet, never mind caulk a seam
on the quinquereme of Nineveh.'

# MADOC: A MYSTERY 1990

I ran into Foley six months ago in a dubbing suite in Los Angeles. He was half-way through post-production on a remake of *The Hoodlum Priest*, a film for which I've a special affection since my cousin Marina McCall was an extra in the first version. She had worked as a nanny for various movie stars, including Tippi Hedren, and seemed to spend half her time in the sky between New York and LA. Though I sat through three or four showings of *The Hoodlum Priest* in the Olympic Cinema, Moy, and carefully scrutinized the crowd scenes, I was never able to point to Marina with anything like conviction.

Foley was working on a sequence involving a police line-up, in which the victim shuffled along, stopped with each suspect in turn, then shuffled on. At a critical moment, she dropped a key on the floor. Foley was having trouble matching sound to picture on this last effect. I was struck by the fact that, just as early radio announcers had worn dinner-jackets, he was wearing an ultramarine tuxedo. After half a dozen attempts, he decided to call it quits, and emerged from his sound booth like a diver from a bathysphere. He offered me a tidbit that tasted only of mesquite.

I wanted to say something about Marina, something about an 'identity parade' in which I once took part, something about the etymology of 'tuxedo', but I found myself savouring the play between 'booth' and 'bathy-', 'quits' and 'mesquite', and began to 'misquote' myself:

> *When he sookied a calf down a boreen*
> *it was through Indo-European.*
> *When he clicked at a donkey carting dung*
> *your grandfather had an African tongue.*
> *You seem content to ventriloquize the surf.*

Foley swallowed whatever it was:

> *Still defending that same old patch of turf?*
> *Have you forgotten that 'hoodlum' is back-slang*
> *for the leader of a San Francisco street-gang?*

He flounced off into his cubicle. Though this, our only exchange, was remarkable for its banality, Foley has had some profound effect on me. These past six months I've sometimes run a little ahead of myself, but mostly I lag behind, my footfalls already pre-empted by their echoes.


## TEA

I was rooting through tea-chest after tea-chest
as they drifted in along Key West

when I chanced on 'Pythagoras in America':
the book had fallen open at a book-mark

of tea; a tassel
of black watered silk from a Missal;

a tea-bird's black tail-feather.
All I have in the house is some left-over

squid cooked in its own ink
and this unfortunate cup of tea. Take it. Drink.


## CAPERCAILLIES

In a deep, in a dark wood, somewhere north of Loch Lomond,
Saint Joan and I should be in our element;
the electroplated bracken and furze
have only gradually given way to pines and firs

in which a—what?—a straggler from Hadrian's
sixth legion squats over the latrine

and casts a die. His spurs suggest a renegade
Norman knight, as does his newly-prinked

escutcheon of sable on a field of sable,
whereas the hens—three, four, five—in fashionable
yellow gum-boots, are meekly back from Harrods.
Once a year (tonight, perhaps) such virtue has its reward;

raising his eyes to heaven—as if about to commit hara-
kiri—the cock will hop on each in turn and, unhurri-
edly, do three or four push-ups,
reaching all too soon for a scuffed Elizabeth Bishop.

'Paul? Was it you put the *pol* in polygamy
or was it somebody else?' While their flesh is notably gamey
even in bilberry-time, their winter tack's
mainly pine-shoots, so they now smack

of nothing so much as turpentine.
Room 233. Through a frosted, half-opened
window I listen to the love-burps and borborygms of a capercaillie
('horse of the woods', the name means in Gaelic)

as he challenges me to mortal combat.
The following morning, Saint Joan has moved into the camp-bed.


## ASRA

The night I wrote your name in biro on my wrist
we would wake before dawn; back to back: duellists.

## THE PANTHER

For what it's worth, the last panther in Massachusetts
was brought to justice
in the woods beyond these meadows
and hung by its heels from a meat-hook
in what is now our kitchen.

(The house itself is something of a conundrum,
built as it was by an Ephraim Cowan from Antrim.)

I look in one evening while Jean
is jelly-making. She has rendered down pounds of grapes
and crab-apples
to a single jar
at once impenetrable and clear:
'Something's missing. This simply won't take.'

The air directly under the meat-hook—
it quakes, it quickens;
on a flagstone, the smudge of the tippy-tip of its nose.


## CAULIFLOWERS

*Plants that glow in the dark have been developed through gene-splicing, in which
light-producing bacteria from the mouths of fish are introduced to cabbage, carrots
and potatoes.*

— THE NATIONAL ENQUIRER

More often than not he stops at the headrig to light
his pipe
and try to regain
his composure. The price of cauliflowers
has gone down
two weeks in a row on the Belfast market.

From here we can just make out
a platoon of Light
Infantry going down
the road to the accompaniment of a pipe-
band. The sun glints on their silver-
buttoned jerkins.

My uncle, Patrick Regan,
has been leaning against the mud-guard
of the lorry. He levers
open the bonnet and tinkers with a light
wrench at the hose-pipe
that's always going down.

Then he himself goes down
to bleed oil into a jerry-can.
My father slips the pipe
into his scorch-marked
breast pocket and again makes light
of the trepanned cauliflowers.

All this as I listened to lovers
repeatedly going down
on each other in the next room . . . 'light
of my life . . .' in a motel in Oregon.
All this. Magritte's
pipe

and the pipe-
bomb. White Annetts. Gillyflowers.
Margaret,
are you grieving? My father going down
the primrose path with Patrick Regan.
All gone out of the world of light.

All gone down
the original pipe. And the cauliflowers
in an unmarked pit, that were harvested by their own light.

# THE BRIEFCASE

*For Seamus Heaney*

I held the briefcase at arm's length from me;
the oxblood or liver
eelskin with which it was covered
had suddenly grown supple.

I'd been waiting in line for the cross-town
bus when an almighty cloudburst
left the sidewalk a raging torrent.

And though it contained only the first
inkling of this poem, I knew I daren't
set the briefcase down
to slap my pockets for an obol—

for fear it might slink into a culvert
and strike out along the East River
for the sea. By which I mean the 'open' sea.

# MADOC: A MYSTERY

[THALES]

When he ventured forth from the smallroom
he activated a sensor-tile
that set off the first in a series of alarms
and sent a ripple through Unitel.

He was running now. A frog
scrawled across a lily-pond.
A kind of hopscotch frug.
There'd be a twenty second

delay. Then he'd almost certainly succumb
to their cotton-candy
scum-foam.
He'd only to whisper 'In Xanadu . . .'

and smile 'did Kubla Khan . . .'
His voice-count
was still good. Then a retina-scan.
On the stroke of three the door opened

and all hell broke loose.
There were Geckoes armed with Zens
to either side. He let go of his old valise.
And since

there was nowhere to turn
he turned to the unruffled, waist-deep hedge
with its furbelow of thorns
and deckle-edged

razor-ribbon.
One or two Geckoes began to applaud.
He took the plunge. Whereupon
he became just another twist in the plot.

[ANAXIMANDER]

'Are you telling me that South was as free as a bird
to wander through the Dome
and it wasn't until he went to take a dump . . .'
'Then we knew something untoward

had happened.' 'How?' 'He weighed more rather than less
when he left the crapper.'
'Much more?' 'Exactly as much as the scrap of paper
we repossessed from his valise.'


[ANAXIMENES]

The Geckoes lowered their stun-guns
and looked askance

when an Omnipod
scuttled

along the scarp
of trifoliate Chinese orange

on which he'd whittled
himself down to size.

They could see this was no saniteam
but a wet-set

out for revenge.
They heard him scream

'The fluted cypresses rear'd up
their living obelisks'

as a whatsit
was clamped to his bod.

Then an oxygen-mask.
And, though one of his eyes

was totally written-off,
he was harnessed to a retinagraph.

## [PYTHAGORAS]

'It looked as if he'd simply xferred the motto
from the Roanoke Rood.'
'The which?' 'The Roanoke Rood or Rule.
A scorch-marked lump of wood

they found somewhere on the Outer Rink
at the turn of the century.
It's under a sheet of imaglass
in West 14.'

'Where South had limited right of entry.'
'Exactly. But other than this motto—"CROATAN"—
it was mud.'

'Until?' 'Until we discovered his gloss
in sympathetic ink:
C[*oleridge*] RO[*bert Southey The S*]ATAN[*ic School*].'


## [HERACLITUS]

So that, though it may seem somewhat improbable,
all that follows
flickers and flows
from the back of his right eyeball.


## [PARMENIDES]

A woodchuck gets up on its hind legs and tail
to check the azimuth
and squinny
down the fork in the trail

where the Way of Seeming and the Way of Truth
diverge. He upsets
his own little tin pot and trivet
to tumble-pour

down the burrow
from which he derived.
September, 1798. What could be more apposite
than that into this vale

a young ass or hinny
bear Samuel Taylor Coleridge?
We see him reach
into his pantaloons for a small, sea-green vial,

then be overwhelmed by another pang of guilt.
A flock of siskins
or some such finches
blunders up from the Susquehanna.

Given the vagaries
and caracoles
of her star-gazing Narragansett colt
it's unlikely that Sara Fricker

will ever make good the yards, feet and inches
between herself and S.T.C. A grackle
blurts out from the choke-cherries.
The colt can no longer suppress a snicker.

[EMPEDOCLES]

The woodchuck has had occasion
to turn into a moccasin.

## [ANAXAGORAS]

—————

For a week now, since he came down with a fever,
Cornplanter and Red Jacket

have kept a vigil by Handsome Lake.
Sassafras. Elder.

Ewe's-milk.
They look at each other. They speculate

on whether his chest might be colder.
They press a rust-speckled,

jagged
glass to his mouth. It refuses to mist over.

—————

In the light of the X Y Z affair
America and France are limbering up for war.

—————

Near Femme Osage creek, on the lower Missouri,
Daniel Boone

comes on a beaver caught in two separate
traps.

It has gnawed both drubs
to the bone.

This beaver, like the woodchuck, is an emissary
from the Great Spirit.

[PROTAGORAS]

At which Alexander Cinnamond, the Scots-
Irish scout,

unbuttons his saddle-holster.
He's undertaken to lead them to Ulster

for a keg of powder and a pair
of ear-rings. They're now half-way there.

De dum, de dum, de dum, de dum,
de dum, de dum, de dum, de dum.

Cinnamond fondles a tobacco-
pouch made from the scrotal sac

of a Conestoga who must, we suppose,
have meddled with the Paxton Boys.

He muses to himself
as he raises it to his mouth

and teases open its gossamerish thongs:
'Mon is the mezjur of all thungs.'

[ZENO]

Perhaps this was indeed a Seneca buck
whose low-pitched chortle

from among the choke-cherries
threw Sara into momentary

disarray.
A life-sized turtle

in red and yellow ochres
scram-

bles aimlessly about his torso.
When he goes to scratch his back

there's a quiver
of fully-fledged arrows.

By which time Sara will have recovered
her perfect equilibrium.


[SOCRATES]

———

While one by one the rest of the cavalcade
draw level
with her in the glade.
Her sisters, Edith Southey and Mary Lovell,

are astride a strawberry roan.
Their man-servant, Shad,
is driving a spanking-new, iron-
shod

wagon in which Lovell himself is laid.
Three days ago, a wood-sprite
worried his shoulder-blade.
The wound has begun to suppurate.

Messrs Allen, Burnett, Le Grice and Favell
dismount and pitch

the first of several
bell-tents. A pure-white spaniel bitch

runs rings round them. Cinnamond builds
a fire, helps Lovell to the shelter of a cairn
of stones and applies another poultice
of hemlock-bark and acorns.

———

A thrum of hooves. If Southey is to Bucephalus
as a flame is to its wick
then Southey is a flame.

He clutches a small, already-battered valise,
a sheaf of quills, a quire of vellum.
He cancels everything in his wake.

[LEUCIPPUS]

And in the twinkling of an eye
the weather-vane
swiggles at its own behest
and the chest

of tools, the great auger,
the plow-sock,
the sacks
of flour and sugar . . .

[DEMOCRITUS]

The rip-saw, sundry axes,
some boxes
of sea-salt,
the cast-iron skillet,

the meal-ark,
the muddle of ropes
and barrel-hoops,
salted herrings, salted pork,

assorted helves and handles,
the tallow candles
and pewter
candle-sticks, the keg of powder,

the griddle,
the dozen-odd bags
of seed, the pearwood box
of tricks, the cradle,

the mahogany desk,
the cask
of rum, the bath with claw feet,
go smattering into the void.

[ANTISTHENES]

Coleridge follows a white spaniel
through the caverns of the Domdaniel.

**[PLATO]**

*My mother said I was mad; if so, she was bit by me, for she wished to go as much as I did. Coleridge and I preached Pantisocracy and Aspheterism everywhere. These are two new words, the first signifying the equal government of all, and the other the generalization of individual property; words well understood in the city of Bristol.*

(Southey)

**[DIOGENES]**

When Sara stretches into the dark
of the meal-ark

her hand is taken by a hand.

———

A tongue-in-cheek snail goes metic-
ulously across a mattock's

blade-end.

———

As Southey squats in the claw-foot tub,
oblivious of the shadow-rub

of horses against his tent.

**[ARISTOTLE]**

*Now, if you are in the mood for a reverie, fancy only me in America; imagine my ground uncultivated since the creation, and see me wielding the ax, now to cut down the tree, and now the snakes that nestled in it. Then see me grubbing up the roots, and building a nice, snug little dairy with them; three rooms in my cottage, and my only companion some poor negro whom I have bought on purpose to emancipate. After a hard day's toil, see me sleep upon rushes, and, in very bad weather, take out my casette and write to you, for you shall positively write to me in America. Do not imagine I shall leave rhyming or philosophizing; till at last comes an ill-looking Indian with a tomahawk, and scalps me—a most melancholy proof that society is very bad, and that I shall have done very little to improve it. So vanity, vanity will come from my lips, and poor Southey will either be cooked for a Cherokee, or oysterized by a tiger.*

(Southey)

**[THEOPHRASTUS]**

De dum, de dum, de dum, de dum, de dum.

**[PYRRHO]**

———

New York. In his closing remarks to the Wigwam
of the Order of Saint Tammany
the Republican mugwump
Aaron Burr, alludes not only to *Timon*

and *Titus Andronicus*
but Milton

by way of Gray; he drinks
to the demise of 'mute, inglorious' Hamilton

and his Federalist chaff:
the Tammanyites respond with a grudging chorus
of 'Aaron, Aaron, Aaron . . .'

———

The spaniel ushers Coleridge along a path
covered with grass
to a belt of blue beads, a bow made of horn.

[EUCLID]

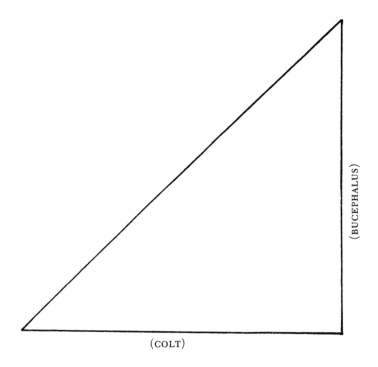

(BUCEPHALUS)

(COLT)

[ZENO]

It had dawned on Shad that something was askew
when he went to draw and hew

and found, under the mottled porch
of a clump of birch,

the water spaniel Cerberus,
her throat slashed like a silk-lined purse

and her eyes
wide-open, world-weary and oddly wise.



[EPICURUS]

They tip
Coleridge into the icy tub

to bring him round.
His ornate

*serge-de-Nîmes*
vest and pantaloons

are laudanum-
mackled. His eyes a raccoon's.

He's coming to
his senses when a toe

stirs, then the right fore-claw,
and the tub begins to cla-

mber like an alligator
towards the birch-bower.

The spaniel reeks of elder-
flowers.

A length of tarred twine
dangles from a twig with (1)

a silver ear-ring
and (2) a salted herring.


[ARCHIMEDES]

Coleridge leaps out of the tub. Imagine that.


[AENESIDEMUS]

We doubt even that we doubt. Why on earth
would Cinnamond, if Cinnamond
it was, abduct one of the 'milliners of Bath'?
Unless, of course,

she did go willingly. If not,
why no ransom-note?
How could Sara so readily
abandon Berkeley and Hartley?

What are we to make of Bucephalus
striking out due north,
the colt
and a pack-horse

due west? In any case, both
trails are already cold,

both almost certainly false.
It remains to be seen what they have in mind.


[SENECA]

———

A woman falls to earth, onto the muddy turtle-back of the earth.

———

There Wind has his way with her, and leaves her two arrows as tokens, one untipped, one tipped with flint.

———

Her sons are Flint and Sapling.

———

Wherever Sapling runs, trees leap up behind him. Whenever he throws a handful of earth, living things rush off in all directions. Each winter, the animals are impounded by Flint in a cave of ice. In spring, Sapling sets them free.

———

Sapling makes two-way rivers for easy canoe-journeys. But Flint undoes the work, causing rivers to flow, like this, in one direction only.

———

And the river flows into Handsome Lake.


[DIONYSIUS]

Who hears his name called by each of three angels.
They are wearing skunk bonnets.
Their jowls
are daubed with lamp-black and vermilion paint.

## [EPICTETUS]

*I carried Epictetus in my pocket till my very heart was ingrained
with it, as a pig's bones become red by feeding him upon madder.*

(Southey)

## [PTOLEMY]

NEW YORK

PENNSYLVANIA

Athens  O

Ulster  O

Susquehanna

[GALEN]

It transpires that Bucephalus is even now
pumping a jet
of spunk into the rowdy-dow-dow
of some hoity-toity little skewbald jade.

[ORIGEN]

A tavern in New Orleans. John Evans drains a glass of port:
'It seemed to me that the Omaha chief, Blackbird,
though he fed his enemies arsenic,
was a gentleman like yourself.' His companion in the snug

is Brigadier-General James Wilkinson,
on whose behalf he raised the Spanish ensign
over the Mandan villages:
'That the Mandans are Welsh is, then, fallacious?'

Evans agitates his dregs:
'They're no more Welshmen than Spaniards,
though time and time again I watched them geld

a yearling colt
with a rawhide lanyard
and a sherd of flint. No. No more Welshmen than Turks.'

[PLOTINUS]

———

The next morning, before they pass under
the mare's tail of a waterfall

where the Way of Reason
narrows to the Way of Faith,

Coleridge and Southey must pause
to draw lots. They wave

to Shad and the rest of their tearful,
much-depleted garrison,

who'll try for Ulster at their own pace
before the onset of winter.

———

Shad waves back, and bends for the mattock
he'll use to dig

a grave for the dog
when it comes to him in a flash—MADOC.

[AUGUSTINE]

May, 1799. The hamlet
of Carthage, New York, into which he has stumbled,

is constantly raided by Senecas.
The only street is a glorified mud-sink

which Southey is about to ford
when he recognizes the star on the forehead

of a shaggy-coated Bucephalus,
who points him in the direction of an ale-house.


[**PROCLUS**]

Might Allen and Favell be discussing metaphysics
as they lean on their bill-hooks?

They've already girdled
five acres of trees to make way for the cattle

and razor-back hogs.
Hartley frolics with one of the young Cayugas

who frequent the gate
of the stockade.

Her name is Bean. Her sisters are Corn and Squash.
The only sound is the swoosh

of a bull-roarer.
Favell spits in his palms: *Laborare est orare.*


[**PSEUDO-DIONYSIUS**]

In a second vision, Handsome Lake meets his favourite dog,
one of many

he saw fit to sacrifice
in last New Year's white dog ceremony.

It carries its own head, like a crest,
between its paws. It wags

its tail in recognition, springs up and licks his face.
Handsome Lake also meets Jesus Christ.


[BENEDICT]

Southey takes its tongue between finger and thumb
and the door-bell is struck dumb, de dum.


[BOETHIUS]

So furious are their grunts and groans, so fierce the blizzard
from a cedar-
bole they're cutting into shakes and studs
Shad and Le Grice have missed the clippety-clop of a letter

for Edith.
As she comes running out to them, the blade
of the rip-saw gives a last spasm
and struggles free. In the shored-up chasm

of the saw-pit, Shad begins to contemplate
one crinkled saw-tooth
as if everything depends on it. He's in such a lather

of sweat and blood and sawdust
that he might easily be mistaken for some kind of satyr
or wood-wizard.

## [SCOTUS ERIUGENA]

We can discern, through the tobacco-fug,
Cinnamond ensconced at a bench
with a stoneware jug

of punch
and a bowl of stew
before him. The floor's a midden

into which he might at any moment spew
potatoes, onions, carrots, mutton.
'What,' he riddles himself, 'is the difference

between an Irishmon and a puddle?'
When a voice pipes up, 'The bottle . . .'
Cinnamond frowns

in disbelief, then squawks and squalls
as Southey rams the sheaf of goose-quills
into his eyes.


## [AVICENNA]

'From his brimstone bed at break of day
a-walking the Devil is gone
to look at his snug little farm the Earth
and see how his stock went on . . .'

[ANSELM]

De dum, Te Deum, de dum, Te Deum, de dum.


[ABELARD]

The letter from Sara to Edith Southey's
stamped with her seal, a coronet

and the legend TOUJOURS GAI;
on a snig of hemp

or linsey-woolsey's
hung a teeny-weeny key;

and a message in her own *Lingo Grande*:
'Signifump. Signifump. Signifump.'


[AVERROES]

———

'He went into a rich bookseller's shop.
Quoth he, We are both of one college
for I sat myself like a cormorant once
hard by the Tree of Knowledge.'

———

Though he's now encumbered by two jennets
laden with pelts
Southey fairly jaunts
through the woods, humming a little ballad.

———

'As he went through Cold Bath Fields he saw
a solitary cell . . .'

[MAIMONIDES]

———

'And the Devil was pleased for it gave him a hint
for improving the prisons of . . .'

———

Coleridge stops in his tracks. A Seneca
wearing only a breech-

clout
and a skunk

bonnet and cradling an arquebus
has just stepped out

from behind a beech.
Coleridge is genuinely perplexed.

He unclasps and dabbles
in the portmanteau

for which Southey and he drew lots.
He brandishes John Eliot's

Algonquian bible
and quaveringly intones the name of 'Manitou'.

The Mohawk, as he turns out to be, goads
and bullies

him through the gateless gates
of Canada

and into
the formal gardens and unfathomable fountains

of this, the summer palace
of the Old Man of the Mountains.

[FIBONACCI]

Up a spiral staircase with precisely two hundred and thirty-three
steps, each conjured from the living rock.

[BACON]

Through the hoopless hoop of a black rainbow.

[AQUINAS]

To the room where Thayendanegea, Joseph Brant,
appears to him as in a dream,

his head shaved but for a scalp-lock
adorned with a white

feather, his bearskin
robe, his shirt a calico

print
set off by a solid brass

gorget, his sword-stick with its brass ferrule.
He offers Coleridge tea and scones,

pres-
erves and clotted cream.

He folds his arms: 'Would
you say you came here of your own free will?'


[DUNS SCOTUS]

Southey has wedged himself between two boulders
by the side of a creek.
His pine-cone fire splutters
out. Bucephalus speaks to him in halting Greek:

'This is indeed a holy place
dedicated to the sun god, Bel.'
Southey can but dimly make out the blaze
on his poll:

'Were the secret of the ogam
script on the edge of this standing stone
known to the Reverend Samson Occom
he would hold it in disdain.

Yet his own people, the Mohegan,
are the seed of the Celtic chieftain, Eoghan.'

[OCCAM]

One or two things we should know about Joseph Brant.

He was born in 1743, the son of a ginseng-gatherer.

His name means 'two sticks tied together'.

In the spring of 1761 he received a good conduct medal from George the Third for his services against the French.

He studied Hebrew, Latin and Greek at Wheelock's Academy, now Dartmouth College.

In 1776 he visited London, where the King presented him with a Mason's apron. He was interviewed by James Boswell for *The London Magazine*.

He sided with the British during the Revolutionary War.

In 1797 he dined with Aaron Burr and his daughter, Theodosia, who considered serving him a human head.

Though he is nominally 'King of the Mohawks' he is plagued by schisms.

Five years ago his son, Isaac, tried to kill him.

This past winter a strangled white dog was slung from a pole just
        outside Brant's Town.

This is enough to be going on with.

## [BURIDAN]

Since Bucephalus is neither more nor less
inclined
to the grey jennet's
shy come-hither

than the chestnut's
blatantly swollen gland
(not to speak of the cross
on her withers)

he'll dilly-dally
and dawdle and dither
until he's utterly
at a loss

as to the whys and wherefores
of either or either or either or either.

## [WYCLIFFE]

Another thing. In 1786 Brant again visited London. He met with the
Archbishop of Canterbury to discuss his new edition of the Mohawk
Prayer Book.

[MANDEVILLE]

It moulders now in the double-dusk
of the valise
along with a copy of Voltaire's
*L'Ingénu*: cowries,

hooks-and-eyes, hawks'-bells;
a matching pair
of conchs;
more roanoke; pig-tails

of tobacco; such bagatelles
as the hank
of Washington's hair
so prized by Thomas Poole;

the apothecary's
array, tsk tsk,
of red and violet and blue phials
and philtres.


[BRANT]

———

When George Burnett climbs
to his thirty-foot-high look-out
post he surveys six cabins caulked
with moss and lime

and the clinkered roof
of their new barn.

The ten-year-old Lord Byron
stamps his cloven hoof.

———

The sword-stick. Its brass ferrule.
'Did you come of your own free will?'

———

Apart from a leak of yellow
from the nail-shop
where Shad is slowly turning a felloe
everything's ship-shape.

[ERASMUS]

Twelve months ago they embarked, de dum, Te Deum,
on a merchantman out of Rotterdam

and were seen off from the Bristol quay
by a bemused citizenry

including Hucks and Cottle, their fellow-
Pantisocrats, who now dismissed the plan as folly.

They would anchor briefly in an Irish harbour
to take on board the usual raparees

and rapscallions;
cattle, pigs, sheep and, of course, the stallion.

[MACHIAVELLI]

Bucephalus gives Southey a knowing look:
'It appears that Shadrach Weeks is in league
with Cinnamond, while Cinnamond is in league
with the Seneca prophet, Handsome Lake.'




[COPERNICUS]

Te Deum. De dum. Te Deum. De dum. Te Deum.
An omnium-gatherum
of stoats
and weasels and other vermin

got up in ermine
or swallow-tail coats
and armed with shillelaghs
and spiked clubs

come at a gallop
through the valley.
When the leader's mount gives way under him,
de dum,

he lights a fire at the critical point
just behind its belly-band.

[MORE]

———

It's a year to the day since Thomas Jefferson
tabled his first version

of 'the mould-board
of least resistance' for a plow

to the American
Philosophical Society.

———

A year, too, since the Unitedman, the MacGuffin,
paid a Dutch captain one hundred guilders

and took passage on a coffin-
ship from Westport.

MacGuffin has now changed his name to 'Smith'.
He is in the service of Aaron Burr.

———

Little does Jefferson know, as he saddles the Morgan
and slopes off down to Mulberry Row

and the less-than-smooth
furrow of his light-skinned Jocasta,

that 'Smith' overhears them link and uncouple.
Little does he think that the world is out of kilter.

[**LUTHER**]

*I was haunted by evil spirits, of whose presence, though unseen, I was aware. At length an arm appeared through a half-opened door, or rather a long hand. I ran up and caught it. I pulled at it with desperate effort, dragged a sort of shapeless body into the room and trampled upon it, crying out the while for horror.*

(Southey)

[**SCALIGER**]

Southey awakes from the nightmare to a hurricane
of hooves, though barely within earshot;

at this distance, not even Bucephalus can reckon
if they're (1) shod or (2) unshod;

he nonetheless strains for effect on his halter:
'*Eadem*, de dum, *sed aliter.*'

[**PARACELSUS**]

What wouldn't Coleridge give for a tipple-tope
of the celebrated Kendal Black Drop?

[CALVIN]

Back on the hill, at Monticello,
a chill

runs down Minerva's spine;
the door of the laundry's

open.
She grips her lantern.

Already scared out of her wits
by the demoniacal

chuckles from the vats,
the involuntary creak of a mangle,

she happens on a bar of lye-soap
and the name ✷ ✷ ✷ ✷ ✷ ✷ ✷ ✷ .


[ASCHAM]

From behind a freshly-scraped, buffalo-hide arras
on which hangs an elk-horn

bow and a brangle of blood-stained arrows
a woman begins to keen:

'Now your snouterumpater is a connoisorrow
who has lost her raspectabilberry.'

An elk-horn bow. A brangle of blood-stained arrows
tipped with chalcedony and jasper.

*The historical facts on which this poem is founded may be related in a few words. On the death of Owen Gwyneth, king of north Wales, A.D. 1169, his children disputed the succession. Yorwerth, the elder, was set aside without a struggle, as being incapacitated by a blemish on his face. Hoel, though illegitimate, and born of an Irish mother, obtained possession of the throne for a while, till he was defeated and slain by David, the eldest son of the late king by a second wife. The conqueror, who then succeeded without opposition, slew Yorwerth, imprisoned Rodri, and hunted others of his brethren into exile. But Madoc, meantime, abandoned his barbarous country, and sailed away to the west in search of some better resting-place. The land which he discovered pleased him: he left there part of his people, and went back to Wales for a fresh supply of adventurers, with whom he again set sail, and was heard of no more.*

*(Southey)*

[SCALIGER]

As he goes to emend a jotting on the flyleaf
of a small morocco-bound tome,
Southey plucks a grey goose-quill from the sheaf;
its nib is stiff with grume, de dum.

[BRAHE]

Once his mast inclines towards the forest
the star in the bucket
from which Burnett slakes his thirst . . .

[BRUNO]

Is momentarily out of true. At the picket,
the alchemy
of horses. A mallet-tap on a spigot.

Not so much as a glimmer
from the nail-shop. Then the cut and thrust
of a double-edged claymore.


[HAKLUYT]

A room over the New Orleans tavern.
John Evans rummages in his lice-ridden shirt
and unfolds a chart
of a river wider than the mouth of the Severn.

Beyond the Mandan
villages, beyond this squalid
ruck in the quilt,
is yet another range of mountains.

There, surely, are the tell-tale
blue eyes and fair skins
of the scions
of the prince of Wales

for whom Evans has searched in vain.
About his neck is hung
a bag of asafetida, or 'devil's dung'.
He bares his arm. The physician gropes for a vein.

A black slave wearing one white glove
opens
a copper chafing-dish.
A boiled
ham studded with cloves.
Broad beans.
Brant is at once outlandish
and polite:
'Only last winter
I went out to stuff a chicken
with snow
so it wouldn't spoil.
I caught an ague
for my trouble. I took it as an omen.
I remembered Cornelius Sturgeon
hacked
to death by his own Onondagas.
He, too, had stuffed himself with whiteness.'
'What of this white woman
in Cornplanter's
Town? Is she British or American?'
'I know
only that her name is Sybil
and that she belongs to Red Jacket.
I know nothing of her origins.
This I swear to you, as God is my witness.'




[GALILEO]

————

The Mohawk braves take off their skunk bonnets.
Other than a statue of the Good Twin

carved from a twenty-foot log
they can see little of Cornplanter's Town,

what with its pall of smoke like a scab
on a wound. Coleridge crawls to his vantage-point.

―――――

When he squints through the telescope
given to Brant by Lord Sydney

in 1786, he suddenly knows all he needs to know:
nailed to the statue is a white dog.


[CAMPANELLA]

An island on the Ohio
where Harman
Blennerhassett
is building a Roman
villa
complete with mosaics
and frescoes
and a modest cupola.

The bog-oak
lintel
was unearthed
on his god-forsaken
family estate
in Kerry.
He had it shipped
from Philadelphia
by barge
and bullock-cart.

It took a dozen
men to hoist
it into position.
One was cut in half,
*eheu*,
when the cable
of the windlass
snapped.

Blennerhassett studies
a marble
bust of himself
above the hearth.
It's ever so slightly
awry.

That rather unsightly
stand
of birch
and sugar-maple
is destined
soon to become a lawn.

An artesian
well. A lily-pond.
The sound of Handel's
*Water Music*
on a spinet
or harpsichord.
A peacock
and a dappled fawn.

This is The New Atlantis.
The City of the Sun.

[KEPLER]

Which is already burning off the fogs
and marsh-gas
from the glen. The halloo of a fox.
The report of geese

from the Lac
Qui Parle. Southey begins to prime
a flint-lock.
A snatch of the now-familiar rhyme:

'An apothecary on a white horse
rode by on his vocation
and the Devil thought of his old friend
Death, in the Revelation.'


[BOEHME]

What a beautiful thing it is, in a pot, urine.

Has Coleridge somehow given Shad offence
by treating him, de dum,
as a mere factotum?

Why do those blue beads, the bow made of horn,
remind him not of Sara, but Mary Evans?

[HARVEY]

Just as he's ramming a wad into the pistol
Southey has the uncanny . . .

a black pustule
or blood-blistereen

roughly the size of a guinea
has erupted on the stallion's pastern.

[HOBBES]

———

Coleridge can no more argue from this faded blue
turtle's splay
above the long-house door to a universal
idea of 'blue' or 'turtle'

than from powder-horns, muskets,
paddles, pumpkins,
thingums, thingammies,
bear-oil against mosquitoes,

hatchets, hoes, digging-sticks,
knives, kettles,
steel combs, brass tacks,
corn-husk masks or ceremonial rattles

to anything beyond their names. The silent drums.
The empty cask of trade-rum.

———

While the white woman is being rogered
by one Seneca tipped with chert

she sap-
sips

a second.
Coleridge turns away, sickened,

snaps shut the telescope
and fumbles for his pony's halter-rope.


[DESCARTES]

———

In 'France', a little child, a limber elf,
pulls a straw bee-skep over himself.

———

Now doubting everything but his own doubt
Southey bites on a weevil-riddled
ship's biscuit
and goes in search of the Pantisocrats.


[MORE]

Though he's self-evidently a leprechaun
who barely comes up to the ankle

of Lord Moira (or the waist
of Lady Donegal)

all London hails
the self-evidently angel-voiced

Tom Moore as the new Anacreon.
This includes the *other* Prince of Wales.


[PASCAL]

Jefferson is so beside himself with glee
that he finishes off a carafe

of his best Médoc;
his newly-modified polygraph

will automatically
follow hand-in-glove

his copper-plate 'whippoorwill'
or 'praise' or 'love':

will run parallel to the parallel
realm to which it is itself the only clue.


[BOYLE]

Before Coleridge has had time to settle
into the saddle
a hunting-party gallops
up through the hickories.

The hides
of the ponies are smeared
with mud from the Allegheny.
Cornplanter's son, Henry O'Bail,

is resplendent
in a cougar-
and-lynx-
skin vest, red leggings

and stove-pipe hat.
Were it not for the Quakers,
Swayne and Simmons,
bringing up the rear

he might well appeal
to his tomahawk.
Just as he's about to vent
his spleen

his bedraggled pony breaks wind
so vehemently
it shakes the rafters
of the metaphysical long-house.

All collapse
in helpless laughter.
This horse-fart smells of newly-cut grass
and, is it nutmeg?


[LOCKE]

Not until he sees the great cloud-eddy
renewing itself in a pond
will Southey have even the faintest idea
of what's happened.

Until he hears
the sobbing of a resinous plank
that's already been shaved of its ears
his mind's a total blank.

## [SPINOZA]

*Brother, I rise to return the thanks of this nation to our ancient friends—if any such we have—for their good wishes towards us in attempting to teach us your religion. Perhaps your religion may be peculiarly adapted to your condition. You say that you destroyed the Son of the Great Spirit. Perhaps this is the merited cause of all your troubles and misfortunes.*

*Brother, we pity you. We wish you to bear to our good friends our best wishes. Inform them that in compassion towards them we are willing to send them missionaries to teach them our religion, habits, and customs. Perhaps you think we are ignorant and uninformed. Go, then, and teach the whites. Select, for example, the people of Buffalo. Improve their morals and refine their habits. Make them less disposed to cheat Indians. Make the whites generally less inclined to make Indians drunk and to take from them their lands. Let us know the tree by the blossoms, and the blossoms by the fruit.*

(Red Jacket)

## [BURNET]

Dangles
by one fretful ankle
over the illustrious dung-hill.

As to holding forth
on the inherent worth
of the earth,

he would surely be on the brink
of speech—were it not for the brank
of his own prong.

[HOOKE]

O spirochete. O spirochete. O spirochete.


[MALEBRANCHE]

Notwithstanding his having a whiff
of a stake burned at the stake of itself
like a lithe and lissome Joan of Arc.

Notwithstanding his having a taste
of tar-water and a sooty crust
Southey will stay completely in the dark.


[NEWTON]

Until it strikes him, as if by some fluke;
this strict, unseasonable, black snowflake.


[BURNET]

Te Deum. Te Deum. Te Deum. Te Deum. Te Deum.

[LEIBNIZ]

Which falls a little too patly into the scheme
of things. It now seems inevitable,
for example, that the pivotal beam
of the barn will topple

at any moment, making a splash
of orange, while the ghosts of individual
log-cabins step, naked, from their ash-
pink farthingales and fiddle

with their hair. Bucephalus hobbles
through what was meant to be the best
of all possible
worlds, hitches himself to a hitching-post

and arches his neck:
'Since we're now approaching the gates of Hell
you should know that the "nock" in Mount Monadnock
is indeed the Gaelic word *cnoc*, a hill.'



[BAYLE]

———

The last thing he remembers is the arc
of his pony's tail

skittering off like a comet
as his own unkempt

head dashes against a rock.

———

It turns out that Henry O'Bail

has had Coleridge and his few belongings
thrown into a rude palanquin

and all conveyed, at a frantic lick,
to Cornplanter's Town and Handsome Lake.


[V I C O]

A hand-wringing, small grey squirrel
plods
along a wicker

treadmill that's attached
by an elaborate
system of levers

and cogs and cranks
and pulleys
and gears

and cams and cinches
and sprags and sprockets
and spindles

and tappets and trundles
and spirochetes
and winches

and jennies and jiggers
and pawls
and pranks

and the whole palaver
of rods
and ratchets

to a wicker
treadmill in which there plods
a hand-wringing, small grey squirrel.


[TOLAND]

Nutmeg. A sizar at Jesus. The smell of laver-bread reveals
Coleridge lying with Mary Evans in the Gog Magog Hills.


[MANDEVILLE]

———

The buffalo-hide arras covers the filthy smoot
of a beehive hut.

———

A gopher mimics from its honeycomb:
'Where's my stumparumper? Where's my sillycum?'


[CLARKE]

Then consoles itself, in the waste of alkali,
with a sprig of the as-yet-unnamed *Clarkia pulchella*.

## [BERKELEY]

That treadmill might have existed only in the mind
of a child, were the child not now a non-entity
under his flower-strewn, almost-imperceptible mound:
BERKELEY COLERIDGE 1798–99


## [BUTLER]

Try as Southey may to reconcile himself
to a whimsical

whirligig going unscathed
while Burnett unravels

from his gibbet,
while Berkeley and Lovell

have met their ends,
he's set upon by, of all things, a sheaf

of corn, by some flibbertigibbet
wielding, in one hand,

a rusty sickle
and, in the other, the sned of a scythe.

[VOLTAIRE]

CORNPLANTER
It goes without saying that Cinnamond
sold her to the Crees, with whom he's made a pact.

HIGGENBOTTOM
And this?

HANDSOME LAKE
            A liniment
of aspen and hawk-weed
for your scalp.

HIGGENBOTTOM
I would be swayed less by your herb tisanes
and juleps
than by your offering me a dozen
warriors who know the ways of the Crees.

RED JACKET
It goes without saying. But you must earn
our trust.

HANDSOME LAKE
            I see a path covered with grass.

HIGGENBOTTOM
A belt of blue beads. A bow made of horn.




[HARTLEY]

Southey's about to blow out the goblin's brains
when the bee-skep
slumps forward to divulge
his three-year-old nephew who escaped,

supposedly, to 'France'.
Four days ago, he determines,
Hartley had stayed with Edith, Shad and Burnett
while the others left for the village

of Athens. There came
ten or twelve men with pails of burning pitch.
They burned and burned.
Uncle Shad went into the fiery furnace

to save the strawberry roan.
Then an angel rescued *him*.
An angel? The angel looked like 'Cindermans',
though he also looked like Daisy.

(By this he must mean the border collie
with one eye-patch.)
Aunt Edith? She, too, has fled to 'France'.
Southey follows him through the smoke

to the shallow gully
overgrown with horse-tail ferns
where he finds Edith, dazed,
wearing only a crumpled, blood-spattered smock.



[FRANKLIN]

That teeny-weeny key. Bear it in mind.

———

None of this impinges as yet on Private Moses Reed.

———

In spite of various qualms and cavils
Coleridge has deemed it the lesser of two evils
to present Handsome Lake with the valise.

———

'At any moment now, the retina will disintegrate.'

[HUME]

September, 1799. They're putting the finishing touches
to the maze of dykes and ditches
beyond the live-oak palisade.
The stone blockhouse is proof against a mortar-blast.

Its roof is of ten-inch-thick sheets of slate
hauled here by mule-sled.
For a weekly ration of grog and a few gew-gaws
Southey has enlisted fifteen disaffected Cayugas.

One of whom guards Edith. She rolls over in her hammock
and twiddles a newly-peeled, sharpened osier
from the bundle by her side. A hummock

under her chemise. Its occasional jitter-jolt.
Her recurrent dream of a shorn and bloody hawser.
And, as always, Bucephalus, niggling: 'Who *owns* the child?'

## [FREDERICK THE GREAT]

September, 1800. A Cayuga wet-nurse dandles
the infant in her lap
while Southey recites from his endless
saga of *Thalaba*

*the Destroyer*: 'the fluted cypresses
rear'd up
their living obelisks . . .'
Hartley sulks as Bean expresses

milk from her diddly-doos,
then resolutely cups
the spout of his tortoise-shell powder-flask:
'Not until you see the whites of their eyes.'


## [ROUSSEAU]

December, 1802. The two Toms, Jefferson and Paine,
look out through the silver birches,
past undulating spruce and pine,
to the illimitabilities of the Louisiana Purchase.


## [DIDEROT]

In the downstairs study, Jefferson's aide-de-camp
makes a tally of blankets, hats and gloves;
opium, laudanum,
cinnamon, oil of cloves;

marlinspikes, wimbles,
gimlets and awls;
needles and thimbles;
fish-hooks; powder and ball;

the theodolite, quadrant, compass and chain . . .
Except for his not as yet having got
to grips with the code

based on the key word 'artichokes',
all's set fair for his clandestine mission.
Meriwether Lewis swaggers up and out to the jakes.


[PUTNAM]

'Not until you see the whites of their eyes.'


[SMITH]

A small gust of wind through the open window.
A gasp on a cello or viola.
A flittering across the portfolio
Lewis has left untied.

A cursory glance
at the ledgers and log books.
Abracadabra. Hocus-pocus.
A thumb through a well-thumbed Linnaeus.

Until, among bills-of-lading and manifests
and almanacs and a Mercator
plan of the heavens,

this: the map drawn up by John Evans
that shows such a vast
unsulliedness the very candle gulps and gutters.

[KANT]

April, 1804. It stands to, well, 'it stands to reason'
that Wilkinson, who's 'in the pay of' Spain,

should 'sow the seeds of treason'
in the 'fertile mind' of Aaron Burr,

of whom Alexander Hamilton holds 'a despicable opinion'.
The tedium, de dum, of it all. The slurry-slur.

[BURKE]

The Envoy Extraordinary and Minister Plenipotentiary
of His Britannic Majesty,

one Anthony Merry
(though 'merry' is hardly *le mot juste*)

laboriously
presents Tom Moore, late of Bermuda,

to Jefferson, the sublime and beautiful, the paragon
of civility, who prompt-

ly turns on his heel and shuffles off in his slippers,
unwittingly slighting the leprechaun.


[DARWIN]

———

Independence Day, 1804. The moment-of-dawn salute
from the swivel-mounted howitzer
in the stern of the flat-boat
sends up a cloud of parakeets.

Though this barquette
draws only three feet of water
it has more than once foundered in the silt
and quicksand of the river-bed.

———

Clark scrutinizes the newly-repaired cordelle
that caught on a submerged tree-trunk.
It's spliced and greased.
Sergeants Pryor and Ordway dispense two gallons

of whiskey. None for Hall or Collins
(both flogged for being drunk)
or the slave, York, who dances a bear-quadrille
to the scraping of Gibson and Cruzatte.

———

By mid-afternoon, a series of sawyers and snags.
Labiche and Shields
have capsized the white pirogue.
It looks as if Floyd may have dysentery.

Meanwhile a sentry,
one of the brothers Fields,
has been bitten by a rattle-snake.
Lewis dresses the wound with nitre and boiled bark.

———

Then strides out behind Willard's makeshift smithy
among cocklebur and wild timothy.


[PRIESTLEY]

———

On the western branch of the Susquehanna,
Putnam Catlin's

intent on guddling
a trout.

———

Only when she's in her last agony
does the trout renege

on a silver ear-ring
and cough it up and spit it out.

———

It lies on the floor of the birch-bark canoe.
Catlin's all of a sudden filled with dread.

[WATT]

Coincidentally, as she charges his porringer
from a piggin of steamed milk,

Edith skites
his immmmmmmmmmmmmmmmmmmmmmaculate

pea-green waistcoat;
this is much more than Southey can endure.


[PAINE]

Exactly a week later, on the banks of the Hudson,
Burr sends a ball through the kidneys

and milty spleen
of Alexander Hamilton.

A blood-trump out of Hamilton's mouth.
Burr's whisked away by William Van Ness and 'Smith'.


[SAUSSURE]

———

August 7th. Lewis has sent a hunting-party
in search of the deserters, Moses Reed and La Liberté.

———

August 11th. The Captains mull
over the tumulus or mole

where the Omaha chief, Blackbird,
was buried

on his white war-horse.

————

August 18th. Reed's brought back and forced

to run a gauntlet of ramrods
and switches. Boils and buboes. Haemorrhoids.

————

August 20th. Floyd dies of colic and melancholia.

————

August 25th. His spirit clambers up the holy

Mound of the Little People, to the moans
of its thousands of eighteen-inch-high demons.

————

October 14th. John Newman is sentenced to seventy-five
lashes for having uttered a mutinous oath.

————

October 25th. Though the sandstone bluffs and spurs
give way, for the most part, to sparsely-

wooded, deeply-fissured mesas
redolent of wormwood, of the artemisia's

turpentine and camphor,
there's still the occasional, delicately-chamfered

column of honey- or salmon-coloured querns
surmounted, as here, by an obsidian cornice.

Camphor and turpentine. Elk-slots. Bear-scats.
Drouillard and Shields, the scouts,

can see directly across the stately saraband
of the Missouri to the corresponding

scumble of mosques and minarets
and the three-hundred-odd Mandans and Minnetarees.

[JEFFERSON]

Has today received (1) a live gopher (2) a magpie (3) a piece of
chequered skin or hide and (4) a cipher that reads . . . 'A-R-T-I-C-H-
O-K-E-S'.

[BENTHAM]

———

*In fancy now, beneath the twilight gloom,*
*come, let me lead thee o'er this 'second Rome',*
*this embryo capital, where fancy sees*
*squares in morasses, obelisks in trees.*

———

October, 1804. A secret letter from Merry to Burr
encloses these lines by Tom 'Little' Moore:

———

*The patriot, fresh from Freedom's councils come,*
*now pleased retires to lash his slaves at home;*
*or woo, perhaps, some black Aspasia's charms,*
*and dream of freedom in his bondsmaid's arms.*

Merry's seal is of ivory set in jade
and reads, predictably, ΙΑϽ ƨЯUOႱUOT .

[MAIMON]

Amidst oohs and ahs and clucks and cackles
the Mandan girls take turns to wet
their fingers and rub the charcoal
from what must be York's underlying white.




[GODWIN]

Needless to say, these are not girls but berdashes
who beckon him into their earth lodge
near a maelstrom

of brood mares; York follows the stream
that back-breakingly portages
itself from ledge

to ledge, past beehive huts, a sweat-house,
a flotilla of bull-boats
(buffalo-

hides on ribs of willow)
to where Joseph Whitehouse,
the Irishman Gass, and the German Potts

have so fortified themselves on dried smelt
and salmon
they're in ecstasy:

to the hub of the Mandan village, the wooden hogshead
containing their most treasured amulets
and secret talismans.

[**WOLLSTONECRAFT**]

February 11th, 1805. Sacajawea nibbles at the quirt of her newly-
born's umbilical cord.

[**COOPER**]

*Strong evidence has been adduced that Madoc reached America, and
that his posterity exist there to this day, on the southern branches of
the Missouri, retaining their complexion, their language, and, in some
degree, their arts.*

(Southey, Preface to *Madoc*, April 1805)

[**SCHILLER**]

*May 5th, 1805*
*We set out verry early and had not proceeded far before the rudder
Irons of one of the Perogus broke which detained us a short time.
Potts gave Capt Lewis to know that we are follied by a man on a Spot-
ted horse. The Countrey on both sides is as yesterday handsom & fer-
tile. The river rising & current strong & in the evening we saw a
Brown or Grisley beare on a sand beech. I went out with one man
Geo Drewyer & killed the bear, which was verry large and a turrible
looking animal, which we found verry hard to kill. We Shot ten Balls
into him before we killed him, & five of those Balls through his lights.*

(Clark)

[FICHTE]

This very morning, a sixty-foot sloop
was seen to put in
at the Island. The dunt
of a light skiff

against the jetty.
While Aaron Burr
mesmerizes his host
with the barbel

of an Idea,
the ubiquitous 'Smith'
hovers about the pier.
He's absorbed by the dent

below his own water-line. A purple
tick-bite no bigger than a button.
Burr raises his glass to Blennerhassett:
'Syllabub. Syllabub. Syllabub.'


[MALTHUS]

*I am startled at the price of* Madoc. *In fact, books are now so dear
that they are becoming rather articles of furniture than any thing else;
they who buy them do not read them, and they who read them do not
buy them. I have seen a Wiltshire clothier who gives his book-seller no
other instructions than the dimensions of his shelves. If* Madoc *obtain
any celebrity, its size and cost will recommend it among those gen-
try*—libros consumere nati—*born to buy quartos and help the rev-
enue.*

(Southey)

[HEGEL]

William Labiche and the boatman Cruzatte
ruminate

on a ten-foot-long buffalo-
gut

coiled
between them, its listless, puce

and amethyst
cloud-

remnant
sporadically a-shiver.

They've already gorged on the raw
liver

laced
with gall and gun-powder.

Each takes an end. And they grumble-
gripe

through the slick
shambles

(*Ametas*
*and Thestylis*

*Making Hay-Ropes*)
until

it's all but lost its
slack

and they're locked in a putter-
buss

stalemate.
So these brave fellows

draw
their bone-handled

knives.
The Bitterroot Valley. September, 1805.


[SMITH]

Madoc *is doing well; rather more than half the edition is sold, which
is much for so heavy a volume. The sale, of course, will flag now, till
the world shall have settled what they please to think of the poem. The
Monthly is all malice, and is beneath all notice; but look at the Edin-
burgh, and you will see that Jeffrey himself does not know what he is
about. William Taylor has criticised it for the Annual very favourably
and very ably. Taylor has said it is the best English poem that has left
the press since Paradise Lost; indeed, this is not exaggerated praise,
for, unfortunately, there is no competition.*

(Southey)


[COLERIDGE]

Labiche and Cruzatte will put up their blades
when an Appaloosa

comes rollicking past in a blur of tricorn
hat and epaulettes

and twill unmentionables
and shrugs off the erstwhile Light Dragoon,

Silas Tomkyn Comberbache,
as though he's one dapple less on her back.



[MILL]

The five-year-old goes truffling with the hogs
and plants an acorn in his mouth.

Southey prestidigitates the key
on its snig of hemp or linsey-woolsey

while Bucephalus goes down on one knee:
'Penguin. From the Welsh

*pen* and *gwynn*, meaning "head" and "white".'
An infusion of charlock

and jimsonweed.
He tugs his forelock:

'As for the white-headed boy under the oaks
you know he's not a Southey. He's a *South*.'



[SCHELLING]

*September 5th, 1805*
*We assembled the Chiefs & warriers and Spoke to them with much*
*dificuelty as what we Said had to pass through Several languages*
*before it got into theirs, which is Spoken much thro the throught.*
(Clark)

*These natives have the Stranges language of any we have ever yet seen. They appear to us as though they had an Impedement in their Speech.*

(Ordway)

*These Savages has the Strangest language of any we have ever Seen. They appear to us to have an Empediment in their Speech or bur on their tongue. We take these Savages to be the Welch Indians if their be any Such.*

(Whitehouse)

[HERBART]

———

While they deliberate on the Flatheads' 'gurgle'
and 'brogue'
Lewis and Clark have him confined to the coracle
at the stern of the red pirogue

———

where Coleridge spies a Croton bug or beetle
making its regal
progress along a paddle.
The water will suddenly give him back a gargoyle

———

with Southey's eyes and mouth. A sniff of aloes.
The iceberg-
bellows, the bleats and brays of a great battle.
The crumble-itch of a periwig.

———

Then, just as suddenly, a child in blue and yellow
creeping unwillingly to Christ's Hospital.

## [GAUSS]

———

The first watch is taken by John Potts
and Patrick Gass,

who seems infatuated with an abacus
of turquoise beads.

———

In St Louis, Burr asks General Wilkinson
to calculate

the cost, in gold,
of an ordnance of two hundred cannons.

———

Coleridge is given his measure of taffy
along with a mash of various

kinds of berry
and the roots of *Lewisia rediviva*.


## [DAVY]

*In Sweden a very curious phenomenon has been observed on certain
flowers, by M. Haggern, lecturer in natural history. One evening he
perceived a faint flash of light repeatedly dart from a marigold. From
the rapidity of the flash, and other circumstances, it may be conjec-
tured that there is something of electricity in this phenomenon.*

(Coleridge)

**[BYRON]**

Again stamps his cloven hoof
as he conjugates the verb 'to have'.

**[SCHOPENHAUER]**

———

'And where did you come by the Nez Percé pony?'

———

Coleridge absentmindedly ties a knot
in the waist-cord of his breeks.

———

'Are you with the Northwest or X Y Companies?'

———

Retina. From the Latin *rete*, a net.

———

'When I struck the "c" from *castor*
I found myself in the company of John Jacob Astor.'

———

In the waist-cord of his breeks
he inextricably tightens the knot.

———

'Billet him with Newman in the red pirogue.'

## [HAMILTON]

September 7th. Might the spectre of Hamilton
playing a *schottische*

on his melodeon

of blood and guts and shit and piss
have been just enough to give Wilkinson pause?

## [FARADAY]

*'Tis said, in Summer's evening hour*
*Flashes the golden-colour'd flower*
  *A fair electric flame:*
*And so shall flash my love-charg'd eye*
*When all the heart's big ecstasy*
  *Shoots rapid through the frame.*
                    (Coleridge)

## [COMTE]

———

Coleridge and Newman have poled their unwieldy dory
up a fast-flowing, narrow tributary.

———

While Gass and Potts slept the sleep of the just
they ransacked the medicine-chest

for calomel, bee-balm
and what little was left of the opium.

A compass and binnacle.
Brooches, bangles

and other knick-knacks.
A Sheffield knife. A calumet. Some kinnikinnick.

————

With first light, they manhandle the red pirogue
on to a sand-bar and throw up a wind-break

of cottonwood boughs. Coleridge wants simply to verify
the opium. Five grains. Tusk. Tongue furfurry.

[NEWMAN]

Would seem to have taken another about-turn
and shown a clean pair of heels. Why, though, had he drawn

the knife? It lies point-upward near a flint, a punk
and a pile of kindling on the sandy bank

where he must have been meaning to build a fire
and where his footprints, see, where they, see, disappear.

[EMERSON]

*Plotinus, a man memorable for corrupting philosophy, was in favour
with Gallienus, and requested his royal highness would give him a
ruined city in Campania, which he might rebuild and people with
philosophers, governed by the laws of Plato, and from whom the city
would be called Platonopolis. The design would certainly have proved
impracticable in that declining and degenerate age—most probably in*

*any age—yet I cannot help wishing the experiment had been tried; I could rhapsodise most delightfully upon this subject, plan out my city, the palaces and hovels of Southeyopolis.*

(Southey)

[FEUERBACH]

———

The tinkle
of an Aeolian harp.

Eels.
Elvers.

An inkle
of black crêpe.

———

His pirogue
reels

through a sulphurous
brook.

———

What if Coleridge were to plait
a geyser's

cobalt-
azure

into a less than ideal
rope whereby

to wheedle-
warp

himself into the well, well, well
of his own fontanelle.


## [MILL]

Hartley and South have created something of a stir
by dropping a rooster
down the flue
of his study. Rather than fling an ink-well

at the devil,
Southey corners it in the ingle-
nook
and unceremoniously wrings its neck.

Rather than haruspicate
its gizzard
for some portent of disaster,

rather than haggle with Zoroaster,
he looks to Bucephalus, who will hazard
only that *Madoc* means 'the greatest, greatest good'.


## [DARWIN]

*September 19th, 1805*
*Set out early proceeded on up the Creek passing through a Small*
*glade at 6 miles at which place we found a horse. I derected him killed*
*and hung up for the party after takeing a brackfast off for our Selves*
*which we thought fine.*

(Clark)

## [KIERKEGAARD]

———

Lewis and Clark have split up, the better to track
Newman and the British spy Comberbache.

———

In Monticello, the snaggle-toothed gopher
tries his paw at the polygraph.

———

As he takes a skelly at the massive gantry
that now dominates the rath,
Bucephalus finds himself in yet another quandary
as to either or either or either or either.

———

Hartley and South spin a teetotum, de dum, de dum.

## [BOOLE]

———

Coleridge is now resigned to the fact that Sara
could be anywhere west of the Missouri.

———

Henry O'Bail has had the icon of the Good Twin
dismantled and dumped in the Allegheny,
though not before sawing off the narrow plank
on which he stands: 'assimilation'.

[THOREAU]

*September 20th, 1805*
*We had proceeded about 2 miles when we found the greater part of a*
*horse which Capt. Clark had met with and killed for us.*

(Lewis)


[MARX]

————

In the Northwest Company post on the Assiniboine,
among bags of flour and bricks of marchpane

and bolts of none-so-pretty and nankeen
and barrels of whiskey garbled with laudanum,

————

a trade-mark fox
cocks an ear from its rifle-stock

————

at the faint de dum, de dum
of the Crows, perhaps, up to their old shenanigans.


[FOUCAULT]

Even as Southey ponders the variables in torque
on the counter-weight and derrick

of the great ballista
he cannibalized

from that vividly-imagined
sky-machine's

wheels within wheels,
Bucephalus hints at the livid welts and weals

on his such-and-such:
'You're already under siege

from within, just as these blenny-blebs and blets
are storming my Bastille.'

[SPENCER]

The trading-post; a gelding hitched to the hitching-rail
and a palfrey hitched to the gelding's tail.

The palfrey's saddle; a fowling-piece; its scrimshandered
mother-of-pearl inlay: a salamander.

[PASTEUR]

The gelding's apishamore, meanwhile, is a languid,
crimson mackinaw blanket.

[KELVIN]

Southey rests on a wannigan. Cams and cinches.
Sprags and sprockets.
Parakeets.
Finches.

Wrens and whimbrels.
Tups and wethers.
Laverocks. Leverets. Levers.
Tumbrils.

Tricoteuses and sans-culottes.
Red-shanks. Her spackled cambric.
Ox-head. Dithyrambic.
Tups and wethers. Boars. Sows. Gilts.

The pike and carnelian sturgeon
that will rise to this, as to every, occasion.

[HUXLEY]

*September 20th, 1805*
*I set out early and proceeded on through a Countrey as ruged as*
*usial. At 12 miles decended the mountain to a leavel pine Countrey.*
*Proceeded on through a butifull Countrey for three miles to a Small*
*Plain in which I found maney Indian lodges, but fiew men a number*
*of women & children. They call themselves Cho pun-nish or Pierced*
*Noses. Their diolect appears verry different from the flat heads, altho*
*origineally the Same people.*

(Clark)

## [MAXWELL]

A tittle-tattle of light on his ax.
Sackbuts. A butt of sack.

The butt of malmsey.
St Elmo's

Fire. Fata Morgana.
Gomeril. Regan.

Will-o'-the-wisp. Jack-o'-lantern.
The seas incarnadine.

Cochineal. Cinnabar. Cinnamond.
Ruby. Rubicon. Rubicund.

The rail. The grouse. The gudgeon.
His escutcheon

is a buckler or targe
of goatskin over staves of larch.


## [BUTLER]

On which Southey has blocked out an inverted chevron
and a pair of gryphons

rampant, blue on grey;
they unfurl a pennant with, so far, the letters 'CRO—'.

[BRENTANO]

*September 22nd, 1805*
*We had proceeded about two and a half miles when we met Reubin*
*Fields whom Capt. Clark had dispatched to meet us with some dryed*
*fish and roots that he had procured from a band of Indians.*

(Lewis)


*I found Capt. Lewis & the party Encamped, much fatigued & hun-*
*gery, much rejoiced to find something to eate of which they appeared*
*to partake plentifully.*

(Clark)


*The pleasure I now felt in having tryumphed over the rockey Moun-*
*tains and decending once more to a level and fertile country where*
*there was every rational hope of finding a comfortable subsistence for*
*myself and party can be more readily conceived than expressed.*

(Lewis)




[MACH]

November 3rd. Bucephalus
is now so at odds with himself

his very stones
keep their distance.

He's completely engrossed
by the rosettes

and ribbons
on his tumid, de dum, Dick Turpin.

## [POPPER]

Beyond the ramparts, a Cayuga grips
the heft of a rattle
made from the carapace
of a mud-turtle.

The jaws
of his poplar-wood false face
are the jaws
of a vice.

The tongue prates
from its garrotte.
The neb is the neb of a prie-dieu
or misericord.

One eye is a wizened fern-
pod,
the other a fat gold sovereign
to airie thinnesse beat.

Its ogle-leer. Its wry perusal
of a field
of mangel-wurzels. A parasol
of horsehair and felt.

The Cayuga adjusts the lambda
of his grotesque
helmet
and grips the rattle-heft, tsk tsk.

## [PUTNAM]

———

As he reads aloud to the boys from *Thalaba*
Southey closes his right
eye and removes a tiny piece of grit
from the eyelid. A finger-flick. A fillip.

———

'Any moment now. The retina. Disintegrate.'

———

This detail will hardly be lost
on Putnam Catlin's nine-year-old, George,
so irresistible in his urge
to sketch Southey on a skiffle of slate.


## [PEIRCE]

———

As the weeks have gone by, Coleridge feels less squeamish
when he finds a blue and yellow grub
in a raw bulb of quamash.

———

However long he maggots upon why the crop
of mangolds should suddenly spoil,
Southey is none the wiser.
He orders them plowed under. Goody-good for the soil.

———

Pike, pickerel. Hog, hoggerel.
Cock, cockerel. Dog, doggerel.

———

Beyond the ramparts, the False Face lifts his visor.

**[JAMES]**

The pile of horse-dung at the heart of Southeyopolis
looks for all the world like a dish of baked apples.

**[HARTMANN]**

———

Coleridge is about to quench his
thirst in an alkali-

tainted pool. An exorbitant,
harum-scarum

head
over his shoulder.

———

Helter-skelter
across the lava-beds.

———

The almost invisible scrim
of a rabbit-net

strung across a gully.

———

From the Latin, *rete*. Unconscious.

[**NIETZSCHE**]

It seems that nothing—be it arsenic or leeches
or an impromptu sweat-lodge

rigged up from an old bell-tent
at one end of the stable—nothing's of any dint

to the stallion, he's so shot-through, so spangled
with the cankers and carbuncles

of syphilis.
Three nights ago, Southey lay down with Bucephalus

and blew in his ear, as if he might fan the embers.
He's held him since in a fast embrace.



[**CANTOR**]

———

The word on the Burr-Blennerhassett cabal?
Quibble, quibble, quibble.

———

With such innnnnnnnnnnnnnnnnnnnnnnnfinite
tenderness, such care,

Southey brushes the glib
from behind the stallion's ear

and takes aim,
de dum. A flash in the pan. A thunder-clap.

Blood-alphabets. Blood-ems.
A babble of blood out of the broken fount.

[BRADLEY]

*November 7th, 1805*
*Great joy in camp. We are in view of the Ocian. This great Pacific*
*Octean which we been so long anxious to See. And the roreing or*
*noise made by the waves brakeing on the rockey Shores (as I suppose)*
*may be heard distictly.*

(Clark)

[EDISON]

———

Coleridge has fallen in with a band of Modocs
who extemporize a sudatory

from the overturned dory.
They ply him with such mild emetics

as yarrow and Oregon
grape. He's tantalized

by the all-pervasive tang of dulse
or carageen.

———

That night the Modocs light a greasewood beacon
and repeatedly sound a conch.

———

The morning brings a party of Spokanes.
Their chief offers Coleridge the use of his wife

in exchange for (1) the kinnikinnick
and (2) the Sheffield knife.

[BELL]

Brant's Town. A communiqué
from Theodosia Burr

to her old friend, the King of the Mohawks.
Brant invites 'Smith'

to stay for supper,
throughout which he swigs

brandy from the mouth
of a nacreous

skull he took somewhere near Fort Stanwix.
Or was it Niagara?


[SOREL]

Southey clears a space on his escritoire
for the bundle of osiers

and the ax;
the teeny-weeny key: the pearwood box.


[FREGE]

The Spokane chief still wants to dicker
for the knife, on the blade of which are etched

the initials 'G' and 'R';
Coleridge has now assumed the name 'George Rex'.

[MEINONG]

———

Inside the pearwood box—hold on a minute—
is an exact replica

of the valise.

———

Its very contents are identical.

———

Down to the hooks-and-eyes, hawks'-bells,
the not-quite-matching pair

of conchs,
the selfsame hank

of Washington's hair
so prized by Thomas Poole.

———

(Southey peers out at the block
and tackle

with which Bucephalus
was this morning lowered into his mound.)

———

All except for a dog-eared letter in cuttle-
ink addressed by Coleridge to 'my dearest Cottle'.

[ROYCE]

First Allen; then Le Grice; Hartley and Mary Lovell:
one by one, they've grown disenchanted.

Now, without so much as a 'by your leave'
or a 'begging your pardon'

(though true at least to his name), Favell
has taken the chestnut jennet

and set out for God-knows-where. The ever-loyal Edith
busies herself in the herb-garden.

[FREUD]

Her recurrent dream of a shorn and bloody hawser.

[SAUSSURE]

Nothing in this could have prepared him for
the bleached tarpaulin

stretched over stays of baleen
where the Spokane woman slinks from the fur

of a sea-otter
and sways before him like a ship's figurine.

His eye is going against the grain
of her weatherbeaten cedar

when, by a blubbering lamp, Coleridge divines
a heart-shaped tattoo

on her left teat
and a Cupid's dart from, this can't be, EVANS.


[HUSSERL]

*July 4th, 1806*
*This being the day of the decleration of Independence of the United*
*States and a Day commonly scelebrated by my Country I had every*
*disposition to selebrate this day and therefore halted early and par-*
*took of a Sumptious Dinner of a fat Saddle of Venison and Mush of*
*Cows (roots). After Dinner we proceeded on about one mile to a very*
*large Creek which we assended some distance to find a foard to cross.*
*Altho' the debth was not much above the horses belly, the water was*
*so strong it passed over the backs and loads of the horses.*

(Clark)


[BERGSON]

A sennet of hautboys. The glint
of afternoon sunlight on the panoply of hauberks and halberds.
An ungainly colonnade
of Cayugas. Chimeras and camelopards

on their antique
livery. Southey's own tunic is of saffron
and indigo,
his cape the fell of a wolverine.

Since he's suffering from a mild case of the flux,
he's couchant on a tavelin
of vairs and minivers. In his right hand is the valise,
in his left a three-tined javelin

with which he admonishes, from his litter,
the Cayuga so slovenly as to have dropped his muzzle-loader.

[DEWEY]

July 29th, 1806. Aaron Burr entrusts a certain Samuel Swartwout with
a letter for General Wilkinson. This letter is written in three ciphers:
one hieroglyphic, another based on a specific edition of *Entick's
Pocket Dictionary*, the third an alphabet cipher devised by Wilkinson
and 'Captain Smith'.

[WHITEHEAD]

———

Southey wakes in a cold sweat;
penguins don't have white heads.

———

*April, 1797*

*My dearest Cottle,*
    *I am fearful that Southey will begin to rely too much on* story &
event *in his poems to the neglect of those* lofty imaginings *that are pe-
culiar to, & definitive of, the* POET.

(S. T. Coleridge)

*The weary statesman for repose hath fled*
*from halls of council to his negro's shed*
*where blest he woos some black Aspasia's grace*
*and dreams of freedom in his slave's embrace.*
(Tom 'Little' Moore, Epistles,<br>Odes and Other Poems)

[SCHILLER]

Hawk-nosed, with a hawk's clumsily seeled eye,
duodenum, de dum, de dum,
Cinnamond fastens the palfrey's reins
to his gelding's tail.

His wrinkled breeks
are of stuff you might take for shagreen.
He's breakfasted on an oatmeal bannock
or scone.

He tilts the whiskey bottle
at Shad, at the featureless, frank, smoked ham
of Shad's face. O for a flitch of salty
pork.

Nothing. Cinnamond coaxes the bung
into the bottle and yanks
at his loose-fitting, shalloon-lined galligaskins:
'Mon is the mezjur of all thungs.'

[UNAMUNO]

This latest jibe sends Jefferson into such a rage
as to make the Guelphs and Ghibellines

seem tame. The gopher chittering from its cage:
'We must have Favell in Favell alone.'

[CROCE]

———

Southey has just overseen the flogging of the Cayuga,
whose yelps resound through the delirium
as echo-echoes.

———

No wonder Cinnamond's trews are so very becoming;
they're made from the epiderms, de dum,
of at least four, maybe five, hapless Gros Ventre women.

[McTAGGART]

Although Burr has suffered a blow—*O tempora, O mores*—
in the recalling of Anthony Merry

and the unlikelihood, now, of British support,
we find him in quite exuberant spirits.

This may have to do with the fact that a brig
laden with one hundred barrels of pork

is already making its way up-river
to Blennerhassett's Island. It's now. It's now or never.

[RUTHERFORD]

The scalp on Cinnamond's saddle-horn
had belonged to a Crow
whose skull he would bombard
with a stone club.

As he'd worked a broken sabre
from temple to temple
and under the sodden divot,
didn't your man leap

to his feet
and begin to run
through the bushes, balancing a caber

of gore,
and leaving behind the greater part
of his wimple.

[RUSSELL]

In the *Edinburgh Review* of July 1806, Moore is categorized as 'a public nuisance' and 'the most licentious of modern versifiers', to which he takes grave exception. Had this happened only a few years later, he would almost certainly have asked Lord John Russell to assist him on the field of honour.

[LOVEJOY]

―――――

August 14th. The ever-hospitable Mandans
don their buffalo-bull
head-dresses and dance a Buffalo Dance
to celebrate the return of the Captains.

―――――

Edith hooks a cedarwood pail
to the windlass
over the well and lets go of the capstan.
A headlong, clanking plummet. Relentless.

―――――

*September 23rd, 1806*
*Set out decended to the Mississippi and down that river to St. Louis at*
*which place we arrived about 12 oClock. we Suffered the party to fire*
*off their pieces as a Salute to the Town. we were met by all the village*
*and received a harty welcom from it's inhabitants.*

*September 26th, 1806*
*a fine morning we commenced wrighting &c.*

(Clark)

[MOORE]

In the meantime, 'Little' and Francis Jeffrey
of the *Edinburgh Review*

will have met at Chalk Farm for a duel.
In as long as it takes their seconds to load

their pistols ('How do you tell a Scot
from a sot?')

these arch-rivals
have become the best of friends

and, in the end, as they say, 'in the end
common sense prevails . . .'

Which is just as well, since Jeffrey's pistol
is found to be short of its bullet.


[MARCONI]

———

October 8th, 1806. Swartwout finally delivers the cryptogram to
Wilkinson: 'Our object, my dear friend, is brought to a point so long
desired. The gods invite us to glory and fortune. It remains to be seen
whether we deserve the boon.'

———

October 20th. Wilkinson informs Jefferson of the conspiracy. The
President issues warrants for the arrest of Burr and Blennerhassett.


[JUNG]

———

Bear-claws; a soap-stone frog; two big-horn fleeces
sewn into their own rumens;

of all the totems, de dum, that might assuage
the Mandan gods, none will speak more eloquently

from the hogshead-shrine than this: this swatch
of a crimson mackinaw blanket.

————

Southey has now proscribed (1) the white dog ceremony
and (2) the society of False Faces.

[EINSTEIN]

December 11th, 1806. When the Wood County militia
led by Colonel Phelps
come at full gallop
across the Island, one breaks his neck, *eheu,*

on a ha-ha.
The jangle of a bayonet
across the spinet.
There's neither hide nor hair of Blennerhassett.

While his men slaughter and roast
a milch-
cow in the ruins

of the garden,
the Colonel pores over a rune
on the bog-oak lintel. Is it 'CROATAN' or 'CROATOAN'?

[HARTMANN]

November 24th, 1807. During yet another squantum
of boiled ham and beans, the skull begins to drink

from the astonished mouth of the King
of the Mohawks, inveigling him into its kingdom.


[SCHLICK]

In years to come, he'll run his hands like quannets
over the Contessa's

breasts and thighs while Douglas Kinnaird
looks on admiringly and strokes his yard.

For now, we may put *Hours of Idleness* down to Byron's
lack of—might one surmise?—'experience'.


[NEURATH]

————

New Year's Day, 1809. At a literary *fol-de-rol* in Edinburgh
Jeffrey's introduced to the bankrupt, exiled Burr,

now travelling under the aegis of Jeremy Bentham.
'Jeremy . . . ?' *'Bentham'*; the name is lost in the pandemonium.

————

Josiah and Thomas Wedgwood's annuity to the Pantisocrats
is unexpectedly cut. 'Any moment now. Disintegrate.'

————

March 1st, 1809. In *English Bards and Scotch Reviewers*
Byron launches a fierce

attack on the 'ballad-monger' Southey and Tom Moore
who, as we know, is not one to demur

from inviting him over to Chalk Farm,
whence (yet again) they return as brothers-in-arms

to drink each other's health from (yet again) a human skull;
Southey henceforth dubs them 'The Satanic School'.

## [LEWIS]

October 11th, 1809. Governor Lewis attempts to cram
the gralloch-grummle
back into the hole in his belly.
The half-ounce ball
from a second heavy-calibre
pistol has clabbered
his brow, leaving part of his brain exposed
to the idle boast
that, since these were his own weapons,
he must have acted himself, and was not acted upon.

## [ORTEGA]

August 10th, 1815. In the course of a game of lacrosse
played in his honour

by the Seneca élite,
Handsome Lake takes a firm hold

of the handle of his valise and sets out on an inner
journey along the path covered with grass.

[HERRIGEL]

Through the hoopless hoop of an elk-horn bow.


[KEYNES]

———

To the Northwest Company post
on the Assiniboine, which is even now beset

by a war-party of Crows.
Their war-chief (that *éminence grise*

in the buffalo rug)
is William Clark's old freed-man, York.

———

While his warriors are gainfully employed
in breaking out barrels, bales and bolts,

York keeps harking back to the mile-high
column of smoke in an otherwise flawless sky.


[BACHELARD]

Six hours ago, and twenty miles away, they had chanced
on a wagon drawn by a mule-team,
de dum,
and driven by a grizzly bear

who levelled his smooth-bore
not at them, but Shad,
and finished him off with a single shot.
He then stood his ground as, one by one, the Crows

charged at him in an elaborate criss-cross
only to cajole
him with their coup-crooks and cudgels.
When York swooped down and caught him by the scruff

of the neck, Cinnamond simply sloughed off
his skin and slithered
under the wagon like a lizard.
Then, as if this might indeed hold them at bay,

he lit a whisper of hay
and set fire to a semi-circle of sage-brush
that shortly engulfed the wagon, where he surely perished.
York's throat still rankles with aniseed.


[BOHR]

He has nothing to show for his morning's exertions
but this caparison
of stuff he still takes for shagreen
and the one-eyed cloud on the distant horizon.

———

September 26th, 1820. At Femme Osage, on the lower Missouri,
Daniel Boone is about to give up the ghost

when the beaver-skeleton on the wall
starts to glow and hum, looks about to make sure the coast

is clear, then drags itself, traps and all,
across the floor, along the bed: 'Put me out of my misery.'

———

None of the paeans and panegyrics
trouble Southey so much as the 'Byron' of Byron, New York.

[COLLINGWOOD]

An even more distressing thought. On August 23rd, 1805, Lewis and
Clark had submerged their boats, weighting them with stones, and
were travelling on horseback when they met the Flatheads. How
might Coleridge have stolen a pirogue, when there was none to steal?

[WITTGENSTEIN]

'Now your stumparumper is a connoisorrow who has lost his ras-
pectabilberry.'

## [HEIDEGGER]

'I wanted merely to assure you that the name "Evans"
is akin to both "Eoghan" and "Owen

Gwyneth", the father of Madoc,
and that Madoc himself is, above all, emblematic

of our desire to go beyond ourselves . . .'
A tousle of loam

from the mausoleum:
'When my own grandsire, another Bucephalus,

surged through a fetlock-bracing creek
at the head of the force led by Partholan the Greek

and shook himself out on that Irish strand
he was confident, too, that his time was at hand.'

## [GRAMSCI]

Coleridge casts a paternoster into the murky stream.
He himself has only a remote

idea of his whereabouts.
A communal hut. A remuda

of skeletal ponies. Rabbits and more rabbits.
Try as he may, he has but a dim

recollection of why he might have cut
these wind-chimes

from a cloudy yellow lump of agate
and strung them like icicles

in the thatch. Still no take
on the line. He opens a rabbit-skin satchel

and starts to hoke
for a buddy-bud-bud of his so-called Paddy Nostrum.


[CARNAP]

———

February 6th, 1822. Byron is on his hands and knees
as he sookies another canto of *Don Juan*
into the daylight, by its nose;
he himself is his own ball-and-chain.

———

*Of all men, saving Sylla the Man-slayer,*
    *Who passes for in life and death most lucky,*
*Of the great names which in our faces stare,*
    *The General Boon, back-woodsman of Kentucky,*
*Was happiest amongst mortals any where;*
    *For, killing nothing but a bear or buck, he*
*Enjoyed the lonely, vigorous, harmless days*
*Of his old age in wilds of deepest maze.*

———

The Contessa, meanwhile, is taking a snooze;
a little dribble down her chin
is the only sign of their earlier antics
when she winkled the 'semen' out of 'semantics'.

## [BENJAMIN]

Later that afternoon, or the next, a filibegged Byron will hobble
through the streets of Pisa
and trip over a cobble.
As he sprawls there, a group of boys
begin to jeer, '*Diavolo*'.
That night, he writes to Southey to propose
he either retract the 'Satanic' canard
or give him satisfaction. (This missive's intercepted by Kinnaird.)

## [HUXLEY]

———

Bearing only his rabbit-skin satchel, five hawks'-bells,
the sacred

calumet,
a smidgin of laver-bread,

Coleridge is himself the blossom in the bud
of peyote.

———

Betimes a cormorant, betimes a white coyote,
will guide

him across the Lava Beds,
the Klamath

mountains, over plains and forests, to the ziggurats
of Southeyopolis.

**[BAKHTIN]**

Where the flossofer
declaims

from Byron;
Coleridge remarks on the glair-

glim
of mica and feldspar

on the collar
of Southey's closely-knit byrnie.


**[MARCUSE]**

*He had written praises of a regicide;*
    *He had written praises of all kings whatever;*
*He had written for republics far and wide,*
    *And then against them bitterer than ever;*
*For pantisocracy he once had cried*
    *Aloud, a scheme less moral than 'twas clever;*
*Then grew a hearty antijacobin—*
*Had turn'd his coat—and would have turn'd his skin.*
          (Byron, *The Vision of Judgement*)


**[LEWIS]**

Coleridge lays a comforting hand on Southey's shoulder.

## [GADAMER]

*He had sung against all battles, and again*
*    In their high praise and glory: he had call'd*
*Reviewing 'the ungentle craft', and then*
*    Become as base a critic as ere crawl'd—*
*Fed, paid, and pamper'd by the very men*
*    By whom his muse and morals had been maul'd:*
*He had written much blank verse, and blanker prose,*
*And more of both than any body knows.*
                    (Byron, *The Vision of Judgement*)

## [RYLE]

———

A twitch at his sleeve. Southey grasps the arm
and, with all his might,
wrangles the fiend across the room
and jerks its face into the candlelight.

———

Three Cayuga women are sorely vexed
by the sight of a phantom hound—
too small for a wolf, too big for a fox—
scrabbling near the stallion's burial-mound.

## [LACAN]

The wraith pokes its tongue in Southey's ear—
'Rhythm in all thought, and joyance everywhere'—
before leaving only a singe on the air.

[TARSKI]

———

The truth is that the phantom hound
was a coyote

the Cayuga women had killed with their bare hands
and tied by its brush to the postern-gate.

———

Southey interprets this as a revival
of the white dog ceremony

and inaugurates a witch-hunt.

———

May, 1826. Catlin steps back from his remarkably accurate
portrait of the Seneca orator Red Jacket.

———

Blennerhassett bumps into Sam Favell:
'Sorry, Sam.' 'You must be Harman.'

'So *this* is the famous chestnut jennet?'

———

Southey draws a circle with his goose-quill pen
around the name of the wet-nurse, Bean.

**[HOOK]**

———

Whom he sentences to twenty strokes of the birch.

———

After ten, her back and buttocks are blood-
smirched.

———

When he attempts to intercede on behalf of Bean,
South takes a blow to his shoulder-blade
for his pains.

———

The rod cuts right through his leather cuirass,
leaving a deep, trifoliate
graze.

———

The Cayugas are now openly in revolt;
that evening, South leads an exodus
through the dykes and ditches and into the shadows.

**[POPPER]**

We last see him crouching in blood like a jugged hare.
As to where he goes? It's a matter of pure conjecture.

## [ADORNO]

———

April 19th, 1824. On the shore at Missolonghi
Byron's ball-and-chain is missing a link.

———

Independence Day, 1826. A gasp on a cello
or viola reverberates through Monticello.

The polygraph at its usual rigmarole.
The gopher pining for a caramel.

———

Jefferson clutches a bar of lye-soap
on which is scratched the name BEELZEBUB.

## [SARTRE]

June, 1830. As he follows General Clark from the main street
of St Louis and down a muddy path
Catlin is suddenly distraught.
Outside a booth

stacked with jiggers and jeroboams
of a patent elixir
based on tincture of opium,
a crowd has gathered

round a quack
and his guy, who has just now bitten the head
off a live pullet.

Something about this geek
reminds Catlin of his childhood.
A tiny piece of grit in the eye. The blebs. The blenny-blets.


[GOODMAN]

*Now I am inclined to believe that the ten ships of Madoc, or Madawc,*
*made their way up the Mississippi and, at length, advanced up the*
*Missouri to the place where they have been known for many years*
*past by the name of the Mandans, a corruption or abbreviation, per-*
*haps, of 'Madawgwys', the name applied by the Welsh to the followers*
*of Madawc.*

(Catlin)


[ARENDT]

September, 1832. Among these Mandan and Minnetaree
sachems and seneschals

who crowd around Catlin's easel
is one chief's daughter, Midday Sun;

her quaint medicine-
bag was taken during a raid on the Snakes:

as was the snig
of hemp about her neck and, yes, the miniature key.

'Where's my stumparumper? My confabulumper?
My maffrum? My goffrum? My swarnish pigglepow?'

*A few miles from Floyd's Bluff, we landed our canoe and spent a day
in the vicinity of Blackbird's Grave. This very noted chief had been
placed astride his horse's back, with his bow in his hand, and every
warrior of his band painted the palm of his right hand with vermilion,
which was stamped on the milk-white sides of his devoted horse. This
all done, turfs were brought and placed around the feet and legs of the
horse, and gradually up to its sides, and over the back and head of the
unsuspecting animal, and last of all, over the head and even the eagle-
plumes of its valiant rider, where altogether have smouldered and re-
mained undisturbed to the present day.*

(Catlin)

July 25th, 1834. A tinkle on an Aeolian harp
across the scrub

and salt-flats.
Coleridge props himself up under a canopy of gnats

and returns their call to a pair of chickadees:
'Quiddities. Quiddities. Quiddities.'

## [LÉVI-STRAUSS]

Since there's . . . since there's no kelp, come lettuce
draw back the flimsy rattan
lattice.

'At any moment now, his retina
will disintegrate.'
The burden

of a hurdy-gurdy
played by one Modoc damozel.
Another proffers him a sweet gourd

from her camisole.
Liver-wort. Bladder-wrack. Sea-kale. Samphire.
Elm. Holm-oak. Mistletoe.

Ash. Beech. Sycamore.
Yew; his self-bow backed with bone and sinew
in the belly of which the sagamore

finds a tiny crysal. Coleridge insinu-
ates himself through this crack into the vaults
of the Domdaniel. His familiar is a coyote made of snow.

## [WEIL]

'For the only society I have left now
is Bumble-Cum-Tumble and Doggy-Bow-Wow.'

[AYER]

September 14th, 1836. Burr is incontrovertibly dead.


[AUSTIN]

Even though the tree-girt auditorium,
de dum,

is deserted but for a troop
of nymphs and gnomes

and nixies,
Southey hikes up his tabard

and mounts the podium,
de dum.

As he warms to a diatribe
against his enemies

he nags
at the filigreed scabbard

of his sword
so as to emmmmmmmmmmmmphasize his words.


[RICOEUR]

*For more than half a century, English literature had been distin-
guished by its moral purity, the effect, and in turn the cause, of an im-
provement in national manners.*

*A father might, without apprehension of evil, have put into the hands of his children any book which issued from the press, if it did not bear, either in its title-page or frontispiece, manifest signs that it was intended as furniture for the brothel.*

*This was particularly the case with regard to our poetry.*

*It is now no longer so, and woe to those by whom the offence cometh. The school which they have set up may properly be called the Satanic School; for though their productions breathe the spirit of Belial in their lascivious parts, and the spirit of Moloch in those loathesome images of atrocities and horror which they delight to represent, they are more especially characterized by a Satanic spirit of pride and audacious impiety, which still betrays the wretched feeling of hopelessness wherewith it is allied.*

(Southey)

[CAMUS]

June 16th, 1837. The Mandan villages are ravaged by smallpox.

[GRICE]

November 16th. The last word on Edith Southey's lips is 'sentiment'.

[BARTHES]

March 20th, 1843. An almost naked 'Mandan' in harlequin
red and black lozenges
manages only one shot from his squirrel-gun
before a raiding-party of 'Shoshones'

rush his buffalo-wallow
and wrestle
him to the ground. His ululations are to no avail.
They take his scalp. The rehearsal

ends with the 'Shoshone' chief returning the pony-tail
wig to his victim
who stuffs it into a buckskin medicine-bundle,
his *vade mecum*,

which is then lodged in a glory-hole
back in his caravan.
This afternoon finds 'Catlin's Indian Gallery'
somewhere in deepest Wales. In the port, say, of Carnarvon.


[STRAWSON]

The 'Shoshone' is indisputably the artist's nephew, Theodore 'Burr'
Catlin. As for the 'Mandan', when he washes off the lamp-black and
vermilion paint, there's a fleur-de-lys on his shoulder-blade.


[FRANKLIN]

———

And those teeny-weeny keys on their toggles
of hemp?

———

And those teeny-weeny keys on their toggles
of hemp?

———

Again, exactly identical.

[GASS]

In that buckskin parfleche decorated with porcupine quills
are item, a 'catlinite' pipe, item, a soap-stone urn,
item, a belt of blue beads, item, a bow made of horn,
and item, de dum, de dum, Blackbird's and his horse's skulls.


[FOUCAULT]

March 21st, 1843. A volley
of grape-shot from two foul-mouthed basilisks
or culverins.
A breach in the live-oak bailey.
Gavelocks. Pole-axes.

In 'France',
a False Face lifts his visor
and looks agog
from the horse-tail ferns
at the capstan's shorn and bloody hawser.

One Cayuga's
ganched on the teeth of a harrow.
Brays. Bleats. Bellows. Burning brands.
Bucephalus kicks
out in his long barrow.

A bloody handprint
on the flank
of the spirit-steed.
The stone blockhouse has borne the brunt
of the onslaught by a phalanx

of the Turtle clan, who form a *testudo*
behind a battering-ram.
One elbows
his way down the flue of the study,
where he finds the Grand Panjandrum

fast asleep
at the mahogany desk.
He blithely
clutches (1) a copy of *Thalaba*
and (2) the tortoise-shell powder-flask.

[PUTNAM]

———

Southey's lime-scaled pate with its scrofulous,
its scabrous diadem,

de dum,
lolls upon the other-worldly valise.

———

They strip him to the waist. The demagogue
is allowed one ladle of rum,

de dum,
from the keg

to help ward off the ram-
rods and switches and taws and tomahawks,

de dum, de dum,
wielded by the ghosts of a thousand Cayugas.

**[CHOMSKY]**

Several of whom begin to applaud.
He takes the plunge. Whereupon

he's in blood
stepp'd in so far . . . A furbelow of razor-ribbon

on which he'll come to grief.


**[HABERMAS]**

His head is swathed in a bloody turban.
The Cayugas remove the bolts

from their Accarbines
while the wet-set lay him on the pallet

and hook him up to the retinagraph.


**[DERRIDA]**

———

A glance back to the great palladium,
de dum,

as it goes up in flames.
Its voluminous

tulles and smoke-taffetas.
The fetid

stink of new-fangled creosote.
Tar-water. Tar-water and a sooty crust.

———

'At any moment now, the retina
will be in smithereens.'

———

The buckler affixed to the mast-head by a cleat
bears this device: a pair of gryphons

on a field of gold;
a scroll emblazoned with the word 'CROTONA'.

[HARMAN]

'Not "CROATAN", not "CROATOAN", but "CROTONA".'

[NOZICK]

———

May, 1843. 'Catlin's Indian Gallery' has now reached Ireland. Half-way between Belfast and Dublin, near the present site of Unitel West, the medicine-bag is either misplaced or stolen.

———

May, 1846. President Polk engages a secret agent against Mexico. His name? 'Magoffin'.

———

May, 1873. The Modocs, led by Captain Jack, are systematically hunted down on the laver-breads of Oregon.

## [KRISTEVA]

'Signifump. Signifump. Signifump.'

## [HAWKING]

———

The Cayugas have shouldered their Lasabers
and smoothed their scalp-locks.

A scrap of paper in a valise
now falls within the range

of a sensor-tile. The corridor
awash in slime. Trifoliate Chinese orange.

One leg held on by a frivolous
blood-garter.

———

It will all be over, de dum,
in next to no time—

long before 'The fluted cypresses
rear'd up their living obelisks'

has sent a shiver, de dum, de dum,
through Unitel, its iridescent Dome.

THE ANNALS OF CHILE 1994

*Book VI, Lines 313–81*

All the more reason, then, that men and women
should go in fear of Leto, their vengeful, vindictive numen,
and worship the mother of Apollo and Artemis
all the more zealously. This last tale of the demise
of Niobe brought others to mind, inspiring no less zeal
among the storytellers. 'On the fertile soil
of Lycia,' one began, 'the peasants, too, would scorn
Leto and pay the price. Since these Lycians were low-born,
the remarkable story of what happened
is scarcely known, though I saw with my own eyes the pond
where the wonder took place. My father, being too frail
to travel far himself, had sent me on the trail
of a string of prime bullocks he'd turned out
in those distant parts. He'd given me a Lycian scout
whom I followed over the rich
pasture till we came on a lake in the midst of which
stood an ancient altar, its stones blackened
by many sacrificial fires, set in a quicken
of reeds. The scout stopped in his tracks and said in a quiet
voice, "Have mercy on us", and I echoed
him, "Have mercy". When I asked my guide
if this was a shrine to the Naiads or Faunus or some such god
he replied, "Not at all, son: no common hill-god or genius
presides over this place but the one whom Juno
sentenced to wander round and round,
never to set foot on solid ground;
the goddess who dwells
here was the one to whom even Delos
gave short shrift,
though Delos itself was totally adrift;
on that unstable island, braced between a palm and a gnarled
olive, she brought her twins into the world,
then, clasping them to her breast,
set off again with Juno in hot pursuit.

By the time she touched down in Lycia, the bailiwick
of the Chimera, she was completely whacked
from her long travail; the intense heat
had left her drained; her breast-milk had run out.
Just then she stumbled upon a fair-to-middling-sized pond
in which some locals were cutting osiers and bent
and sawgrass and sedge.
Leto knelt by the water's edge
and made to cup her hands. But these local yokels
shook their reaping-hooks and sickles
and wouldn't let her drink. 'Why,' she begged them, 'why
would you deny me what's not yours to deny
since water, along with air and light,
is held by all in common, as a common right?
It's not as if I'm about to throw
myself headlong into your pool. My throat's so dry
and my tongue so swollen I can barely utter
this simple request for a life-giving drink of water.
If not for mine, then for my children's sakes,
I implore you to let us slake
our thirsts.' At that moment, the twins stretched
out their little hands. Who could fail to be touched
by such entreaties? These begrudgers, though, were moved
only to renew their threats and foul oaths:
then, to add insult
to injury, they began to stomp about and stir up the silt
on the bottom of the pond, muddying the water
out of no motive other than sheer spite.
That was it: that was as much as the Titan's daughter
could take; 'Since you've shown,' she cried, 'no soft spot
for me, in this soft spot you'll always stay.'
And stay they have: now they love nothing more than to play
in water, giving themselves over to total
immersion or contentedly skimming the surface; they dawdle
on the bank only to dive back in; now, as ever,
they work themselves into a lather
over some imagined slight; since they continually curse
and swear their voices are hoarse

while their necks, in so far as there's anything between
their heads and shoulders, are goitred; with their yellow
paunches set off by backs of olive-green,
they go leaping about the bog-hole with their frog-fellows." '

## BRAZIL

———

When my mother snapped open her flimsy parasol
it was Brazil: if not Brazil,

then Uruguay.
One nipple darkening her smock.

My shame-faced *Tantum Ergo*
struggling through thurified smoke.

———

Later that afternoon would find
me hunched over the font

as she rinsed my hair. Her towel-turban.
Her terrapin

comb scuttling under the faucet.
I stood there in my string vest

and shorts while she repeated, '*Champi* . . . ?
*Champi* . . . ? *Champi* . . . ?' Then,

that bracelet of shampoo
about the bone, her triumphant '*Champi*ÑON'.

———

If not Uruguay, then Ecuador:
it must be somewhere on or near the equator

given how water
plunged headlong into water

when she pulled the plug.
So much for the obliq-

uity of leaving *What a Boy Should Know*
under my pillow: now *vagina* and *vas*

*deferens* made a holy show
of themselves. 'There is inherent vice

in everything,' as O'Higgins
would proclaim: it was O'Higgins who duly

had the terms 'widdershins'
and 'deasil' expunged from the annals of Chile.

## OSCAR

———

Be that as it may, I'm wakened by the moans
not of the wind
nor the wood-demons

but Oscar MacOscair, as we call the hound
who's wangled himself
into our bed: 'Why?' 'Why not?'

He lies between us like an ancient quoof
with a snout of perished gutta-
percha, and whines at something on the roof.

—

I'm suddenly mesmerized
by what I saw only today: a pair of high heels
abandoned on the road to Amherst.

—

And I've taken off, over the towns of Keady
and Aughnacloy and Caledon—
*Et in Arcadia*—

to a grave lit by acetylene
in which, though she preceded him
by a good ten years, my mother's skeleton

has managed to worm
its way back on top of the old man's,
and she once again has him under her thumb.

## MILKWEED AND MONARCH

—

As he knelt by the grave of his mother and father
the taste of dill, or tarragon—
he could barely tell one from the other—

filled his mouth. It seemed as if he might smother.
Why should he be stricken
with grief, not for his mother and father,

but a woman slinking from the fur of a sea-otter
in Portland, Maine, or, yes, Portland, Oregon—
he could barely tell one from the other—

and why should he now savour
the tang of her, her little pickled gherkin,
as he knelt by the grave of his mother and father?

He looked about. He remembered her palaver
on how both earth and sky would darken—
'You could barely tell one from the other'—

while the Monarch butterflies passed over
in their milkweed-hunger: 'A wing-beat, some reckon,
may trigger off the mother and father

of all storms, striking your Irish Cliffs of Moher
with the force of a hurricane.'
Then: 'Milkweed and Monarch "invented" each other.'

———

He looked about. Cow's-parsley in a samovar.
He'd mistaken his mother's name, 'Regan', for 'Anger':
as he knelt by the grave of his mother and father
he could barely tell one from the other.

## TWICE

It was so cold last night the water in the barrel grew a sod
of water: I asked Taggart and McAnespie to come over
and we sawed and sawed
for half an hour until, using a crowbar as a lever

in the way Archimedes always said
would shift the balance, we were somehow able to manoeuvre
out and, finally, stand on its side
in the snow that fifteen- or eighteen-inch-thick manhole cover:

that 'manhole cover' was surely no more ice
than are McAnespie and Taggart still of this earth;
when I squinnied through it I saw 'Lefty' Clery, 'An Ciotach',

grinning from both ends of the school photograph,
having jooked behind the three-deep rest of us to meet the Kodak's
leisurely pan; 'Two places at once, was it, or one place twice?'


## INCANTATA

*In memory of Mary Farl Powers*

I thought of you tonight, *a leanbh*, lying there in your long barrow
colder and dumber than a fish by Francisco de Herrera,
as I X-Actoed from a spud the Inca
glyph for a mouth: thought of that first time I saw your pink
spotted torso, distant-near as a nautilus,
when you undid your portfolio, yes indeedy,
and held the print of what looked like a cankered potato
at arm's length—your arms being longer, it seemed, than Lugh's.

Even Lugh of the Long (sometimes the Silver) Arm
would have wanted some distance between himself and the army-
        worms
that so clouded the sky over St Cloud you'd have to seal
the doors and windows and steel
yourself against their nightmarish *déjeuner sur l'herbe*:
try as you might to run a foil
across their tracks, it was to no avail;
the army-worms shinnied down the stove-pipe on an army-worm rope.

I can hardly believe that, when we met, my idea of 'R and R'
was to get smashed, almost every night, on sickly-sweet Demarara
rum and Coke: as well as leaving you a grass widow
(remember how Krapp looks up 'viduity'?),
after eight or ten or twelve of those dark rums
it might be eight or ten or twelve o'clock before I'd land
back home in Landseer Street, deaf and blind
to the fact that not only was I all at sea, but in the doldrums.

Again and again you'd hold forth on your own version of Thomism,
your own *Summa*
*Theologiae* that in everything there is an order,
that the things of the world sing out in a great oratorio:
it was Thomism, though, tempered by *La Nausée*,
by His Nibs Sam Bethicket,
and by that Dublin thing, that an artist must walk down Baggott
Street wearing a hair-shirt under the shirt of Nessus.

*'D'éirigh me ar maidin,'* I sang, *'a tharraingt chun aoinigh mhóir'*:
our first night, you just had to let slip that your secret amour
for a friend of mine was such
that you'd ended up lying with him in a ditch
under a bit of whin, or gorse, or furze,
somewhere on the border of Leitrim, perhaps, or Roscommon:
'gamine,' I wanted to say, 'kimono';
even then it was clear I'd never be at the centre of your universe.

Nor should I have been, since you were there already, your own *Ding
an sich*, no less likely to take wing
than the Christ you drew for a Christmas card as a pupa
in swaddling clothes: and how resolutely you would pooh-pooh
the idea I shared with Vladimir and Estragon,
with whom I'd been having a couple of jars,
that this image of the Christ-child swaddled and laid in the manger
could be traced directly to those army-worm dragoons.

I thought of the night Vladimir was explaining to all and sundry
the difference between *geantrai* and *suantrai*
and you remarked on how you used to have a crush
on Burt Lancaster as Elmer Gantry, and Vladimir went to brush
the ash off his sleeve with a legerdemain
that meant only one thing—'Why does he put up with this crap?'—
and you weighed in with 'To live in a dustbin, eating scrap,
seemed to Nagg and Nell a most eminent domain.'

How little you were exercised by those tiresome literary intrigues,
how you urged me to have no more truck

than the Thane of Calder
with a fourth estate that professes itself to be *'égalitaire'*
but wants only blood on the sand: yet, irony of ironies,
you were the one who, in the end,
got yourself up as a *retiarius* and, armed with net and trident,
marched from Mount Street to the Merrion Square arena.

In the end, you were the one who went forth to beard the lion,
you who took the DART line
every day from Jane's flat in Dun Laoghaire, or Dalkey,
dreaming your dream that the subterranean Dodder and Tolka
might again be heard above the *hoi polloi*
for whom Irish 'art' means a High Cross at Carndonagh or Corofin
and *The Book of Kells*: not until the lion cried craven
would the poor Tolka and the poor Dodder again sing out for joy.

I saw you again tonight, in your jump-suit, thin as a rake,
your hand moving in such a deliberate arc
as you ground a lithographic stone
that your hand and the stone blurred to one
and your face blurred into the face of your mother, Betty Wahl,
who took your failing, ink-stained hand
in her failing, ink-stained hand
and together you ground down that stone by sheer force of will.

I remember your pooh-poohing, as we sat there on the *Enterprise*,
my theory that if your name is Powers
you grow into it or, at least,
are less inclined to tremble before the likes of this bomb-blast
further up the track: I myself was shaking like a leaf
as we wondered whether the I.R.A. or the Red
Hand Commandos or even the Red
Brigades had brought us to a standstill worthy of Hamm and Clov.

Hamm and Clov; Nagg and Nell; Watt and Knott;
the fact is that we'd been at a standstill long before the night
things came to a head,
long before we'd sat for half the day in the sweltering heat

somewhere just south of Killnasaggart
and I let slip a name—her name—off my tongue
and you turned away (I see it now) the better to deliver the sting
in your own tail, to let slip your own little secret.

I thought of you again tonight, thin as a rake, as you bent
over the copper plate of 'Emblements',
its tidal wave of army-worms into which you all but disappeared:
I wanted to catch something of its spirit
and yours, to body out your disembodied *vox*
*clamantis in deserto*, to let this all-too-cumbersome device
of a potato-mouth in a potato-face
speak out, unencumbered, from its long, low, mould-filled box.

I wanted it to speak to what seems always true of the truly great,
that you had a winningly inaccurate
sense of your own worth, that you would second-guess
yourself too readily by far, that you would rally to any cause
before your own, mine even,
though you detected in me a tendency to put
on too much artificiality, both as man and poet,
which is why you called me 'Polyester' or 'Polyurethane'.

That last time in Dublin, I copied with a quill dipped in oak-gall
onto a sheet of vellum, or maybe a human caul,
a poem for *The Great Book of Ireland*: as I watched the low
swoop over the lawn today of a swallow
I thought of your animated talk of Camille Pissarro
and André Derain's *The Turning Road, L'Estaque*:
when I saw in that swallow's nest a face in a mud-pack
from that muddy road I was filled again with a profound sorrow.

You must have known already, as we moved from the 'Hurly Burly'
to McDaid's or Riley's,
that something was amiss: I think you even mentioned a homeopath
as you showed off the great new acid-bath
in the Graphic Studio, and again undid your portfolio
to lay out your latest works; I try to imagine the strain

you must have been under, pretending to be as right as rain
while hearing the bells of a church from some long-flooded valley.

From the Quabbin reservoir, maybe, where the banks and bakeries
of a dozen little submerged Pompeii reliquaries
still do a roaring trade: as clearly as I saw your death-mask
in that swallow's nest, you must have heard the music
rise from the muddy ground between
your breasts as a nocturne, maybe, by John Field;
to think that you thought yourself so invulnerable, so inviolate,
that a little cancer could be beaten.

You must have known, as we walked through the ankle-deep clabber
with Katherine and Jean and the long-winded Quintus Calaber,
that cancer had already made such a breach
that you would almost surely perish:
you must have thought, as we walked through the woods
along the edge of the Quabbin,
that rather than let some doctor cut you open
you'd rely on infusions of hardock, hemlock, all the idle weeds.

I thought again of how art may be made, as it was by André Derain,
of nothing more than a turn
in the road where a swallow dips into the mire
or plucks a strand of bloody wool from a strand of barbed wire
in the aftermath of Chickamauga or Culloden
and builds from pain, from misery, from a deep-seated hurt,
a monument to the human heart
that shines like a golden dome among roofs rain-glazed and leaden.

I wanted the mouth in this potato-cut
to be heard far beyond the leaden, rain-glazed roofs of Quito,
to be heard all the way from the southern hemisphere
to Clontarf or Clondalkin, to wherever your sweet-severe
spirit might still find a toe-hold
in this world: it struck me then how you would be aghast
at the thought of my thinking you were some kind of ghost
who might still roam the earth in search of an earthly delight.

You'd be aghast at the idea of your spirit hanging over this vale
of tears like a jump-suited jump-jet whose vapour-trail
unravels a sky: for there's nothing, you'd say, nothing over
and above the sky itself, nothing but cloud-cover
reflected in a thousand lakes; it seems that Minne-
sota itself means 'sky-tinted water', that the sky is a great slab
of granite or iron ore that might at any moment slip
back into the worked-out sky-quarry, into the worked-out sky-mines.

To use the word 'might' is to betray you once too often, to betray
your notion that nothing's random, nothing arbitrary:
the gelignite weeps, the hands fly by on the alarm clock,
the '*Enterprise*' goes clackety-clack
as they all must; even the car hijacked that morning in the Cross,
that was preordained, its owner spread on the bonnet
before being gagged and bound or bound
and gagged, that was fixed like the stars in the Southern Cross.

The fact that you were determined to cut yourself off in your prime
because it was *pre*-determined has my eyes abrim:
I crouch with Belacqua
and Lucky and Pozzo in the Acacacac-
ademy of Anthropopopometry, trying to make sense of the '*quaquaqua*'
of that potato-mouth; that mouth as prim
and proper as it's full of self-opprobrium,
with its '*quaquaqua*', with its 'Quoiquoiquoiquoiquoiquoiquoiq'.

That's all that's left of the voice of Enrico Caruso
from all that's left of an opera-house somewhere in Matto Grosso,
all that's left of the hogweed and horehound and cuckoo-pint,
of the eighteen soldiers dead at Warrenpoint,
of the Black Church clique and the Graphic Studio claque,
of the many moons of glasses on a tray,
of the brewery-carts drawn by moon-booted drays,
of those jump-suits worn under your bottle-green worsted cloak.

Of the great big dishes of chicken lo mein and beef chow mein,
of what's mine is yours and what's yours mine,

of the oxlips and cowslips
on the banks of the Liffey at Leixlip
where the salmon breaks through the either/or neither/nor nether
reaches despite the temple-veil
of itself being rent and the penny left out overnight on the rail
is a sheet of copper when the mail-train has passed over.

Of the bride carried over the threshold, hey, only to alight
on the limestone slab of another threshold,
of the swarm, the cast,
the colt, the spew of bees hanging like a bottle of Lucozade
from a branch the groom must sever,
of Emily Post's ruling, in *Etiquette*,
on how best to deal with the butler being in cahoots
with the cook when they're both in cahoots with the chauffeur.

Of that poplar-flanked stretch of road between Leiden
and The Hague, of the road between Rathmullen and Ramelton,
where we looked so long and hard
for some trace of Spinoza or Amelia Earhart,
both of them going down with their engines on fire:
of the stretch of road somewhere near Urney
where Orpheus was again overwhelmed by that urge to turn
back and lost not only Eurydice but his steel-strung lyre.

Of the sparrows and finches in their bell of suet,
of the bitter-sweet
bottle of Calvados we felt obliged to open
somewhere near Falaise, so as to toast our new-found *copains*,
of the priest of the parish
who came enquiring about our 'status', of the hedge-clippers
I somehow had to hand, of him running like the clappers
up Landseer Street, of my subsequent self-reproach.

Of the remnants of Airey Neave, of the remnants of Mountbatten,
of the famous *andouilles*, of the famous *boudins
noirs et blancs*, of the barrel-vault
of the Cathedral at Rouen, of the flashlight, fat and roll of felt

on each of their sledges, of the music
of Joseph Beuys's pack of huskies, of that baldy little bugger
mushing them all the way from Berncastel through Bacarrat
to Belfast, his head stuck with honey and gold-leaf like a mosque.

Of Benjamin Britten's *Lachrymae*, with its gut-wrenching viola,
of Vivaldi's *Four Seasons*, of Frankie Valli's,
of Braque's great painting *The Shower of Rain*,
of the fizzy, lemon or sherbet-green *Rana*
*temporaria* plonked down in Trinity like a little Naugahyde pouffe,
of eighteen soldiers dead in Oriel,
of the weakness for a little fol-de-rol-de-rolly
suggested by the gap between the front teeth of the Wife of Bath.

Of *A Sunday Afternoon on the Island of La Grande Jatte*, of Seurat's
piling of tesserae upon tesserae
to give us a monkey arching its back
and the smoke arching out from a smoke-stack,
of Sunday afternoons in the Botanic Gardens, going with the flow
of the burghers of Sandy Row and Donegal
Pass and Andersonstown and Rathcoole,
of the army Landrover flaunt-flouncing by with its heavy furbelow.

Of Marlborough Park, of Notting Hill, of the Fitzroy Avenue
immortalized by Van 'His real name's Ivan'
Morrison, 'and him the dead spit
of Padraic Fiacc', of John Hewitt, the famous expat,
in whose memory they offer every year six of their best milch cows,
of the Bard of Ballymacarrett,
of every ungodly poet in his or her godly garret,
of Medhbh and Michael and Frank and Ciaran and 'wee' John
        Qughes.

Of the Belfast school, so called, of the school of hard knocks,
of your fervent eschewal of stockings and socks
as you set out to hunt down your foes
as implacably as the *tóraidheacht* through the Fews

of Redmond O'Hanlon, of how that 'd' and that 'c' aspirate
in *tóraidheacht* make it sound like a last gasp in an oxygen-tent,
of your refusal to open a vent
but to breathe in spirit of salt, the mordant salt-spirit.

Of how mordantly hydrochloric acid must have scored and scarred,
of the claim that boiled skirrets
can cure the spitting of blood, of that dank
flat somewhere off Morehampton Road, of the unbelievable stink
of valerian or feverfew simmering over a low heat,
of your sitting there, pale and gaunt,
with that great prescriber of boiled skirrets, Dr John Arbuthnot,
your face in a bowl of feverfew, a towel over your head.

Of the great roll of paper like a bolt of cloth
running out again and again like a road at the edge of a cliff,
of how you called a Red Admiral a Red
*Admirable*, of how you were never in the red
on either the first or the last
of the month, of your habit of loosing the drawstring of your purse
and finding one scrunched-up, obstreperous
note and smoothing it out and holding it up, pristine and pellucid.

Of how you spent your whole life with your back to the wall,
of your generosity when all the while
you yourself lived from hand
to mouth, of Joseph Beuys's pack of hounds
crying out from their felt and fat 'Atone, atone, atone',
of Watt remembering the '*Krak! Krek! Krik!*'
of those three frogs' karaoke
like the still, sad *basso continuo* of the great quotidian.

Of a ground bass of sadness, yes, but also a sennet of hautboys
as the fat and felt hounds of Beuys O'Beuys
bayed at the moon over a caravan
in Dunmore East, I'm pretty sure it was, or Dungarvan:
of my guest appearance in your self-portrait not as a hidalgo

from a long line
of hidalgos but a hound-dog, a *leanbh*,
a dog that skulks in the background, a dog that skulks and stalks.

Of that self-portrait, of the self-portraits by Rembrandt van Rijn,
of all that's revelation, all that's rune,
of all that's composed, all composed of odds and ends,
of that daft urge to make amends
when it's far too late, too late even to make sense of the clutter
of false trails and reversed horseshoe tracks
and the aniseed we took it in turn to drag
across each other's scents, when only a fish is dumber and colder.

Of your avoidance of canned goods, in the main,
on account of the exceeeeeeeeeeeeeeeedingly high risk of ptomaine,
of corned beef in particular being full of crap,
of your delight, so, in eating a banana as ceremoniously as Krapp
but flinging the skin over your shoulder like a thrush
flinging off a shell from which it's only just managed to disinter
a snail, like a stone-faced, twelfth-century
FitzKrapp eating his banana by the mellow yellow light of a rush.

Of the 'Yes, let's go' spoken by Monsieur Tarragon,
of the early-ripening jargonelle, the tumorous jardon, the jargon
of jays, the jars
of tomato relish and the jars
of Victoria plums, absolutely *de rigueur* for a passable plum baba,
of the drawers full of balls of twine and butcher's string,
of Dire Straits playing 'The Sultans of Swing',
of the horse's hock suddenly erupting in those boils and buboes.

Of the Greek figurine of a pig, of the pig on a terracotta frieze,
of the sow dropping dead from some mysterious virus,
of your predilection for gammon
served with a sauce of coriander or cumin,
of the slippery elm, of the hornbeam or witch-, or even wych-,
hazel that's good for stopping a haemor-
rhage in mid-flow, of the merest of mere
hints of elderberry curing everything from sciatica to a stitch.

Of the decree *condemnator*, the decree *absolvitor*, the decree *nisi*,
of *Aosdána*, of *an chraobh cnuais*,
of the fields of buckwheat
taken over by garget, inkberry, scoke—all names for pokeweed—
of *Mother Courage*, of *Arturo Ui*,
of those Sunday mornings spent picking at sesame
noodles and all sorts and conditions of dim sum,
of tea and ham sandwiches in the Nesbitt Arms Hotel in Ardara.

Of the day your father came to call, of your leaving your sick-room
in what can only have been a state of delirium,
of how you simply wouldn't relent
from your vision of a blind
watch-maker, of your fatal belief that fate
governs everything from the honey-rust of your father's terrier's
eyebrows to the horse that rusts and rears
in the furrow, of the furrows from which we can no more deviate

than they can from themselves, no more than the map of Europe
can be redrawn, than that Hermes might make a harp from his
                *harpe*,
than that we must live in a vale
of tears on the banks of the Lagan or the Foyle,
than that what we have is a done deal,
than that the Irish Hermes,
Lugh, might have leafed through his vast herbarium
for the leaf that had it within it, Mary, to anoint and anneal,

than that Lugh of the Long Arm might have found in the midst of
                *lus*
*na leac* or *lus na treatha* or *Frannc-lus*,
in the midst of eyebright, or speedwell, or tansy, an antidote,
than that this *Incantata*
might have you look up from your plate of copper or zinc
on which you've etched the row upon row
of army-worms, than that you might reach out, arrah,
and take in your ink-stained hands my own hands stained with ink.

## THE SONOGRAM

Only a few weeks ago, the sonogram of Jean's womb
resembled nothing so much
as a satellite-map of Ireland:

now the image
is so well-defined we can make out not only a hand
but a thumb;

on the road to Spiddal, a woman hitching a ride;
a gladiator in his net, passing judgement on the crowd.


## FOOTLING

This I don't believe: rather than take a header
off the groyne
and into the ground-swell,
yea verily, the *ground-swell* of life,

she shows instead her utter
disregard—part diffidence, but mostly scorn—
for what lies behind the great sea-wall
and what knocks away at the great sea-cliff;

though she's been in training all spring and summer
and swathed herself in fat
and Saran-

Wrap like an old-time Channel swimmer,
she's now got cold feet
and turned in on herself, the phantom 'a' in Cesarian.

## THE BIRTH

Seven o'clock. The seventh day of the seventh month of the year.
No sooner have I got myself up in lime-green scrubs,
a sterile cap and mask,
and taken my place at the head of the table

than the windlass-women ply their shears
and gralloch-grub
for a footling foot, then, warming to their task,
haul into the inestimable

realm of apple-blossoms and chanterelles and damsons and eel-
        spears
and foxes and the general hubbub
of inkies and jennets and Kickapoos with their lemniscs
or peekaboo-quiffs of Russian sable

and tallow-unctuous vernix, into the realm of the widgeon—
the 'whew' or 'yellow-poll', not the 'zuizin'—

Dorothy Aoife Korelitz Muldoon: I watch through floods of tears
as they give her a quick rub-a-dub
and whisk
her off to the nursery, then check their staple-guns for staples.

## CÉSAR VALLEJO: *TESTIMONY*

I will die in Paris, on a day the rain's been coming down hard,
a day I can even now recall.
I will die in Paris—I try not to take this too much to heart—
on a Thursday, probably, in the Fall.

It'll be like today, a Thursday: a Thursday on which, as I make
and remake this poem, the very bones

in my forearms ache.
Never before, along the road, have I felt more alone.

César Vallejo is dead: everyone used to knock him about,
they'll say, though he'd done no harm;
they hit him hard with a rod

and, also, a length of rope; this will be borne out
by Thursdays, by the bones in his forearms,
by loneliness, by heavy rain, by the aforementioned roads.

## COWS

*For Dermot Seymour*

————

Even as we speak, there's a smoker's cough
from behind the whitethorn hedge: we stop dead in our tracks;
a distant tingle of water into a trough.

————

In the past half-hour—since a cattle-truck
all but sent us shuffling off this mortal coil—
we've consoled ourselves with the dregs

of a bottle of Redbreast. Had Hawthorne been a Gael,
I insist, the scarlet 'A' on Hester Prynne
would have stood for 'Alcohol'.

————

This must be the same truck whose tail-lights burn
so dimly, as if caked with dirt,
three or four hundred yards along the boreen

(a diminutive form of the Gaelic *bóthar*, 'a road',
from *bó*, 'a cow', and *thar*
meaning, in this case, something like 'athwart',

'boreen' has entered English 'through the air'
despite the protestations of the O.E.D.):
why, though, should one tail-light flash and flare,

then flicker-fade
to an after-image of tourmaline
set in a dark part-jet, part-jasper or -jade?

———

That smoker's cough again: it triggers off from drumlin
to drumlin an emphysemantiphon
of cows. They hoist themselves on to their trampoline

and steady themselves and straight away divine
water in some far-flung spot
to which they then gravely incline. This is no Devon

cow-coterie, by the way, whey-faced, with Spode
hooves and horns: nor are they the metaphysicattle of Japan
that have merely to anticipate

scoring a bull's-eye and, lo, it happens;
these are earth-flesh, earth-blood, salt of the earth,
whose talismans are their own jaw-bones

buried under threshold and hearth.
For though they trace themselves to the kith and kine
that presided over the birth

of Christ (so carry their calves a full nine
months and boast liquorice
cachous on their tongues), they belong more to the line

that's tramped these cwms and corries
since Cuchulainn tramped Aoife.
Again the flash. Again the fade. However I might allegorize

some oscaraboscarabinary bevy
of cattle there's no getting round this cattle-truck,
one light on the blink, laden with what? Microwaves? Hi-fis?

———

*Oscaraboscarabinary*: a twin, entwined, a tree, a Tuareg;
a double dung-beetle; a plain
and simple hi-firing party; an off-the-back-of-a-lorry drogue?

Enough of Colette and Céline, Céline and Paul Celan:
enough of whether Nabokov
taught at Wellesley or Wesleyan.

Now let us talk of slaughter and the slain,
the helicopter gun-ship, the mighty Kalashnikov:
let's rest for a while in a place where a cow has lain.


## YARROW

Little by little it dawned on us that the row
of kale would shortly be overwhelmed by these pink
and cream blooms, that all of us

would be overwhelmed, that even if my da
were to lose an arm
or a leg to the fly-wheel

of a combine and be laid out on a tarp
in a pool of blood and oil
and my ma were to make one of her increasingly rare

appeals to some higher power, some *Deo*
this or that, all would be swept away by the stream
that fanned across the land.

———

All would be swept away: the altar where Montezuma's
daughter severed her own aorta
with an obsidian knife; where the young Ignatius

of Loyola knelt and, raising the visor of his bucket,
pledged himself either *Ad Major*
or *Ad Majorem Dei Gloriam*, I can't quite remember which.

———

For all would be swept away: the barn where the Pharaohs
had buried Tutankhamen;
where Aladdin found the magic lamp and ring;

where Ali Baba
watched the slave, Morgiana,
pour boiling oil on the thieves in their jars;

where Cicero smooth-talked the senators;
where I myself was caught up in the rush
of peers and paladins who ventured out with Charlemagne.

———

All would be swept away, all sold for scrap:
the hen-house improvised from a high-sided cattle-truck,
the coils of barbed wire, the coulter

of a plough, the pair of angle-iron
posts between which she'll waver, one day towards the end,
as she pins the clothes on the clothes-line.

For the moment, though, she thumbs through a seed-catalogue
she's borrowed from Tohill's of the Moy
while, quiet, almost craven,

he studies the grain in the shaft of a rake:
there are two palm-prints in blue stone
on the bib of his overalls

where he's absentmindedly put his hands
to his heart; in a den in St John's, Newfoundland, I browse
on a sprig of *Achillea millefolium*, as it's classed.

———

*Achillea millefolium*: with its bedraggled, feathery leaf
and pink (less red
than mauve) or off-white flower, its tight little knot

of a head,
it's like something keeping a secret
from itself, something on the tip of its own tongue.

———

Would that I might take comfort in the vestigial scent
of a yarrow-sprig, a yarrow-spurt
I've plucked from the somewhat unorthodox

funerary vase
that fills one grate:
from the other there's a chortle of methane-gas

(is it methane
that's so redolent of the apple-butt?)
through a snow-capped sierra of non-combustible coal.

———

Would that I might as readily follow
this nosegay of yarrow as Don Junipero Serra
led us all the way back

along *El Camino Real*
by the helter-skelter path
of poppies we'd sown in the sap-sweet April rain.

———

I zap the remote control: that same poor elk or eland
dragged down by a bobolink;
a Spanish *Lear*; the umpteenth *Broken Arrow*;

a boxing-match; Robert Hughes dismantling Dada;
a Michael Jackson video
in which our friends, the Sioux, will peel

the face off a white man whose metacarp-
al bones, with those of either talus,
they've already numbered; the atmosphere's so rare

that if Michael's moon-suit of aluminium foil
were suddenly to split at the seams
he'd not only buy, but fertilize, the farm.

———

Again and again I stare out across the fallow
where a herd of peccaries
(white-lipped musk-

pigs, as they're sometimes known) have beaten
a path through what was the cabbage-field
to where they wallow in whiskey and *bainne clabair*.

———

Again and again I find myself keeping watch from the bridge
across the Callan: a snatch of hazel-wood
gives on to the open

range in which, once Jimmy McParland would turn
them out of the byre,
his cattle would cross-fade to Elmer Kelton's

stampeding herd
from *The Day the Cowboys Quit*, or *The Oklamydia Kid*,
or, hold on, something by Jack Schaefer.

———

After Cavafy and Elytis and Ritsos and Seferis
and Sikelianos and Vassilis Vassilikos come R.E.S. Wyatt's
*The Inns and Outs of Cricket* and *Bridge*

*from A to Z* by George S. Coffin: an 'insult to the heart'
was Livesey's diagnosis to the Squire
when Trelawney flew in from the Philippines

to visit S——in Hazelden;
across the drumlins of Aughnacloy and Caledon and Keady
I myself flap like a little green heron.

———

Would that I might have put on hold
what must have sounded like a condemned man's last request
for a flagon of ale

while mine host was explaining how in some final over
he himself was the short slip
who caught that fiendish Gagoogly from *King Solomon's Mines*.

———

*King Solomon's Mines*; *The Sign of Four*; *The Lost
World*; *Rob Roy*;
I would steady myself with Lancelot du Lac

as I grasped with both hands
my sword in the stone
(this was the rusted blade of a griffawn

embedded in a whitewashed wall);
I would grit my teeth and brace
myself against the plunge into Owl Creek.

—————

I grit my teeth. I brace myself. It's 1:43
by the clock
on the V.C.R.: with one bound

Peyton Farquhar and I will break free and swim across
to Librium
with a leisurely crawl and flutter-kick.

—————

*An Occurrence at Owl Creek Bridge, The Ox-Bow Incident*:
I've never been able to separate
'occurrence' from 'incident', 'owl' from 'ox';

in the first, I know, the narrative device
begins to—how shall I put it?—grate
a little, just as *un petit soupçon* of auteurism goes

a hell of a long way for myself, even,
despite my predilection for pushing out the boat,
never mind Pauline Kael.

—————

The bridge. The barn. The all-too-familiar terrain.
I hear McParland's cattle low
as they plumb their murky bath

for a respite from their cattle-sorrow:
they're not to notice, taped to the trough, an aerial
and a battery-pack.

—————

This looks suspiciously like a prize-fighter's arm
mounted behind glass. I drink
to Goneril's bland-

ishments and Cordelia's smart-ass 'Nada'
from a tot of fusel oil.
My supper of cod-tongues and seal-

flipper pie repeats on me as I flipper through a Harp-
er and Row
first edition of cod-tongues and moose, medium rare,

washed down by the best beer in the U.S.,
the nonesuch 'Anchor Steam',
and remember one who did herself in *utcunque placuerit Deo*.

―――――

That must have been the year old Vladimir Vladimirovich
smoked kief all the way from *Alamein to mon Zem-
Zemblable* with *The Bride of Lammermoor*

and *Ada, or Ardor*:
that was the year, while Plath found solace in *The Bhagavad
Gita*, Jim Hawkins and I were putting in at Nassau.

―――――

While Jim and I were plundering the Spanish Main
from the Grenadines to Grand Cayman
she knew that even amidst fierce

flames she might yet plant centaury:
while Jim and I were sailing with Teach and Morgan
she was fixing the rubber ring

on a Mason jar;
even amidst fierce flames, the expiapiaratory rush
of poppies in July, October poppies.

―――――

To appease a *moon*-goddess, no? How to read that last line
in that last poem? Does it describe
the moon or the woman? I mean at the very end

of 'Edge'; 'Her blacks crackle and drag.'
Whose 'blacks'? Is it the woman on the funeral urn
or the moon? Are they both 'masturbating a glitter'?

———

I crouch with Jim in the apple-butt on the *Marie Celeste*
while my half-eaten pomeroy
shows me its teeth: a fine layer of talc

has bandaged my hands;
it's Mexico, 1918;
this arm belongs to the pugilist-poet, Arthur Cravan;

it's enshrined now on the wall
of the den between a plaster of Paris
cow's skull and a stuffed ortolan, or Carolina crake.

———

It's Mexico, 1918, and I'm leaning out over the strake
with the inconsolable Myrna Loy,
whose poet-pugilist's

yawl
has almost certainly sunk like a stone:
'J'y avais trouvé une combinaison idéal et idyllique—

mon Artilutteur Ecrivain';
the label on the rake reads 'Pierce';
I'm thinking of those who have died by their own hands.

———

The scent of new-mown hay (it may be the scent of tonka)
pervades the 1848 edition of Clough's
*The Bothie of Tofer-na-Fuosich*: I know that ash-girt

well where a red
bullock with a stunningly white head
will again put its shoulder to the water like hardy Canute.

———

In a conventional sestina, that plaster of Paris skull
would almost certainly reveal the dent
where my da took a turf-spade to poleaxe

one of McParland's poley cows
that had run amuck on our spread,
bringing it to its knees by dint of a wallop so great

it must have ruptured a major vein,
such was the spout
of, like, blood that hit him full in the face.

———

When John L. Sullivan did for Jake Kilrain
in the seventy-fifth round, it was with such a blow
as left them both

utterly winded (note the caesura)
though no less so than Prince Peter and Mary O'Reilly
when they made the beast with two backs.

———

To find a pugilist-poet who'd tap his own prostate gland
for the piss-and-vinegar ink
in which he'd dash off a couple of 'sparrow-

songs', then jump headfirst into her fine how-d'-ye-do
heedless of whether she'd used a deo-
dorant, that was S——'s ideal:

after a twelve-hour day at Skadden, Arps
she wanted me to play Catullus
to her, like, Clodia; even now I savour her *arrière-*

*goût* of sweat and patchouli oil
and see, as she reaches for *The Interpretation of Dreams*,
that tattoo on her upper arm.

———

Even as I tug at the rusted blade of Excalibur
I can hear the gallant six hundred ride into the valley
and the Assyrian come down on the fold:

beyond the cattle-crush, beyond the piggery,
I fall headfirst with Peyton
Farquhar through doeskin and denim and dimity and damask.

———

Even now, after eight—almost ten—years, I savour
the whiff of patchouli oil and sweat:
from Avenue A, her view of Brooklyn Bridge

inspired her to 'kingdoms naked in the trembling heart—
*Te Deum laudamus* O Thou Hand of Fire';
and, should it happen

that He's lost his bit of Latin,
she would nevertheless have been understood by God,
to whom she appealed at every twist and turn.

———

'For your body is a temple,' my ma had said to Morholt,
'the temple of the Holy Ghost':
even now I see Morholt raise the visor of his pail

as he mulled this over;
the memory of an elk, or eland, struggling up a slope
must have been what darkened his dark mien.

———

Even now I savour her scent of jacaranda—jasmine:
even now I try to catch hold
of her as she steps from her diaphanous half-slip

with its lime-white gusset
and turns to me as if to ask, with the Lady Guinevere,
'What is the meaning of the Holy Grail?'

———

While my da studies the grain in the shaft of his rake
and I tug at the rusted blade of the loy
my ma ticks off a list

of seeds: Tohill, from *tuathal*,
meaning 'withershins'—with its regrettable overtones
of sun-worship—in our beloved Goidelic;

even as I head up a straggling caravan
of ragamuffins and rapparees
my rocking-horse's halter fast-forwards through my hands.

———

To the time I hunkered with Wyatt Earp and Wild Bill Hickok
on the ramparts of Troy
as Wild Bill tried to explain to Priam

how 'saboteur' derives from *sabot*, a clog:
to the time we drove ten thousand head from U-Cross
to Laramie with Jimi and Eric riding point.

———

Even as I lean forward to slacken Roland's martingale
the moonlit road from Ghent
to Aix

goes up in smoke and mirrors and marsh-gas
and a hound-spirit
can be heard all the way from the Great

Grimpen to Fitzroy Road; not since 1947
had a winter been so bad;
it seemed as though ice burned and was but the more ice.

If only Plath had been able to take up the slack
of the free rein
lent her so briefly by Ariel:

all I remember of that all-time low
of January 1963 was a reprieve from Cicero
and the weekly hair-wash and bath.

That must have been the year they shut down Armagh
College: the Moy road was a rink;
all we had to eat was a bland

concoction of bread and milk known as 'panada'.
Though her mouth was smoother than oil,
the mouth of Christine Keel-

er, her end was sharp
as a two-edged sword, as the arrow
that flieth by day. Rich and rare

were the gems Dedalus
gave the Countess Irina, despite the *tempus edax rerum*
of that bloody-nosed 'Venus' clerk, Ovide'.

That was the year I stumbled on Publius Ovidius Naso
vying with Charlie Gunn in an elegiac distich:
the year Eric and Jimi rode picket

on the Chisholm
Trail and Mike Fink declaimed from his Advanced Reader
the salascient passages from *Amores*.

That was the year my da would find the larvae, or pupae,
of cabbage-whites on the acumen
of a leaf: my rocking-horse with the horse-hair mane

stopped in its tracks, giving me such a jar
I fell off, just as Utepandragun
himself was trotting by; 'How come you Fenians are so averse

to buying plants in Comber, that's loyal to the King,
instead of smuggling them in from Rush?
Buy stalwart plants from a stalwart Prod, albeit a dissenter.'

———

All I remember is how my da drew himself up like Popeye
as he gave a tight-lipped 'C'mon'
and by sheer might and main

stuffed Utepandragun into a spinach-jar:
'I'll have you know, you clouricane,
that I force

my own kale every Spring';
all I remember was the sudden rush
of blood from his nose, a rush of blood and snatters.

———

All I remember was a reprieve from 'seachain droch-chómhluadar'
as she last rinsed my hair: she'd sung 'Eileen Aroon'

or some such ditty and scrubbed and scrubbed
till the sink was full of dreck;
'Stay well away from those louts and layabouts at the loanin'-end.'

———

Was it not now time, they urged, to levy the weregild, the *éiric*,
on the seed and breed of that scum-bag, Mountjoy,
that semioticonoclast

who took it upon himself to smash Shane O'Neill's
coronation-stone
on the chalky slopes of Tullahogue?

Was it not now time for the Irish to break the graven
image of a Queen whose very blotting-paper
was black, black with so much blood on her hands?

———

Like a little green heron, or 'fly-up-the-creek',
I flap above Carrickmore and Pomeroy
with volume one of Burton's translation of *The Lusiads*:

'One for all,'
I hear a cry go up, 'and all for one,'
followed by '*S'é tuar oilc*

*an t-éan sin, agus leabhar in a chroibhín*';
that was the year I did battle with Sir Bors
for Iseult the Fair (not Iseult of the White Hands).

———

That was the year Deirdre watched Jimi cut the tongue
from a Hereford calf
while a raven drank its blood: she pulled on her cigarette;

'Is there no man with snow-white skin and cheeks red
as blood and a crow-black head
in all of Ulster and Munster and Leinster and Connaught?'

———

That was the year my ma gave me a copy of Eleanor Knott's
*Irish Classical Poetry* and I first got my tongue
around *An Craoibhín Aoibhinn* (Douglas Hyde):

I was much less interested in a yellowed copy of *An Claidheamh
Soluis* than *Tschiffley's Ride* or *The Red
Rover* or *A Connecticut Yankee in King Arthur's Court*.

———

That was the year of such frost and snow and burning ice
I was kept home from school
for almost two weeks:

the year the stork or some such great
bird was blown off course and loitered with intent
on the west spire of the twin-spired

Armagh cathedral; my ragamuffins
and rapparees, meanwhile, were champing at the bit
for the slightest *belli casus*.

———

Surely the time had come for the Irish to strike back
at the *Defensor Fidei*, the peerless Oriana,
by whose command Patrick Pearse and The O'Rahilly

were put up against a wall? Was that not a *casus belli*?
Put up against a wall, like this ortolan, or sora,
and shot at the whim of Elizabloodybeth.

———

The day S—— came back with the arrow
through a heart tattooed on her upper arm, it made me think
of the fleur-de-lys

on Milady's shoulder (not Milady Clark, who helped the U.D.A.
run a shipment of Aramis
into Kilkeel

but Milady *Clarik*, whose great-great-grandfather led the I.R.B.
invasion of Canada, the one who helped foil
the plot in which the courier

was none other than herself, her): she shrugs off her taffeta
wither-band and begs me to, like, rim
her for Land's sakes; instead of 'Lord', she says 'Land'.

Throughout all this she wears some kind of ski-hood or -mask
(what she terms her 'clobber-clobber'):
as the peyote-button

begins to take effect, she shrugs off her *feileadh*
*beag* and turns up Jean Michel Jarre's loathsome hocus-pokery;
Jean Michel Jarre or the loathsome Mike Oldfield.

———

'Wither' as in 'widdersinnes', meaning to turn
against the sun: she ticks off 'carrots', 'parsnips', 'swedes'
while I suffer

the tortures of the damned, imagining myself a Shackleton
frozen by fire;
'parsnips', 'swedes'; for, unless I manage to purge

myself of concupiscent thoughts and keep a weather-eye open
for the least occasion of sin, the Gates
of Glory will be barred to me, not being pure of heart.

———

While I skellied up and down the ward in the South Tyrone
Hospital she toyed with her cream of wheat
with its scallop-shell of Chivers:

of all the peers and Paladins
who'd been entangled in a coil of barbed wire
at the battle of Bearosche,

Gawain mourned none more than his war-dobbins
Mancho and Gato
and Ingliart 'With the Short Ears', his dear Ingliart.

Mother o'mine. Mother o'mine. That silver-haired mother o'mine.
With what conviction did she hold
that a single lapse—from *lapsus*, a slip

or stumble—would have a body cast
into the outer dark. Dost thou know Dover?
The foul fiend haunts poor Tom in the voice of a nightingale.

———

Since every woman was at heart a rake
and the purest heart itself marred by some base alloy
and whosoever looketh on a woman to lust

after her would go the way of Charles Stewart Parnell,
'*Ná bac*,' she would intone,
'*ná bac leis an duilleog*

*rua ar an craoibhín*
*aoibhinn álainn óg*,' and, rummaging in her purse,
'For Satan finds some mischief still for idle hands.'

———

'May your word be as good as or better than your bond,'
my ma was saying to Queequeg
as she made a sign of the Cross

over the tray:
when would we Irish find our *lán glaice*
of nutmeg to sweeten our barium?

———

That was the year there blew such an almighty gale
it not only bent
our poplars out of shape but downed one of the few oaks

left standing after Cill Cais.
We heated a saucepan of milk on a spirit-
stove and dreamed of the day when we Irish might grate

a little nutmeg over our oatmeal. The reek of paraffin.
When might we sweeten our stirabout
with *un petit soupçon* of nutmeg or some such spice?

———

'*Non,*' I heard from the depths of the barn, '*Je ne regrette rien*':
Edith Piaf, I thought, but lo
and behold, if it wasn't Sir Reginald Front-de-Boeuf

and Ben Gunn, fresh from the battle of Zara;
Ben had armed himself with a hurley
and both *Wisden's Cricketer's* and *Old Moore's* almanacs.

———

Now that the whole country, Ben volunteered, was going to rack,
*faraoir*, to rack and ruin,
now that the bird had perched for a week on the west oriel,

was it not now time to take down the hogweed blow-
gun that had stood me in such good stead against Assyria?
(Hogweed was perfect, having no pith.)

———

It might have been hogweed, or horehound, perhaps even arum,
that would inundate this rinky-dink
bit of land

on which a mushroom-mogul has since built a hacienda:
our own *Defensor Fidei* is somewhat reminiscent of Olyve Oyl
as she continues to reel

off in her own loopy version of R.P.
'parsnips', 'swedes', and, I guess, 'vegetable marrow';
hers is a sensibility so rare

that I'll first know Apuleius
as the author of *The Golden Beam*;
'It should be *Fidei Defensor*, by the way, not *Defensor Fidei*.'

———

That must have been the year I stood by the wheel-barrow
with Davy Crockett and Mike Fink
to recite the Angelus:

we followed that with a rousing medley of 'Me and Me Da',
'Believe Me If All Those Endearing Young Charms',
'Do Ye Ken John Peel?'

and, to round it off, 'An Arab's
Farewell to His Steed'; Mike opened a packet wrapped in foil
and shook out on to a piece of Carrara

a kilo of black powder he then divvied
up into charges of exactly eleven drachms,
admirable for medium-sized game—sable antelope or eland.

———

Mike was holding forth to Virgil Earp on how Dido and Aeneas
sometimes got so close you couldn't tell which
was which and that was how they 'begat'

in olden days, though things had changed some,
mostly for the worse: Mike fancied himself as an orator;
'*O tempora!*' he would extemporise, '*O mores!*'

———

'*Sé mo mhíle brón*' Ben wept, '*tu bheith sínte fuar i measc
na dtom*' as Rashleigh and Caleb, er,
Balderstone gave his brother, Charlie, a sup of poteen:

that was the year Armagh would lose to Offaly
and my band of buccaneers and buckaroos
would weep openly over the corpse of poor, poor, poor Foulata.

That must have been the year S—— and the mighty Umbopa
were playing mah-jong or backgammon
with Allan Quatermain

and myself when a fey curled out of the jar
and spoke to her: this, of course, was the Fata Morgana,
the Great Queen of the Fairies,

who recognized Umbopa as her once and future king;
it looked as if S—— was still having a cocaine-rush
after almost a month in the rehab centre.

———

That was the year Mike Fink—'half-horse, half-alligator'—
appealed to *The First Oration against Catiline*
as he mused on the times that were in it when a Grey Heron

or a Great Crested Grebe
or, more likely than not, a White Stork
could have the country debating what evil it might portend.

———

The blow-gun was still sleek with Wright's Coal Tar:
there was a hair-line
crack from the fall I took when an Assyrian

ran me through; we'd held the bridge against Sennacherib,
of course, despite his trick
of torching the barn, which was where Aladdin met his end.

———

That was the year, after the Caliph of Baghdad, Haroun,
had forced him to eat his own weight
in emeralds and sapphires,

the doughty Aladdin
had a Michelin-man spare tyre:
it was Aladdin who gave Prince Peter the salamander brooch

Prince Peter gave the Countess Irina, whereupon
Popeye exclaimed to Quatermain and Curtis and Captain Good,
'Somebody here is gonna get hurt.'

———

The bridge. The barn. The all-too-familiar seal-flipper terrine
with the hint of seaweed
(carrageen? samphire?)

that lent it the texture of gelatin.
Again and again S—— turns up 'The Unforgettable Fire'
and shrugs off her halter of buckram or barege

and holds herself open;
my ma hands me the carbon-slip; 'But to the girdle do the gods,'
she repeats, 'but to the girdle do the gods inherit.'

———

That night I dreamed—*Te Deum laudamus, In Nomine Domini*—
that the hornless doe, *an eilit
mhaol*, came to me as a slip

of a girl and laid her exquisite
flank beside me under the covers
and offered me her breast, her breast *chomh bán le haol*.

———

'How much longer,' she cajoled, 'must we rant and rail
against the ermine
yoke of the House of Hanover?

When might the roots of Freedom take hold?
For how much longer must we cosset
Freedom's green shoot and Freedom's little green slip?'

The following morning I got up at the scrake
of dawn and struggled into my corduroy
breeks and packed the blow-gun and the cobbler's last

and awl
into the trunk of the two-tone
(pink and cream) '62 Cadillac

with a gryphon
rampant on its hood, switched on the windshield wipers
and sped away, look, no hands.

———

Little did I know, as I began to rake
across the snowy yard, how short-lived would be my joy:
for I had unwittingly entered the lists

against John Ridd and Jack McCall
and Rashleigh Osbaldistone
and other villains of that ilk;

this is not to speak of Agravain
and his little platoon of pirries
and djinns; I mean the dastardly 'Agravain of the Hard Hand'.

———

Little did I know that Agravain was weighing his knobkerrieknout:
not even the tongue
of fire that will-o'-the-wisped above my head

would save me; 'I'd as lief,'
Agravain was muttering, 'I'd as lief you'd stay and help me redd
up after the bluestone barrels are scoured.'

Little did I think that S—— would turn to me one night:
'The only Saracen I know's a Saracen tank
with a lion rampant on its hood;

from Aghalane to Artigarvan to Articlave
the Erne and the Foyle and the Bann must run red';
that must have been the year Twala's troops were massacred.

———

Now I took the little awl I'd used with such consummate skill
to scuttle *The Golden Vanitee*
and picked the locks

on the old suitcase
in which was hidden the two-page spread
from *The News of the World*: after stopping by the cattle-grid

to pick up Laudine and Yvain
I smiled as I thought of the awl (was it a brace and bit?)
wrapped in a photo of Mandy Rice Davies.

———

The two-tone Cadillac's engine-block was a vice
lapped in a coil
of barbed wire and wedged between an apple-box

and a packing-crate:
as I crossed the bridge, I was so intent
on Freedom's green slip and Freedom's green sprout

her '*Ná bac leis an craoibhín aoibhinn*'
and 'Stay clear of those louts and layabouts'
were quite lost on me; I promptly stepped on the gas.

———

'O come ye back,' I heard her sing, 'O come ye back
to Erin':
I was somewhat more exercised by the fact that my yourali

supply was running so low
I might well have to spend my last cruzeiro
on an ounce of civet, or resort to my precious *Bufo bufo*.

———

The magical toad entrusted to me by Francisco Pizarro
might still be good against this bird that continued to prink
itself, alas,

even as we left Sitanda's
kraal and struck out, God between us and all harm,
for the deep north: that was the year Jack McCall would deal

the dead man's hand to Earp,
the year Captain Good was obliged to shave in inco-oil
and S—— got hooked on 'curare';

the year Scragga and Infadoos
joined Quatermain in reciting 'The Jackdaw of Rheims'
as we plunged deeper into Kukuanaland.

———

Only yesterday, as I shlepped out to Newark on the PATH
whom should I spot but two Japanese guys wearing fanny-packs:
I recognized them as 'Basho' and 'Sora'

from Avenue A; I knew by the tags on their mule-train
that they were just getting back from the Lowlands Low;
'Tooralooraloora,' Basho gave me a stupid grin, 'tooralooralay.'

———

'Tirra lirra,' S—— sang when we were stopped by the 'fuzz'
as she drove back to school:
she was reading, it seemed, as deeply into Maalox

as Malebranche, Rennies as René Descartes:
I helped her move into a 'pad', as she styled her apartment,
in which Herrick's *Hesperides* and a can of Sprite

and Duchamp's 'The Bride Stripped Bare by Her Bachelors, Even'
all said one thing—'I masturbate';
she was writing now on *Ulster: From C. S. Lewis to C. S. Gas*.

———

'Tirra lirra lirra,' was what she sang to Umslopogaas
and myself to, like, break the ice
when we first went to see her in detox:

an albino ginko, or some such sport;
she was now deeply into Lloyd Cole
and Julio Cortázar and, *Dios me libre*, Fuentes;

Lloyd 'King' Cole, she'd dubbed him; Warren Zevon;
as for U2's Edge, his 'Bad'
put him up there with Jimi and Eric, a 'Guitar Great'.

———

Five days north of Sitanda's kraal we were joined by Sigurd,
his twin cousins, Hrut and Knut,
and Lieutenant Henry Ark, also known as Eric the Red:

it was Eric who cut us each a strip of biltong
from the shield carried by his son, Leif;
Leif Ericson's shield was covered with chlordiazepoxide.

———

'How dare you,' began Milady Clarik, 'how dare you desecrate
the memory of Connolly and Clarke and Ceannt':
she brandished *The Little Red*

*Book* of Mao Tse-tung;
'How dare you blather on about the Caliph
of Baghdad when you should strike while the iron's hot.'

————

'Surely,' S—— chimed in, 'surely the time is at hand
for the Hatfields and McCoys
to recognize their common bond?' (It was Milady *Clark*

who'd given her a copy of Ian Adamson's *The Cruthin*,
of which she'd bought a thousand tonnes
for 'intellectual ballast'.)

Together they'd entered into dialogue
with the first mate of a ship registered in Valparaiso
who had 'connections' in the Transvaal.

————

Ben Gunn would now gladly have red-hewed his right hand
for a piece of mouse-trap cheese, when the fairy Terdelaschoye
rustled up some *Caprice des Dieux*: so it was that Erec

and Enid and I hoisted the main-sail (complete with raven)
and hung the lodestone
by an elast-

ic band; *Caprice*, for Land's sake, from the 'goat-like'
caprioles and capers
of those Athenian galleys with their tu-whit-tutelary owls.

————

Only moments later, I was bending over to tie a slip-
knot when I looked up suddenly and the rough tree rail
had been superseded by the coast

of Africa; it struck me then that the limpet-mine
in the *Hispaniola*'s hold
had been planted there by the pesky Pedro Navarro.

That must have been from our last trip up the Guadalquivir:
we'd given the Athenian galleys the slip
and put in at Seville rather than try to hold

our course for Dover, its cliffs *chomh bán le haol,*
with our cargo of calomel (or calamine);
the Guadalquivir had been our Rubicon; the die was cast.

———

To make matters worse, Ben reported that he'd just heard
the unmistakable tu-whit
tu-whoo of the *gubernaculum* in the stern

of a Roman galley. We were getting ready to open
fire
on anything that moved when 'Vamos, muchachos, vamos a ver'

came out of nowhere, followed by a barge
with a triangular sail—a jib, to be precise—cut
from a single piece of lateen.

———

From the cut of their jib we took the crew for a horde
of Cruthin dyed with woad:
it hadn't occurred to us that we ourselves might turn

blue after a month in an open
boat; it transpired
these legionnaires had been set adrift by Septimius Severus

in 211 A.D.; we shared what was left of our porridge,
then joined them in a game of quoits
on the deck of the *Caledonia.*

———

Who should hove into view, with a boy-troop from St Enda's,
but Pearse himself: together with the gallioteers,
we went ashore and began the long trek

north from St Enda's kraal; when the tree-line
gave way to unfamiliar scrub
we knew we'd rounded not the Cape of Good Hope but Cape Horn.

———

That was the year Mike Fink was a bouncer at 'The Bitter End'
on Bleecker Street: 'The times are out of kilter,'
he remarked to S——, eyeing the needle-tracks

on her arms; that was the year she would mainline
so much 'curare' they ran up two flags over her wing at Scripps.
(By 'curare', or 'yourali', she meant heroin.)

———

In view of these square red flags with square black centres
we turned back and fell to right away to gammon
the bow-sprit with baobab-

ropes and secure the cat's-head and the catharping
against the impending hurricane:
we'd already stowed the sails (fore-, mizzen- and main-)

and breamed the hull with burning furze
and touched up the figurehead—an angel carved by William Rush
from the sturdiest of mahoganies, the Australian jarrah.

———

All I remember is a thunder-cloud of dust across the veldt
(much like the rattle of Twala's Massagais
on shields) and Ben's 'Bejasus' and 'Begorrah'

as the dust-cloud engulfed the rigging of our clipper;
the courage, then, with which he and one or two other fellows
crawled from hatch to hatch to check the battens.

———

For a whole week we survived on pages torn from *Old Moore*
or *Wisden* and flavoured with star anise:
this was a trick Israel had picked up from a short-order

cook who'd sailed with Flint: Israel used a switch-
blade to peel and portion our last satsuma;
that year MacNeice and Frost and Plath all kicked the bucket.

———

The storm blew over, of course, and with the help of Arrow,
the first mate, and Nemo and Livesey, her shrinks,
we bundled S—— into the *Nautilus*

and set off for Grenada:
many's the old salt would swing from the yard-arm,
many's the sea-dog be keel-

hauled for failing to keep a sharp
lookout for Carthaginian hydrofoils;
after a month, she was transferred to the *Fighting Téméraire*

despite objections from the 'perfidious'
Trelawney having to do with her 'low self-esteem'
and her 'unhealthy interest' in Henri de Montherlant.

———

The next thing I knew, we were with Gonzalo Fernandez de Oviedo,
discombobulated by the clink
of mutinous men-at-arms,

upon a peak in Da-
rien: we'd been watching *The Irish in Us*
when the projector must have broken down during the third reel

and thrown me into a time-warp;
not only was S—— the dead spit of Olivia de Havilland
playing Liadan to my, like, Cuirithir

but (this chilled me to the marrow)
her face in the freeze-frame
was not unlike Maud Gonne's, swathed in a butterfly-net voile.

———

As we hunkered there in the projection-booth
the projector had gone, like, totally out of whack:
the freeze-frame of Maud Gonne from *Mise Eire*

had S—— strike up her all-too-familiar refrain;
'The women that I picked spoke sweet and low
and yet they all gave tongue, gave tongue right royally.'

———

Maud Gonne was explaining how 'San Graal' was a pun on '*Sang
real*'
to 'Diana Vernon' and Constance Gore-Booth
when 'Blow me,' Popeye roared, 'blow

me down if I can't put my hand on the knapsack-
sprayer': Constance Gore-Booth was back from a trip to the Ukraine
with Milady Clarik, the aforementioned 'emissary'.

———

That was the year Yeats said to Plath, '*Mi casa es su casa*':
all the way from Drumcliff old 'Hound Voice'
could be heard; 'How much longer will the House of Saxe-

Coburg-Gotha try to break the spirit
of the Gael?
How much longer must we Irish vent

our spleen against their cold, their rook-delighting heaven?
When will we have at last put paid
to Milady's great-grandfather's foes?' (He meant 'great-great'.)

———

So it was that every year for thirty years I'd bream
its clinkered hull, lest horehound or cuckoo-pint
or dandelion-clocks

should swamp my frail caïque:
for thirty years we ran before the wind from Monterey
to San Diego by way of Santa Cruz.

———

For thirty years I would serve on *The Golden Hind*:
thirty years, man and boy,
I sailed with Sir Humphrey Gilbert and Drake;

thirty years that led to the, like, raven-
stone
where Mary Queen of Scots herself lost

her head because she, too, was a 'Catlick';
thirty years before I understood what Lady Percy
and Hotspur meant by Milady's 'howl'.

———

It was thirty years till I reached back for the quiver
in which I'd hidden the carbon-slip
from Tohill's of the Moy: my hand found the hilt

of the dirk I confiscated from Israel;
the carbon-slip was gone; what with those 'persimmons'
and 'swedes', I'd been diverted from my quest.

———

In addition to missing the carbon-slip I was getting hard:
not since our family outing to White
and Boa Islands on Lower Lough Erne

(where a *Síle na gcíoch* held herself wide open)
had I been so mortified; it was then I noticed the command-wire
running all the way from behind a silver

birch
to the drinking-trough; that trough was my Skagerrak, my Kattegat,
its water a brilliant celadon.

———

As we neared Armagh, the Convent of the Sacred Heart
was awash in light: nor galloped less steadily Roland a whit
than when S—— ran

those five red lights in downtown New Haven: 'George Oppen,'
she announced, 'there's a poet with fire
in his belly'; this was to the arresting 'officiffer'

who had her try to walk a straight line back to the Porsche;
after calling him 'the unvoiced "c" in Connecticut',
she gave our names as Cuirithir and Liadan.

———

Even now a larva was gnawing at her 'most secret and inviolate'
rose of Damascus:
as we neared Armagh, I could still hear her pecky, pecky, peckery

though it was drowned out by Mike's 'Cruise of the Calabar';
little did we know, as we galloped along the Folly,
that S—— had broken the seal on the little box marked *Verboten*.

———

As we neared Armagh, she'd dipped the tip of each little arrow
in the blood of an albino skink
or some such *lusus*

*naturae*: that must have been the year we ran cattle from Nevada
to Wyoming; the year, as we rode into Laramie
with Jimi and Eric and Shane (*the* Shane, not Shane O'Neill)

we heard from behind us, '*Manos arriba*';
'Parsnips,' I kept saying, 'parsnips and parzleval';
little did we know that a whole raree-

show led by Agravain and the Agraviados
had been on our case since S—— had dallied with Wolfram,
much to the chagrin—remember?—of Roland.

———

I seem to recall that she was even more into Barthes
than Wolfram von Eschenbach:
largely because of *Writing Degree Zero*

she now ran with a flock of post-Saussureans
who leapt about from 'high' to 'low'
like so many dyed-in-the-wool serows or oorials.

———

'Dyed-in-the-wool'; 'serow'; 'oorial': in the midst of chaos,
she would say, the word is a suspect device,
a Pandora's—that's it—*box*;

and she leaned over me the way a bow-sprit
(bow-sprit? martingale?)
leans over the water in search of a 'referent';

this last time I saw her, in New Haven,
she leaned over, so, and whispered, 'This darling bud,
this bud's for you,' then settled back on the packing-crate.

———

As we neared the Convent of the Sacred . . . of the Sacred
Heart, our way was blocked by a Knight
of the Red

Branch astride a skewbald mustn'tang:
I noticed, as he threw down his glove,
something familiar about his ski-mask, or his ski-hood.

'How dare you suggest that his "far-off, most secret,
and inviolate rose" is a cunt:
how dare you misread

his line about how they "all gave tongue";
how dare you suggest that *Il Duce* of Drumcliff
meant that "Diana Vernon" and Maud Gonne gave good head.'

———

It was now too late for Erec to pull out of Enid
while she masturbated her clitoris
and S—— and I, like, outparamoured the Turk

in the next room: the scent of Vaseline;
her fondness for the crop;
the *arrière-goût* of patchouli oil and urine.

———

There was nothing for it, after Ben had dispatched the sentry
with a tap of his trusty *camán*,
but to load the breech of the drain-pipe

with Richardson's Two-Sward: just then I heard the Lorelei sing
to an American
bomber sweeping the Rhine and the Main;

even now I smell the phosphorus
when I lit the fuse—the terminal spike of a bulrush
I'd kept tinder-dry in a sealed jam-jar.

———

For the time was now ripe, S—— had vowed, to 'make a *Sendero
Luminoso* of our *Camino
Real*': along with the tattoo, she'd taken to wearing a labiaba-

ring
featuring a salamander, a salamander being the paragon
of constancy; it was twenty years to the month the water-main

froze
on Fitzroy Road and the *T.L.S.* had given the bum's rush
to *The Bell Jar.*

———

It was now too late, as I crouched with Cuchulainn and Emer,
to feel anything much but nausea
as again and again S—— cast about for an artery:

I'd not be surprised if this were some kind of time-switch
taped to the trough, that the click of a zoom;
such nausea (from *navis,* a ship) as I'd not felt since the *Pequod.*

———

For I'd not be surprised if this were a video
camera giving me a nod and a wink
from the blue corner, if it were hooked up not to an alarm

but the TV, that I myself am laid out on a da-
venport in this 'supremely Joycean object, a nautilus
of memory jammed next to memory', that I'll shortly reel

with Schwitters and Arp
through our *Kathedrale des erotischen Elends*
while the bobolink, rare

bird that she is, feeds on the corpse from *Run of the Arrow,*
leaving off only fitfully to scream
in Gaelakota, '*Ná bac leis. Ná bac leis, a Phóil.*'

———

This is some goddess of battle, Macha or Badhbh,
whose '*Ná bac
leis, a Phóil*' translates as 'Take heed, sirrah:

you must refrain
from peeking down my dress, though it's cut so low
you may see my areolae.'

This is Badhbh, or Macha, or Morrigan—the greatest of great
queens—whose cackle-caws
translate as *tempus rerum edax*:

'Where on earth,' she croaks, 'where on earth have you spent
the past half-hour?' 'I've just lit the fuse
on a cannon,' I begin, sticking the glowing coal

in my pocket. 'What in under heaven
did we do to deserve you, taking off like that, in a U-boat,
when you knew rightly the spuds needed sprayed?'

―――――

At first it seemed that the louts and layabouts at the cross
might have stolen the prime
from my touch-hole and sold it to, like, Henry of Ballantrae

and the acumen, or point,
of the bulrush had been lost on the powder-keg;
the deelawg was not so much an earwig, I suspect, as a clock.

―――――

'Take Neruda,' S―― volunteered, 'a poet who dirtied his hands
like a *bona fide* minstrel boy
gone to the wars in Tacna-Arica:

if he's not to refine
himself out of existence, if he's not to end up on methadone,
the poet who wants to last

must immerse himself in Tacna-Arica and Talca';
the larva, meanwhile, of *Pieris
brassicae* was working through kale and cauliflower *et al.*

―――――

I crouch with Schwitters and Arp in the house in Hanover
that stands like a ship on the slips
when, lo and behold,

the sky opens and it begins to hail
codeine and amyl nitrate and sulphides and amphetamines
and Mike Oldfield and Jean Michel Jarre cassettes.

———

'Vengeance is mine,' proclaimed my armchair anarchist
to the pesky Ramon Navarro,
'mine and mine

alone'; even now the hounds were straining at their slips
as the hornless doe, *an eilit mhaol*,
stumbles out of *A Witness Tree*; New York, 1942; Henry Holt.

———

Again and again I flap through Aughnacloy and Caledon:
Tray, Blanche and Sweet-
heart

are dogs that must to kennel while Milady's brach
doth stand by the fire
with the red-eyed towhee, turn, turn, turn;

Don Junipero, meanwhile, weighed down with silver,
finds his way back from codeine to *kodeia*,
the 'poppy-head' much loved by the towhee, or marsh robin.

———

Again and again the maudlin towhee flaps over Bonn or Baden-
Baden
like an American bomber on a night-flight
along the Rhine valley

as Salah-ed-din holds the larva (from *larva*, a ghost or mask)
in forceps, maybe, or catticallipillers;
he holds it close to his chest like Hickok's last hand in baccarat.

S—— would detect the mating-call of Fine Gael or Fianna Fáil
in that red-eyed chewink's
'*Fadó, fadó*':

'*Ní fiú liom sin*,' she would say, '*Ní fiú sin dada*';
now her tattoo of a heart and arrow
was all but crowded out by those cochineal

sores not unlike those of herp-
es or chlamydia; I should have known this was no boxer's arm,
*faraoir, faraoir*,

about to land
a haymaker, but a prize carp, or a prize bream,
or the dreaded *Dracunculus*.

———

That last time I stood by her side, like some latterday Uriel,
she sang the praises of 'The Shining Path'
while she cut a line of coke with a line of Sweet 'n Low:

then she lay down by the tracks
and waited for the train
that would carry Deirdre and Naoise back to Assaroe.

———

All I remember is a lonesome tu-whit tu-whoo from the crate
and her bitter 'What have *you* done for the cause?
You're just another Sir Pertinax

MacSycophant,
brown-nosing some Brit who's sitting on your face
and thinking it's, like, really cool.'

She brandished a bottle of Evian;
'Thing is, *a Phóil*, your head's so far up your own fat butt
you've pretty much disappeared.'

Ten years after Plath set the napkin under her head
I got out from under S——'s cheese-cloth skirt
where what I'd taken for a nutmeg-clove

tasted now of monk's-hood, or aconite:
'*No tengo,*' the salamander fumed, '*no tengo
mas que darte*'; and I saw red, red, red, red, red.

———

'Nevermore,' my ma chipped in, 'will the soul clap its hands
for sheer joy
as it did for Yeats and William Blake:

the legacy of Arthur Griffin'
(she meant Griffi*th*) 'and Emmet and Wolfe Tone
is lost, completely lost

on our loanin'-end ideologues,
while the legacy of Connolly and, God help us, Pearse
is the latest pell-mell in Pall Mall.'

———

Again and again I'm about to touch down by the pebble-dashed wall
(by way of Keady and Aughnacloy)
when it hits me that the house has changed hands:

the original of that salamander dalk
such as might have graced the lime-white throat of Etain
was recovered near Dunluce or Dunseverick

or wherever the *Girona* was Dunsevericked or Dunluced;
in the 1931 *Connecticut Yankee* Myrna Loy appears
as Morgan the Fay; my ma is now in the arms of Sister Morphine.

———

'For every Neruda,' mused the bloody-nosed Countess Irina,
'must have his, like, Allende':
with that she handed back to Prince Peter the scarab

for which he'd paid a thousand guilders
and went back to cutting the line of coke with the line
of dalk, from the Anglo-Saxon *dalc* or *dolc*, a brooch or torc.

———

In due course Prince Peter sent a tape of Jean Michel Jarre's
*Equinoxe* to the commune
in Portland and, though it was returned to sender,

he realized from the thuriferous
scent that S—— must have gone off to Portland, Oregon,
with Yogi Bear and Boo-Boo

rather than Portland, like, Maine;
he realized, moreover, that she'd scrawled 'RUSH'
on the packet, which now contained a carbon-slip and a ring.

———

A carbon-slip? A ring? As he slipped it back in the packet
the salamander's double-edged 'nothing more'
cut him in two like a scim-

itar and he crouched with Naoise
after the limestone slab had crushed both Deirdre and the witch,
that being it, as they say, for the old Gagoolic order.

———

The ring? The carbon-slip? It's 1:49 and the video's
now so wildly out of synch
there's no telling *Some Experiences of an Irish R.M.*

from *The Shaggy D.A.*:
in Frost's great poem, 'The Most of It', the 'talus'
refers not to a heel,

of course, but the cliff-face or scarp
up which his moose or eland
will so memorably rear—'rare',

my da would have said—while the Cathedral of Ero-
tic Misery, like that of Rheims,
will soon be awash in blood, in blood and sacred oil.

———

For that bobolink was no more your common oriole
than was Barton Booth
your common bletherskite: his 'Blow,

winds, and crack
your cheeks! Spit, fire! Spout, rain!'
would cut through the cackle like the mark of Zorro.

———

I crouch with Jim and Ben and our black-cloaked desperado
in a high-sided, two-wheeled *carreta*
full of hides and tallow and what must be retted flax.

Chlamydia: from *chlamys*, a cloak or cowl;
the filthy mantle on the gas;
again she renews her vows

to the moon-goddess; again she turns on the oven;
again the Agraviados begin to lay about
them while their Captain cries, 'Avaunt ye curs, avaunt.'

———

Now Father McEntaggart flings off his black, black cloak:
'This, Brigid, is a cross
you must bear with fortitude': as he gives her a cake

from the pyx (the mini-ciborium)
the dogs, for some reason, stand at point;
she calls to them in turn, to Sweetheart, Blanche and Tray.

Through Caledon and Aughnacloy the little dogs and all
are hard on my heels: they're led by that no good hobbledehoy
by the name of Israel Hands

who again clambers out of an Edmund Dulac
half-tone
to launch his Blitzkrieg

on Jim and myself; again the *Hispaniola* will take a sudden list
and Israel's dirk-blade pierce
my shoulder-muscle and its tendons be rent and riven.

———

The bridge. The barn. Again and again I stand aghast
as I contemplate what never
again will be mine:

'Look on her. Look, her lips.
Listen to her *râle*
where ovarian cancer takes her in its strangle-hold.'

———

Sharp was her end as the scimitar of Salah-ed-din
with which he cut through . . . what?
A cushion? A pillow? That was the year Richard the Lionheart

floated barrage-
balloons all along the coast between Jaffa and Tyre;
the year Lionheart smote an iron

bar with such force as so far,
so good, while Salah-ed-din, ever the more delicate,
sliced through the right Fallopian.

———

And there lay the mare—after they sliced her open—
there lay the mare with her nostril all wide
while Badhbh, daughter of Cailidin,

cried out on her behalf, 'Whosoever
looketh upon a woman with carnal desire
as after the water brooks panteth the hart . . .'

'Ovarian,' did I write? Uterine.
Salah-ed-din would slice through in his De Havilland Mosquito.
'American,' did I write? British.

———

All I remember was the linen cloth, at once primped and puckery,
where her chin rested on the patten:
'I'm living in Drumlister,' she says, 'in clabber

to the knee'; that was the year Salah-ed-din took the field
at Acre and with the fine edge of his damask
blade lopped off the right arm of Caius Mucius Scaevola.

———

Salah-ed-din would now seem poised to run a foil
through the weakest link
in the moon-suit wrought by some vidua

or whidah
bird while the scald crow,
Badhbh, latches on to the wheals

on the broken body of Tarp-
eia on whom, alas, the Sabines dumped their arms
as decisively as a bomber sweeping the Ruhr

would dump on Childe Roland:
an ampoule of Lustau's port, another of Bristol Cream,
are jittery in their tantalus.

I crouch with Schwitters and Arp, with Tristan Tzara,
as the Lorelei
lillibullabies from the Rhine,

thus affording the bomber a clear flight-path
through the ack-ack, or flak,
by which a dozen Spitfires have already been laid low.

———

Only yesterday I heard the cry go up, 'Vene sancti Spiritu,'
as our old crate
overshot the runway at Halifax,

Nova Scotia: again I heard Oglalagalagool's
cackackle-Kiowas
as blood gushed from every orifice;

an ampoule of Lustau's port; a photograph of Godfrey Evans
who used to keep wicket—perhaps even went to bat—
for the noble and true-hearted Kent.

———

And here lies the mare with her nostril all wide and red
as I sit with her head
'twixt my knees: still appealing to Wakantanka,

our friends the Sioux, as they excoriate
Michael Jackson; all that's left of him is his top note;
'Why should a dog, a horse, a rat have life?'

———

There's not even an arm, not an arm left of Arthur Cravan,
for whom the disconsolate Mina Loy
would howl, howl, howl

when he upped and went; after the bomb-blast
has rained down clay and stones
and arms and legs and feet and hands,

I should, I guess, help Mina rake
over these misrememberings for some sign of Ambrose Bierce,
maybe, if not her own Quetzalcoatliac.

———

Again and again, I hover in Bierce's 'good, kind dark'
while a young R.N.
hooks an I.V. into her arm: it must have been 'The Bottom Line'

rather than 'The Bitter End':
that must have been the year S—— wrote 'Helter-skelter'
in her own blood on the wall; she'd hidden a razor in her scrubs.

———

All would be swept away: the T'ang chamber-pot and the Ming;
again and again I wedge my trusty Camoëns
in the barn-door to keep it ajar

lest Agravyn à la Dure Mayn
mistake me for Ladon or some apple-butt dragon
and come after me; even now I hear his shuffle-saunter

through the yard, his slapping the bib
of his overalls; even now he stops by the cattle-crush
from which the peers and paladins would set out on their forays.

———

Again and again I look out over the bridge where Deirdre
dashed her head against the 'Begad,
I'll teach him not to mitch

when the spuds need spraying'; again and again the cruel Emir
stops with the High King, Connor MacNessa,
at the barn-door; again and again they cry out, 'Open, Sesame.'

The bridge, the barn: the tongue of a boot once lus-
trous with mink-
oil;

a rocking-horse's hoof; the family tree from *Ada*;
all swept away in the bob and
wheel

of the sonata for flute and harp,
the wild harp hanged on a willow by Wolfgang Amadeo;
again and again Lear enters with a rare

and radiant maiden in his arms
who might at any moment fret and fream,
'I am the arrow that flieth by day. I am the arrow.'

———

In a conventional tornada, the strains of her *'Che sera, sera'*
or 'The Harp That Once' would transport me back
to a bath resplendent with yarrow

(it's really a sink set on breeze- or cinder-blocks):
then I might be delivered
from the rail's monotonous 'alack, alack';

in a conventional envoy, her voice would be ever
soft, gentle and low
and the chrism of milfoil might over-

flow
as the great wheel
came full circle; here a bittern's bibulous *'Orinochone O'*

is counterpointed only by that corncrake, by the gulder-gowl
of a nightjar, I guess, above the open-cast mines,
by a quail's

indecipherable code; of the great cog-wheel, all that remains
is a rush of air—a wing-beat,
more like—past my head; even as I try to regain

my equilibrium, there's no more relief, no more respite
than when I scurried, click, down McParland's lane
with my arms crossed, click, under my armpits;

———

I can no more read between the lines
of the quail's 'Wet-my-lips' or his 'Quick, quick'
than get to grips with Friedrich Hölderlin

or that phrase in Vallejo having to do with the 'ache'
in his forearms; on the freshly-laid asphalt
a freshly-peeled willow-switch, or baton, shows a vivid mosaic

of gold on a black field, while over the fields
of buckwheat it's harder and harder to pin down a gowk's
poopookarian *ignis fatuus*;

though it slips, the great cog,
there's something about the quail's 'Wet-my-foot'
and the sink full of hart's-tongue, borage and common kedlock

that I've either forgotten or disavowed;
it has to do with a trireme, laden with ravensara,
that was lost with all hands between Ireland and Montevideo.

**HAY 1998**

## THE MUDROOM

We followed the narrow track, my love, we followed the narrow
track through a valley in the Jura
to where the goats delight to tread upon the brink
of meaning. I carried my skating rink,
the folding one, plus
a pair of skates laced with convolvulus,
you a copy of the feminist Haggadah
from last year's Seder. I reached for the haggaday
or hasp over the half door of the mudroom
in which, by and by, I grasped the rim
not of a quern or a chariot wheel but a wheel
of Morbier propped like the last reel
of *The Ten Commandments* or *The Robe*.
When she turned to us from high along the scarp
and showed us her gargoyle-
face stained with red-blue soil,
I could have sworn the she-goat was walking on air,
bounding, vaulting, pausing in mid-career
to browse on a sprig of the myrtle of which she's a devotee,
never putting a foot
wrong as she led us through the atrium's
down jackets, bow and quiver, jars of gefilte fish and garum,
to the uplands
where, at dusk, a farmer spreads a layer of bland
curds on the blue-green seam
of pine ash that runs like a schism
between bland dawn-milk and bland dusk-milk, along a corridor
smoking with the blue-green ordure
of cows, to yet another half door that would issue
onto the altar of Jehovah-nissi.
There our kittens, Pangur Ban and Pyewacket,
sprawled on the horsehair blanket I bought in Bogotá
along with the horsehair hackamore.
There a wheel felloe of ash or sycamore
from the quadriga to which the steeds had no sooner been hitched
than it foundered in a blue-green ditch

with the rest of the Pharaoh's
war machine was perfectly preserved between two amphoras,
one of wild birdseed, the other of Kikkoman.
It was somewhere in this vicinity that I'd hidden the afikomen
at last year's Seder. I looked back down the Valley of the Kings
that was flooded now by the tears of things
and heard again that she-goat pipe
home a herd of cows, their hullabaloo and hubbub
at dawn or dusk, saw again her mouth stained with fraochans
(for she is of blaeberry browsers the paragon)
and followed her yet again through gefilte fish and garum jars,
crocks, cruses, saucepans, the samovar
from turn-of-the-century
Russia, along the blue-green path of pine cinders
through the myrtleberry—myrtle- or whortleberry?—underbrush
from which an apprehensive thrush
gave over its pre-emin . . . pre-emin . . . pre-emin . . .
its preeminent voice to *une petite chanson d'Allemagne.*
There, in the berry-laden scrub,
was a brangle of scrap
that had once been the body of that quadriga.
Yet again I stood amid the dreck
and clutter
of the mudroom, the cardboard boxes from K-mart and Caldor,
the Hoover, the ironing board, the ram's horn
on which Moses called to Aaron, a pair of my da's boots so worn
it was hard to judge where the boots came to an end
and the world began, given how one would blend
imperceptibly into the other, given that there was no fine
blue-green line
between them. Virgil's *Georgics*. Plato's *Dialogues*.
Yet again the she-goat reared up on her hind legs
in the Jura or the Haute-Savoie
and perched on top of that amphora of soy
and stared across the ravine
that, imperceptibly, intervenes
between the stalwart curds of daybreak
onto which the farmer rakes

the pine coals from the warm hearthstone
and the stalwart curds of dailygone.
She reared up on her hind legs as if to see, once and for all,
the children of Israel negotiate the water wall
on their right hand
and on their left—"Look, no hands"—
as if a she-goat might indeed pause in mid-career to browse
on some horsehair blanket I bought in Valparaíso,
on a whirligig, a scythe and strickle, a cobbler's last.
They weighed on me now, the skating rink and the skates laced
with convolvulus as we followed the narrow track, my love,
to that rugged enclave
in the Jura, to where a she-goat might delight to tread
upon the middle cake of matzo bread
that runs as neat as neat
between unleavened morning and unleavened night.
Yet again that she-goat had run ahead
and yet again we followed her through the Haute-
Savoie past a ziggurat
of four eighty-pound bags of Sakrete,
on the top of which she paused to expose her red-blue tongue,
past the hearth set of brush, tongs
and poker bent
out of shape, past a shale outcrop of some of the preeminent
voices of the seventies—*The Pretender*, *Desperado*, *The Best of
       Spirit*,
box after cardboard box
of all manner of schmaltz and schlock from Abba to Ultravox,
till we heard the she-goat's own preeminent voice
from across the blue-green crevasse
that ran between the cohorts of dawn and the dusk cohorts,
heard her girn and grate
upon the mishegaas
of the brazen-mouthed cows
of morn and the brazen-mouthed cows of even,
their horns summoned up by a seven-
branched candlestick itself once or twice summoned up at Shabbat.
The candelabrum, the whirligig, those boots

with their toes worn through from the raking of pine coals
at crack of dawn and crepuscule,
the whirr of the bellows
and the dull glow
of pine ash, the hubcap from a Ford Sierra
blown up in—yes, siree—
a controlled explosion in Belfast, the Kaliber six-pack,
the stack of twenty copies of *The Annals of Chile* ($21 hardback).
Again the she-goat would blare down the trail
when we paused to draw breath, as the children of Israel
might draw breath on the Sabbath,
again exhort us to follow the narrow path
that runs like a blue-green membrane
between the amphoras of soy and assorted small-headed grains,
exhort us yet again to follow
through the valley
"the narrow track to the highest good" as set forth by Epicurus,
past the hearth set of brush, tongs, and poker
bent out of shape, the ever-so-faint scent of musk,
till I happened upon the snow-swatch of damask
in which I'd wrapped the afikomen. The bag of pitons.
The medicinal bottle of poteen.
Yet again something had come between
the she-goat poised on a slope on which the cattle batten
and ourselves, that rivulet
or blue-green fault
between the clabber of morn and the stalwart even-clabber.
It was time, I felt sure, to unpack the Kaliber
into the old Hotpoint fridge
in which the she-goat was wont to forage,
to toss the poster tube—Hopper, Magritte, Grant Wood—
and clear a space in the dew-wet
underbrush in which, at long last, I might open
my folding skating rink and, at long last, tread upon
the hubcap of that old Sierra that could itself turn
on a sixpence, could itself turn
as precipitously as a bucket of milk in a booley-byre,
to roll up the strand of barbed wire

hand-wrought by the King of the Chaldeans,
the one and only Joseph Glidden,
that had run between the herd
of morn and the herd
of even, when you found the little *shuinshu* covered with black brocade
I bought for two Zuzim our last day in Kyoto
and it struck me that the she-goat
had somehow managed to acquire what looked like your skates
and your *gants en chevreau*
and was performing *grands jetés* on the hubcap of the Ford Zephyr.
I, meanwhile, was struggling for a foothold.
Even as I drove another piton to the hilt
in the roughcast
of a bag of Sakrete, the she-goat executed an exquisite
*saut de l'ange* from an outcrop of shale,
pausing to browse on a sprig of myrtle or sweet gale
in the vicinity of the bow and quiver, down jackets, Hoover,
where I hid the afikomen last Passover,
bounding, vaulting, never making a slip
as I followed her, then as now—though then I had to schlep
through the brush of skirts (maxi- and mini-)
my folding rink plus my skates laced with scammony
*plus* the middle of the three
cakes of matzo bread that had, if you recall, since gone astray.
It was time, I felt sure, to unpack the Suntory
into the old fridge, to clear a space between *De Rerum Natura*
and Virgil's *Eclogues*,
a space in which, at long last, I might unlock
the rink, so I drove another piton into an eighty-pound
bag of Sakrete and flipped the half door on the dairy cabinet
of the old Hotpoint
and happened, my love, just happened
upon the cross
section of Morbier and saw, once and for all, the precarious
blue-green, pine-ash path along which Isaac followed Abraham
to an altar lit by a seven-branched candelabrum,
the ram's horn, the little goat whirligig
that left him all agog.

## THE POINT

Not Sato's sword, not Sato's "consecrated blade"
that for all its years in the oubliette
of Thoor Ballylee is unsullied, keen,
lapped yet in the lap of a geisha's gown.

Not the dagger that Hiroo Onoda
would use again and again to undo
the froufrous, the fripperies, the Fallopian
tubes of a dead cow in the Philippines.

What everything in me wants to articulate
is this little bit of a scar that dates
from the time O'Clery, my schoolroom foe,

rammed his pencil into my exposed *thigh*
(not, as the chronicles have it, my calf)
with such force that the point was broken off.


## NIGHTINGALES

I

"In great contrast to the nightingale's preeminent voice
is the inconspicuous coloration of its plumage,"
as Alfred Newton so winningly puts it

in his *Dictionary of Birds*. I fell in love with a host face
that showed not the slightest blemish.
They tell me her makeup was powdered nightingale shit.

II

They tell me the Japanese nightingale's not a nightingale
but a Persian bulbul. Needless to say, it's the male bird

that's noted for opening the floodgates
and pouring out its soul, particularly during nesting season.


### III

Now they tell me a network of wedges and widgets and wooden nails
has Nijojo Castle's floorboards
twitter "like nightingales." This twittering warned the shogunate
of unwelcome guests. Wide boys. Would-be assassins.


## PLOVERS

The plovers come down hard, then clear again,
for they are the embodiment of rain.


## THE BANGLE

### I

Between the bream with cumin and the beef with marrow
in Le Petit Zinc
a bangle gleamed. Aurora Australis.
Many a bream, my darling, and many a luce
in stew.


### II

Not unlike the magpie and the daw,
the emu loves a shiny doodah,
a shiny doodlebob.

**III**

       So a harum-scarum
Bushman, hey, would slash one forearm
with a flint, ho, or a sliver of steel
till it flashed, hey ho, like a hel-
iograph.

**IV**

       By dribs, hey, by dribs and drabs
the emu's still lured from its diet of fruit and herbs
with a bottle cap, ho, or a bit of tinfoil
till it's in the enemy's toils.

**V**

Its song ranges from a boom to a kerplink
reminiscent of the worst excesses of Conlon Nancarrow.

## THE PLOT

*He said, my pretty fair maid, if it is as you say,*
*I'll do my best endeavors in cutting of your hay,*
*For in your lovely countenance I never saw a frown,*
*So, my lovely lass, I'll cut your grass, that's ne'er been trampled down.*
—TRADITIONAL BALLAD

```
a  l  f  a  l  f  a  l  f  a  l  f  a  l  f  a  l  f  a
l  f  a  l  f  a  l  f  a  l  f  a  l  f  a  l  f  a  l
f  a  l  f  a  l  f  a  l  f  a  l  f  a  l  f  a  l  f
a  l  f  a                                a  l  f  a
l  f  a  l                                l  f  a  l
f  a  l  f                                f  a  l  f
a  l  f  a           a  l  p  h  a        a  l  f  a
l  f  a  l                                l  f  a  l
f  a  l  f                                f  a  l  f
a  l  f  a                                a  l  f  a
l  f  a  l  f  a  l  f  a  l  f  a  l  f  a  l  f  a  l
f  a  l  f  a  l  f  a  l  f  a  l  f  a  l  f  a  l  f
a  l  f  a  l  f  a  l  f  a  l  f  a  l  f  a  l  f  a
```

## TRACT

I cleared the trees about my cabin, all
that came within range of a musket ball.

## RAINER MARIA RILKE: *THE UNICORN*

This, then, is the beast that has never actually been:
not having seen one, they prized in any case
its perfect poise, its throat, the straightforward gaze
it gave them back—so straightforward, so serene.

Since it had never been, it was all the more
unsullied. And they allowed it such latitude
that, in a clearing in the wood,
it raised its head as if its essence shrugged off mere

existence. They brought it on, not with oats or corn,
but with the chance, however slight,
that it might come into its own. This gave it such strength

that from its brow there sprang a horn. A single horn.
Only when it met a maiden's white with white
would it be bodied out in her, in her mirror's full length.

## WHITE SHOULDERS

My heart is heavy. For I saw Fionnuala,
"The Gem of the Roe," "The Flower of Sweet Strabane,"
when a girl reached down into a freezer bin
to bring up my double scoop of vanilla.

# GREEN GOWN

*In the afternoon my wife and I had a little quarrel which I reconciled with a
flourish. Then she read a sermon in Dr. Tillotson to me. It is to be observed that the
flourish was performed on the billiard table.*
        —WILLIAM BYRD, *a diary entry for July 30, 1710*


Again and again, when it came her turn
to take a shot,
Marie's first inclination had been to pass
for she knew full well that as soon as she bent low
over the table I would draw
closer to glimpse her "two young roes

that were twins" and the "ivory
tower" of her neck and shoulder and side
and the small of her back
and maybe even the flat
of her belly . . . "The poets of *Sir Gawayne
and the Grene*

*Knight* and *The Romance of the Rose*
were among those to whom Spenser would turn
and upon whom he would draw . . ."
It was the week after the Aldershot
bomb and we were all lying low
for fear of reprisals from Donegall Pass

and Sandy Row . . . "The description of a 'greene
gowne' sported by Lecherie in *The Faerie
Queene*,
for example . . ." That vodka on the side
gave my glass of Heineken, which had fallen flat,
a little bit of pep . . . Knock it back . . .

Knock it back, Rainer, till you pass
out on a breast dripping Liebfraumilch or Mateus Rosé
or Hirondelle . . . "If John Livingston Lowes

is to be believed, Coleridge's turn
of mind was that of a man who's half-shot
most of the time . . ." The main draw-

back,
then, of her house on College Green
had been that it was indeed a house, not a flat,
so that a gay Lothario
had to contend with the snide asides
of her Derry duennas . . . Again and again

Dolores and Perpetua would gallop down a draw
and cut me off at the pass . . .
Again and again I'd been shot
down in flames . . . Until this evening, when I rose
to find my Princess Marie von Thurn
und Taxis-Hohenlohe

sitting on the stately pile of old issues of *Gown*
they used, I'm quite sure, for wiping their back-
sides,
tipping a bottle of green
stuff onto her left palm . . . "Be it Fauré's
Andante for Violin and Piano in B flat

or his *Au bord de l'eau,*
his music fills me with longing . . ." You must draw
your own conclusions as to why things took this turn
after a month-long impasse,
but I suspect that I rose
in her estimation that afternoon when shot

after shot had rung out from Divis Flats
and I kept right on drinking my glass of Heineken
in the public bar of Lavery's
as if this were nothing more than a car back-
firing . . . In any event, I was slumped, green
at the gills, over the side

of the toilet bowl, when she shot
me a glance such as Daphne might shoot Apollo:
"We must gather the Rose
of love, whilst yet is time." "Time?" "To withdraw . . ."
It had already given her a little pizzazz,
that vodka, emboldened her to turn

the cue, hard, as she struck the ball, lending it such side
that it hurtled across the bogs, fens, flats
of chalky green
all the way from Aquinas to (if I may) Quine
at whom it balked, wheehee, did some class of a back-
flip, then rebounded off Porphyry

and Averroes . . . "I use 'withdraw'
in the Marvellian sense . . ." Spermicide, was it, or aloe vera?
"You'll be lucky to get an 'allowed pass' . . ."
She lay on the flat of her back
in a haze of shot silk . . . "Since you've not done a hand's turn . . ."
Her breast . . . "Not a stroke . . ." The green of her green gown.

## NOW, NOW

### I

A sentence of death, my love, as if we were destined to squint
into the glint
of a firing party, going down on one knee
the better to see
their hearts a-flutter with swatches of lint.

### II

Seeing, instead, a pig's back all tinges and tints
merely by dint

of its having been handed down, under an apple-heavy tree,
a sentence of death.


### III

For we hold in our heart of hearts, as the frizzens strike their flints,
what we hitherto took as a hint—
that the rider whom we so eagerly
awaited will leap from the saddle now, now to issue the decree
that life is indeed no more than "a misprint
in the sentence of death."


## LONGBONES

When she came to me that night in Damascus Street
she was quite beside herself. Her father was about to die
and his mirror was covered with a sheet

so his spirit might not beat
against it but fly as spirits fly.
When she came to me that night in Damascus Street

Longbones had driven through freezing rain or sleet
all the way from Lurgan. The Lurgan sky
was a mirror covered with a sheet

or a banner trailed by an army in defeat.
Though Longbones was already high
when she came to me that night in Damascus Street

she immediately shook out a neat
little blue or red cartouche until, by and by,
she had covered a mirror with a sheet

of that most valiant dust. Then she would entreat
me not to leave her, as if I
had come to her that night in Damascus Street,

as if I had asked if I might turn up the heat
and tested if the spare bed was dry
by slipping the mirror between the sheets.

Only when she turned to greet
me, wistful and wry,
that night of nights in Damascus Street,

did I remark on the discreet
blue or red teardrop tattooed under her left eye.
She covered the mirror with a sheet

and whispered, "Come, my sweet,"
in a tone as sly as it was shy:
"Come to me now." That night in Damascus Street

was the last time Longbones and I would meet.
Only later did it strike me why
she would cover the mirror with a sheet.

Only when I looked back on her snow-white feet
and her snow-white thigh
did it come to me, next morning in Damascus Street,
that she herself was the mirror covered with a sheet.

## LAG

We were joined at the hip. We were joined at the hip
like some latter-day Chang and Eng,
though I lay in that dreadful kip
in North Carolina while you preferred to hang

loose in London, in that selfsame
"room in Bayswater." You wrapped yourself in a flag
(the red flag, with a white elephant, of Siam)
and contemplated the time lag.

It was Chang, I seem to recall, who tried to choke
Eng when he'd had one over the eight.
It was Chang whose breath was always so sickly-sour.

It was Chang who suffered a stroke.
Eng was forced to shoulder his weight.
It was Chang who died first. Eng lived on for five hours.


## SYMPOSIUM

You can lead a horse to water but you can't make it hold
its nose to the grindstone and hunt with the hounds.
Every dog has a stitch in time. Two heads? You've been sold
one good turn. One good turn deserves a bird in the hand.

A bird in the hand is better than no bread.
To have your cake is to pay Paul.
Make hay while you can still hit the nail on the head.
For want of a nail the sky might fall.

People in glass houses can't see the wood
for the new broom. Rome wasn't built between two stools.
Empty vessels wait for no man.

A hair of the dog is a friend indeed.
There's no fool like the fool
who's shot his bolt. There's no smoke after the horse is gone.

## BETWEEN TAKES

I was standing in for myself, my own stunt double,
in a scene where I was meant to do a double

or maybe even a triple back somersault
off the bed. In one hand she held a glass of Meursault,

in the other something akin to a Consulate.
When she spoke, she spoke through the consolette

in a diner booth where Meatloaf and The Platters
still larded it over those meat-loaf platters

with all the trimmings. This was a moment,
it seemed, of such moment

that she felt obliged to set down both cigarette and glass
and peer as through the limo's tainted glass

for a glimpse of the mountain stream that, bolder and bolder,
did its little bit of laundry among the boulders.

## SLEEVE NOTES

MICK JAGGER: *Rock music was a completely new musical form. It hadn't been around for ten years when we started doing it. Now it's forty years old.*
JANN S. WENNER: *What about your own staying power?*
MICK JAGGER: *I have a lot of energy, so I don't see it as an immediate problem.*
JANN S. WENNER: *How's your hearing?*
MICK JAGGER: *My hearing's all right. Sometimes I use earplugs because it gets too loud on my left ear.*
JANN S. WENNER: *Why your left ear?*
MICK JAGGER: *Because Keith's standing on my left.*
— "Jagger Remembers," *Rolling Stone*, MARCH 1996

## THE JIMI HENDRIX EXPERIENCE: *Are You Experienced?*

"Like being driven over by a truck"
was how Pete Townshend described the effect
of the wah-wah on "I Don't Live Today."

This predated by some months the pedal
Clapton used on "Tales of Brave Ulysses"
And I'm taken aback (jolt upon jolt)
to think that Hendrix did it all "by hand."

To think, moreover, that he used *four*-track
*one*-inch tape has (jolt upon jolt) evoked
the long, long view from the Senior Study
through the smoke, yes sir, the smoke of battle
on the fields of Laois, yes sir, and Laos.

Then there was the wah-wah on "Voodoo Child
(Slight Return)" from *Electric Ladyland*.


## CREAM: *Disraeli Gears*

As I labored over the "Georgiks and Bukolikis"
I soon learned to tell thunder from dynamite.


## THE BEATLES: *The Beatles*

Though that was the winter when late each night
I'd put away Cicero or Caesar
and pour new milk into an old saucer
for the hedgehog which, when it showed up right

on cue, would set its nose down like that flight
back from the U.S. . . . back from the, yes sir . . .
back from the . . . back from the U.S.S.R. . . . .
I'd never noticed the play on *"album"* and *"white."*

## THE ROLLING STONES: *Beggar's Banquet*

Thanks to Miss Latimore,
I was "coming along nicely" at piano

while, compared to the whoops and wild halloos
of the local urchins,

my diction
was im-pecc-a-ble.

In next to no time I would be lost
to the milk bars

and luncheonettes
of smoky Belfast,

where a troubadour
such as the frontman of Them

had long since traded in the lute
for bass and blues harmonica.


## VAN MORRISON: *Astral Weeks*

Not only had I lived on Fitzroy Avenue,
I'd lived there with Madame Georgie Hyde Lees,
to whom I would rather shortly be wed.

Georgie would lose out to The George and El Vino's
when I "ran away to the BBC"
as poets did, so Dylan Thomas said.


## ERIC CLAPTON: *461 Ocean Boulevard*

It's the house in all its whited sepulchritude
(not the palm tree against which dogs piddle

as they make their way back from wherever
it was they were all night) that's really at a list.

Through the open shutters his music, scatty, skewed,
skids and skites from the neck of a bottle
that might turn on him, might turn and sever
an artery, the big one that runs through his wrist.

## ELVIS COSTELLO AND THE ATTRACTIONS: *My Aim is True*

Even the *reductio ad absurdum*
of the *quid pro quo* or "tit for tat"
killing (For "Eilis" read "Alison")

that now took over from the street riot
was not without an old-fashioned
sense of decorum, an unseemly seemliness.

## WARREN ZEVON: *Excitable Boy*

Somewhere between *Ocean Boulevard* and *Slowhand*
I seemed to have misplaced my wedding band
and taken up with waitresses and usherettes
who drank straight gins and smoked crooked cheroots.

Since those were still the days when more meant less
Georgie was herself playing fast and loose
with the werewolf who, not so very long before,
had come how-howling round our kitchen door

and introduced me to Warren Zevon, whose hymns
to booty, to beasts, to bimbos, boom boom,
are inextricably part of the warp and woof
of the wild and wicked poems in *Quoof*.

**DIRE STRAITS: *Dire Straits***

There was that time the archangel ran his thumb along the shelf
and anointed, it seemed, his own brow with soot.


**BLONDIE: *Parallel Lines***

It had taken all morning to rehearse
a tracking shot

with an Arriflex
mounted on a gurney.

The dream of rain
on the face of a well.

"Ready when you are, Mr. DeMilledoon."
Another small crowd

on the horizon.
We should have rented a Steadicam.


**BRUCE SPRINGSTEEN: *The River***

So it was I gave up the Oona for the Susquehanna,
the Shannon for the Shenandoah.


**LLOYD COLE AND THE COMMOTIONS: *Easy Pieces***

Though not before I'd done my stint on the Cam.
The ceilings taller than the horizon.

The in-crowd
on the outs with the likes of Milton

and Spenser while Cromwell
still walked through the pouring rain.

In graveyards from Urney
to Ardglass, my countrymen laying down some *Lex*

*talionis*: "Only the guy who's shot
gets to ride in the back of the hearse."

**TALKING HEADS: *True Stories***

You can take the man out of Armagh but, you may ask yourself,
can you take the Armagh out of the man in the big Armani suit?

**U2: *The Joshua Tree***

When I went to hear them in Giants Stadium
a year or two ago, the whiff
of kef
brought back the night we drove all night from Palm

Springs to Blythe. No Irish lad and his lass
were so happy as we who roared
and soared
through yucca-scented air. Dawn brought a sense of loss,

faint at first, that would deepen and expand
as our own golden chariot
was showered
with Zippo spears from the upper tiers of the stands.

**PINK FLOYD: *A Momentary Lapse of Reason***

We stopped in at a roadhouse on the way back from Lyonesse
and ordered a Tom Collins and an Old-Fashioned.
As we remounted the chariot

the poplar's synthesized alamo-alamo-eleison
was counterpointed by a redheaded woodpecker's rat-tat-tat
on a snare, a kettledrum's de dum de dum.


PAUL SIMON: *Negotiations and Love Songs*

Little did I think as I knelt by a pothole
to water my elephant with the other elephant drivers,
little did I think as I chewed on some betel

that I might one day be following the river
down the West Side Highway in his smoke-glassed
limo complete with bodyguard-cum-chauffeur

and telling him that his lyrics must surely last:
little did I think as I chewed and chewed
that my own teeth and tongue would be eaten by rust.


LEONARD COHEN: *I'm Your Man*

When I turn up the rickety old gramophone
the wow and flutter from a scratched LP
summons up white walls, the table, the single bed

where Lydia Languish will meet her Le Fanu:
his songs have meant far more to me
than most of the so-called poems I've read.


NIRVANA: *Bleach*

I went there, too, with Mona, or Monica.
Another shot of Absolut.

"The Wild Rover" or some folk anthem
on the jukebox. Some dour

bartender. I, too, have been held fast
by those snares and nets

off the Zinc Coast, the coast of Zanzibar,
                                    lost

                    able
                        addiction

            "chin-chins"
                            loos,

"And it's no,
nay, never, no nay never no more . . ."


BOB DYLAN: *Oh Mercy*

All great artists are their own greatest threat,
as when they aim an industrial laser
at themselves and cut themselves back to the root

so that, with spring, we can never ever be sure
if they shake from head to foot
from an orgasm, you see, sir, or a seizure.


R.E.M.: *Automatic for the People*

Like the grasping for air by an almighty mite
who's suffering from a bad case of the colic.


THE ROLLING STONES: *Voodoo Lounge*

Giants Stadium again . . . Again the scent of drugs
struggling through rain so heavy some young Turks
would feel obliged to butt-hole
surf across those vast puddles

on the field. Some might have burned damp faggots
on a night like this, others faked
the ho-ho-hosannas and the hallelujahs
with their *"Tout passe, tout casse, tout lasse."*

The Stones, of course, have always found the way
of setting a burning brand
to a petrol-soaked stack of hay

and making a "Thou Shalt"
of a "Thou Shalt Not." The sky over the Meadowlands
was still aglow as I drove home to my wife and child.

## HAY

This much I know. Just as I'm about to make that right turn
off Province Line Road
I meet another beat-up Volvo
carrying a load

of hay. (More accurately, a bale of lucerne
on the roof rack,
a bale of lucerne or fescue or alfalfa.)
My hands are raw. I'm itching to cut the twine, to unpack

that hay-accordion, that hay-concertina.
It must be ten o'clock. There's still enough light
(not least from the glow

of the bales themselves) for a body to ascertain
that when one bursts, as now, something takes flight
from those hot-and-heavy box pleats. This much, at least, I know.

## APPLE SLUMP

The bounty-threat of snow
in October. Our apple mound
some boxer fallen foul
of a right swing

waiting for his second to throw—
*the sound, turn up the sound—*
that mean little towel
into the ring.


## THE TRAIN

I've been trying, my darling, to explain
to myself how it is that some freight train
loaded with ballast so a track may rest
easier in its bed should be what's roused

us both from ours, tonight as every night,
despite its being miles off and despite
our custom of putting to the very
back of the mind all that's customary

and then, since it takes forever to pass
with its car after car of coal and gas
and salt and wheat and rails and railway ties,

how it seems determined to give the lie
to the notion, my darling,
that we, not it, might be the constant thing.

## THREE DEER, MOUNT ROSE, AUGUST 1995

How about that? As I stepped outside, the doe and her twin fawns
stopped midway across the yard. They were so laid-back. So serene.
This insouciance might have been enough to evince
their reputation for popping nitroglycerine

to keep their heart rates steady, had we not known already from the
        mounds
of coffee beans that caffeine is their drug of choice.
Not only were they strung out on caffeine but Oscar MacOscair, the
        hound
whose name means "deer favorite," now favored giving chase.

The doe and one fawn got away. The other he caught by a Bakelite
hock as it knocked its head against chicken wire. The Pleiades
had fallen higgledy-piggledy
along its back. All heat of the moment. I could tell from its bleats

this black-tongued fawn wanted to free itself, to make a clean breast
of something, to blurt
out something to the effect, perhaps, that these were the Perseids
rather than the Pleiades, to blurt it out like a Polaroid.


## HOPEWELL HAIKU

I

The door of the shed
open-shuts with the clangor
of red against red.

**II**

A muddle of mice.
Their shit looks like caraway
but smells like allspice.

**III**

From whin-bright Cave Hill
a blackbird might . . . *will* give thanks
with his whin-bright bill.

**IV**

For now, we must make
do with a thumb-blowing owl
across the firebreak.

**V**

A stone at its core,
this snowball's the porcelain
knob on winter's door.

**VI**

Our wild cat, Pangur,
spent last night under the hood
of my old banger.

**VII**

I tamped it with hay,
the boot that began to leak
Thursday or Friday.

## VIII

Snow up to my shanks.
I glance back. The path I've hacked
is a white turf bank.

## IX

Cheek-to-cheek-by-jowl,
from the side of the kettle
my ancestors scowl.

## X

A crocus piss stain.
"There's too much snow in my life,"
my daughter complains.

## XI

Pennons in pine woods
where the white-tailed stag and doe
until just now stood.

## XII

For most of a week
we've lived on a pot of broth
made from a pig's cheek.

## XIII

Burst pipes. Solder flak.
Now she sports a copper ring
with a hairline crack.

## XIV

Though cast in metal,
our doorstop hare finds no place
in which to settle.

## XV

The changeless penknife.
The board. The heavy trestles.
The changeless penknife.

## XVI

Teasel, that lies low,
aspires to raising the nap
on your woolen throw.

## XVII

The finer the cloth
in your obi, or waist piece,
the finer the moth.

## XVIII

The first day of spring.
What to make of that bald patch
right under the swing?

## XIX

A mare's long white face.
A blazed tree marking a trail
we'll never retrace.

**XX**

The razzle-dazzle
of a pair of Ratatosks
on their Yggdrasill.

**XXI**

Jean stoops to the tap
set into a maple's groin
for the rising sap.

**XXII**

The Canada geese
straighten a pantyhose seam,
press a trouser crease.

**XXIII**

When I set a match
to straw—Whiteboys, Bootashees,
pikestaffs in the thatch.

**XXIV**

From the white-hot bales
Caravats and Shanavests
step with white-hot flails.

**XXV**

A hammock at dusk.
I scrimshaw a narwhal hunt
on a narwhal tusk.

**XXVI**

I, too, nailed a coin
to the mast of the *Pequod*.
A tiny pinecone.

**XXVII**

The yard's three lonesome
pines are hung with such tokens.
A play by Zeami.

**XXVIII**

Good Friday. At three,
a swarm of bees sets its heart
on an apple tree.

**XXIX**

While the goldfinch nest
in the peach tree's eye level
with a stallion's crest.

**XXX**

That peach bears the brunt
of the attacks by mildew,
black rot, smuts, and bunts.

**XXXI**

Twilight. Pyewacket
ambles along the ridgepole
with a tar bucket.

## XXXII

We buy flour, bacon
and beans with pollen we pan
here in the Yukon.

## XXXIII

The wide boulevard
where a window-shopping deer
goes by fits and starts.

## XXXIV

None more disheveled
than those who seemed most demure.
Our ragweed revels.

## XXXV

Raspberries. Red-blue.
A paper cut on the tongue
from a billet-doux.

## XXXVI

Now the star-nosed mole
looks back down his long tunnel.
I scrape my boot soles.

## XXXVII

The bold Pangur Ban
draws and quarters a wood thrush
by the garbage can.

**XXXVIII**

It seems from this sheer
clapboard, fungus-flanged, that walls
do indeed have ears.

**XXXIX**

A worm for a lure.
The small-mouthed black bass recoil
from my overtures.

**XL**

Had the thrush not flung
itself at the gin-and-lime.
Had the trap not sprung.

**XLI**

Jean paints one toenail.
In a fork of the white ash,
quick, a cardinal.

**XLII**

Nowadays I flush
a long-drawn-out cry, at most,
from the underbrush.

**XLIII**

A giant puffball.
The swelled, head-hunted, swelled head
of a king of Gaul.

## XLIV

A Saharan boil.
Oscar stretched under a hide
by the toilet bowl.

## XLV

There's a trail of slime
that runs from the lady's-smock.
I'll show you sometime.

## XLVI

At my birthday bash,
a yellow bin for bottles
and a green for trash.

## XLVII

Sunflower with fenceposts.
Communion rail. Crozier. Cope.
The monstrance. The host.

## XLVIII

From under the shed
a stench that's beyond belief.
Pangur Ban is dead.

## XLIX

I lean to one side
to let a funeral pass.
It leans to one side.

**L**

Now I must take stock.
The ax I swaggered and swung's
split the chopping block.

**LI**

In a slow puddle
two dragonflies, Oxford blues,
rest on their paddles.

**LII**

Saturday night. Soap.
Ametas and Thestylis
still making hay ropes.

**LIII**

A lady's-smock thief's
made off with five pairs of smalls
and two handkerchiefs.

**LIV**

An airplane, alas,
is more likely than thunder
to trouble your glass.

**LV**

On the highest rung
of my two-pointed ladder
a splash of bird dung.

### LVI

Immediately you
tap that old bell of millet
it somehow rings true.

### LVII

While from the thistles
that attend our middle age
a goldfinch whistles.

### LVIII

A small, hard pear falls
and hits the deck with a thud.
Ripeness is not all.

### LIX

Wonder of wonders.
The plow that stood in the hay's
itself plowed under.

### LX

Take off his halter
and a horse will genuflect
at a horse altar.

### LXI

Bivouac. Billet.
The moon a waning of lard
on a hot skillet.

**LXII**

For I wrote this page
by the spasm . . . The spasm . . .
A firefly . . . A cage.


**LXIII**

The boiler room floods.
Old apple trees lagged with moss.
Live coals in the mud.


**LXIV**

It's as if he plays
harmonica, the raccoon
with an ear of maize.


**LXV**

No time since we checked
our scythe blades, our reaping hooks
that are now rust-flecked.


**LXVI**

Two trees in the yard
bring neither shade nor shelter
but rain, twice as hard.


**LXVII**

A bullfrog sumo
stares into his bowl of wine.
Those years in Suma.

**LXVIII**

Now he swims across
a swimming pool. His breaststroke
leaves me at a loss.

**LXIX**

Such sallies and swoons.
A starling flock. A total
eclipse of the moon.

**LXX**

Beyond the corn stooks
the maples' firewood detail.
Their little red books.

**LXXI**

A sudden swelter.
A furnace door throwing light
on the ore smelters.

**LXXII**

Like a wayside shrine
to itself, this sideswiped stag
of the seven tines.

## LXXIII

The leaves of the oak
were boons on a hero's booth.
They've gone up in smoke.

## LXXIV

Night. The citadel
gives off carbolic and bleach.
Jeyes' Fluid. Dettol.

## LXXV

I've upset the pail
in which my daughter had kept
her five—"No, *six*"—snails.

## LXXVI

And her homemade kite
of less than perfect design?
Also taken flight.

## LXXVII

Is that body bag
Cuchulainn's or Ferdia's?
Let's check the dog tag.

**LXXVIII**

Fresh snow on the roof
of a car that passed me by.
The print of one hoof.

**LXXIX**

Though the cankered peach
is felled, the bird's nest it held
is still out of reach.

**LXXX**

That stag I sideswiped.
I watched a last tear run down
his tear duct. I wept.

**LXXXI**

There's such a fine line
between freezing rain and sleet.
The stag's narrow chine.

**LXXXII**

A horse farts and farts
on the wind-tormented scarp.
A virtuoso.

**LXXXIII**

A sang-de-boeuf sky
reflected in a cold frame
gives the earth the lie.

**LXXXIV**

The old stag that belled
all night long, tail end of rut.
How my own heart swelled.

**LXXXV**

On the road to town
a raccoon in party mask.
Gray shawl. Gray ballgown.

**LXXXVI**

Winter time, my sweet.
The puppy under our bed
licking salt-raw feet.

**LXXXVII**

Not a golden carp
but a dog turd under ice.
Not a golden carp.

**LXXXVIII**

That wavering flame
is the burn-off from a mill.
Star of Bethlehem.

## LXXXIX

Fishermen have cut
a hole in the frozen lake.
No smoke from their hut.

## XC

The maple's great cask
that once held so much in store
now yields a hip flask.

## ANONYMOUS: *MYSELF AND PANGUR*

Myself and Pangur, my white cat,
have much the same calling, in that
much as Pangur goes after mice
I go hunting for the precise

word. He and I are much the same
in that I'm gladly "lost to fame"
when on the *Georgics*, say, I'm bent
while he seems perfectly content

with his lot. Life in the cloister
can't possibly lose its luster
so long as there's some crucial point
with which he might by leaps and bounds

yet grapple, into which yet sink
our teeth. The bold Pangur will think
through mouse snagging much as I muse
on something naggingly abstruse,

then fix his clear, unflinching eye
on our lime-white cell wall, while I
focus, insofar as I can,
on the limits of what a man

may know. Something of his rapture
at his most recent mouse capture
I share when I, too, get to grips
with what has given me the slip.

And so we while away our whiles,
never cramping each other's styles
but practicing the noble arts
that so lift and lighten our hearts,

Pangur going in for the kill
with all his customary skill
while I, sharp-witted, swift, and sure,
shed light on what had seemed obscure.

## RAINER MARIA RILKE: *BLACK CAT*

Despite its being invisible, a ghost has enough mass
to take your glance and give it glancingly back;
here, though, your sternest look will pass
not through but *into* her fur, fur as dense and black
as the walls against which a madman pounds
his fists, the padded
cell against which, all night long, he expends
himself until his fury has abated.
For it seems that she has somehow been able to keep
within herself every glance that's ever been cast
at her as, bristling, up for battle,
she gives them the once-over before falling asleep.
Then, as if starting from slumber,

she turns her face directly toward your own
and you see yourself, held fast
in the yellow stone
of her eye like a bug, like a long-extinct beetle
set in a lump of amber.


## PAUNCH

Barefoot, in burgundy shorts and a salmon-pink
T-shirt, I pad across the deck
and sink
into one of four old Adirondack

chairs that themselves slump into themselves. There's a flare
from the citronella bucket
as, there,
our eight-week-old stray kitten, Pyewacket,

ventures across what might have seemed a great divide
between her and me, had she not
now begun to nag and needle

and knead
my paunch for milk. The bucket fills with human fat.
The chair takes a dim view through a knothole.


## LONG FINISH

Ten years since we were married, since we stood
under a chuppah of pine boughs
in the middle of a little pinewood
and exchanged our wedding vows.

Save me, good thou,
a piece of marchpane, while I fill your glass with Simi
Chardonnay as high as decency allows,
and then some.

Bear with me now as I myself must bear
the scrutiny of a bottle of wine
that boasts of hints of plum and pear,
its muscadine
tempered by an oak backbone. I myself have designs
on the willow-boss
of your breast, on all your waist confines
between longing and loss.

The wonder is that we somehow have withstood
the soars and slumps in the Dow
of ten years of marriage and parenthood,
its summits and its sloughs—
that we've somehow
managed to withstand an almond-blossomy
five years of bitter rapture, five of blissful rows
(and then some

if we count the one or two to spare
when we've been firmly on cloud nine).
Even now, as you turn away from me with your one bare
shoulder, the veer of your neckline,
I glimpse the all-but-cleared-up eczema patch on your spine
and it brings to mind not the Schloss
that stands, transitory, tra la, Triestine,
between longing and loss

but a crude
hip trench in a field, covered with pine boughs,
in which two men in masks and hoods
who have themselves taken vows
wait for a farmer to break a bale for his cows
before opening fire with semi-

automatics, cutting him off slightly above the eyebrows,
and then some.

It brings to mind another, driving out to care
for six white-faced kine
finishing on heather and mountain air,
another who'll shortly divine
the precise whereabouts of a land mine
on the road between Beragh and Sixmilecross,
who'll shortly know what it is to have breasted the line
between longing and loss.

Such forbearance in the face of vicissitude
also brings to mind the little "there, theres" and "now, nows"
of two sisters whose sleeves are imbued
with the constant douse and souse
of salt water through their salt house
in *Matsukaze* (or *Pining Wind*), by Zeami,
the salt house through which the wind soughs and soughs,
and then some

of the wind's little "now, nows" and "there, theres"
seem to intertwine
with those of Pining Wind and Autumn Rain, who must forbear
the dolor of their lives of boiling down brine.
For the double meaning of "pine"
is much the same in Japanese as English, coming across
both in the sense of "tree" and the sense we assign
between "longing" and "loss"

as when the ghost of Yukihira, the poet-courtier who wooed
both sisters, appears as a ghostly pine, pining among pine boughs.
Barely have Autumn Rain and Pining Wind renewed
their vows
than you turn back toward me, and your blouse,
while it covers the all-but-cleared-up patch of eczema,
falls as low as decency allows,
and then some.

Princess of Accutane, let's no more try to refine
the pure drop from the dross
than distinguish, good thou, between mine and thine,
between longing and loss,
but rouse
ourselves each dawn, here on the shore at Suma,
with such force and fervor as spouses may yet espouse,
and then some.


## THE THROWBACK

Even I can't help but notice, my sweet,
that when you tuck your chin
into your chest, as if folding a sheet
while holding a clothespin

between your teeth, or when, a small detail,
you put your hands like so
on your little potbelly and twiddle
your thumbs like so, it's as if you're a throw-

back to the grandmother you never met,
the mother whom I sight
in this reddish patch of psoriasis

behind your ear that might
suddenly flare up into the helmet
she wore when she stood firm against Xerxes.

# THEY THAT WASH ON THURSDAY

She was such a dab hand, my mother. Such a dab hand
at raising her hand
to a child. At bringing a cane down across my hand
in such a seemingly offhand
manner I almost have to hand
it to her. "Many hands,"
she would say, "spoil the broth." My father took no hand
in this. He washed his hands
of the matter. He sat on his hands.
So I learned firsthand
to deal in the off-, the under-, the sleight-of-hand,
writing now in that great, open hand
yet never quite showing my hand.
I poured myself a drink with a heavy hand.
As for the women with whom I sat hand-in-hand
in the Four-in-Hand,
as soon as they were eating out of my hand
I dismissed them out of hand.
Then one would play into my hands—
or did she force my hand?—
whose lily-white hand
I took in marriage. I should have known beforehand
it wouldn't work. "When will you ever take yourself in hand?"
"And give you the upper hand?"
For things were by now completely out of hand.
The show of hands
on a moonlit hill under the Red Hand.
The Armalite in one hand
and the ballot box in the other. Men dying at hand.
Throughout all of which I would hand
back to continuity as the second hand
came up to noon. "On the one hand . . .
On the other . . ." The much-vaunted even hand
of the BBC. Though they'd pretty much given me a free hand
I decided at length to throw in my hand
and tendered my resignation "by hand."

I was now quite reconciled to living from hand
to mouth. (Give that man a big, big hand.)
My father was gone. My mother long gone. Into Thy hands,
O Lord . . . Gone, too, the ink-stained hands
of Mary Powers. Now I'd taken another lily-white hand
put in by the hole of the door. A hand
no bigger than a cloud. Now she and I and the child of my right
        hand
stand hand in hand,
brave Americans all, and I know ("The bird in the hand
is the early bird . . .") that the time is at hand
for me to set my hand
to my daughter's still-wet, freehand
version of the Muldoon "coat of arms" that came to hand
in a heraldry shop on Nassau Street—on a green field a white hand.


## BLISSOM

The thing is, when Agnieszka and I lay like bride and groom
in the refuse-tip
of her six-by-eight-by-six-foot bed-sitting room

I awoke as a Prince of Serendip
between her legs,
given how my mind would skip

from pegs to kegs to tegelmousted Tuaregs
while I peered through the skylight as if from an open tomb
at those five ewe and three wether-tegs.

# THE LITTLE BLACK BOOK

It was Aisling who first soft-talked my penis tip between her legs
while teasing open that Velcro strip between her legs.

Cliona then. A skinny country girl.
The small stream, in which I would skinny-dip, between her legs.

Born and bred in Londinium, the standoffish Etain,
who kept a stiff upper lip between her legs.

Grainne. Grain goddess. The last, triangular shock of corn,
through which a sickle might rip, between her legs.

Again and again that winter I made a beeline for Ita,
for the sugar-water sip between her legs.

The spring brought not only Liadan but her memory of Cuirithir,
his ghostly one-upmanship between her legs.

(Ita is not to be confused with her steely half sister, Niamh,
she of the ferruginous drip between her legs.)

It was Niamh, as luck would have it, who introduced me to Orla.
The lost weekend of a day trip between *her* legs.

It was Orla, as luck would have it, who introduced me to Roisin.
The bramble patch. The rosehip between her legs.

What ever became of Sile?
Sile, who led me to horse-worship between her legs.

As for Janet from the Shankill, who sometimes went by "Sinead,"
I practiced my double back flip between her legs.

I had a one-on-one tutorial with Siobhan.
I read *The Singapore Grip* between her legs.

And what ever became of Sorcha, Sorcha, Sorcha?
Her weakness for the whip between her legs.

Or the big-boned, broad-shouldered Treasa?
She asked me to give her a buzz clip between her legs.

Or the little black sheep, Una, who kept her own little black book?
I fluttered, like an erratum slip, between her legs.

## ERRATA

For "Antrim" read "Armagh."
For "mother" read "other."
For "harm" read "farm."
For "feather" read "father."

For "Moncrieff" read "Monteith."
For *"Beal Fierste"* read *"Beal Feirste."*
For "brave" read "grave."
For "revered" read "reversed."

For "married" read "marred."
For "pull" read "pall."
For "ban" read "bar."
For "smell" read "small."

For "spike" read "spoke."
For "lost" read "last."
For "Steinbeck" read "Steenbeck."
For "ludic" read "lucid."

For "religion" read "region."
For "ode" read "code."
For "Jane" read "Jean."
For "rod" read "road."

For "pharoah" read "pharaoh."
For *"Fíor-Gael"* read *"Fíor-Ghael."*
For "Jeffrey" read "Jeffery."
For "vigil" read "Virgil."

For "flageolet" read "fava."
For "veto" read "vote."
For "Aiofe" read "Aoife."
For "anecdote" read "antidote."

For "Rosemont" read "Mount Rose."
For "plump" read "plumb."
For "hearse" read "hears."
For "loom" read "bloom."

## HORSES

### I

A sky. A field. A hedge flagrant with gorse.
I'm trying to remember, as best I can,
if I'm a man dreaming I'm a plowhorse
or a great plowhorse dreaming I'm a man.

### II

Midsummer eve. St. John's wort. Spleenwort. Spurge.
I'm hard on the heels of the sage, Chuang Tzu,
when he slips into what was once a forge
through a door in the shape of a horseshoe.

# A JOURNEY TO CRACOW

As we hightailed it across the meadows
toward what might have been common ground
we were dragged down by our own shadows
through a dance floor near Wanda's mound

toward what might have been. Common ground?
Only when a black horse plunges
through a dance floor near Wanda's mound
do they take the barn door off its hinges,

only when a black horse plunges
into the Vistula swollen with rain
do they take the barn door off its hinges
to beat out the black grain.

Into the Vistula swollen with rain
you and I might have plunged and found a way
to beat out the black grain
as our forefathers did on threshing day,

you and I might have plunged and found a way
to set a cigarette on the barn door
as our forefathers did on threshing day
and dance rings around it forevermore,

to set a cigarette on the barn door
wherever it might be, for an instant even,
and dance rings around it forevermore
in some polka or Cracovienne,

whatever that might be. For an instant, even
we were dragged down by our own shadows,
my love, in some polka or mazurka or Cracovienne
as we hightailed it across the meadows.

## AFTERMATH

### I

"Let us now drink," I imagine patriot cry to patriot
after they've shot
a neighbor in his own aftermath, who hangs still between two
        sheaves
like Christ between two tousle-headed thieves,
his body wired up to the moon, as like as not.

### II

To the memory of another left to rot
near some remote beauty spot,
the skin of his right arm rolled up like a shirtsleeve,
let us now drink.

### III

Only a few nights ago, it seems, they set fire to a big house and it got
so preternaturally hot
we knew there would be no reprieve
till the swallows' nests under the eaves
had been baked into these exquisitely glazed little pots
from which, my love, let us now drink.

## WIRE

As I roved out this morning at daybreak
I took a shortcut
through the pine forest, following the high-tension wires
past the timberline

till I stumbled upon a makeshift hide or shooting box
from which a command wire seemed to run

intermittently along the ski run
or firebreak.
I glanced into the hideout. A school lunchbox.
A pear so recently cut
I thought of Ceylon. A can of Valvoline.
Crocodile clips. Sri Lanka, I mean. A hank of wire

that might come in handy if ever I'd want to hot-wire
a motor and make a run
for the border. From just beyond my line
of vision I glimpsed something, or someone, break
cover for an instant. A shaved head, maybe, or a crew cut.
Jumping up like a jack-in-the-box

before ducking back down. Then a distant raking through the gearbox
of a truck suddenly gone haywire
on this hillside of hillsides in Connecticut
brought back some truck on a bomb run,
brought back so much with which I'd hoped to break—
the hard line

yet again refusing to toe the line,
the bullet and the ballot box,
the joyride, the jail break,
Janet endlessly singing "The Men Behind the Wire,"
the endless rerun
of Smithfield, La Mon, Enniskillen, of bodies cut

to ribbons as I heard the truck engine cut
and, you might have read as much between the lines,
ducked down here myself behind the hide. As if I myself were on
        the run.
The truck driver handing a box
cutter, I'm sure, to the bald guy. A pair of real live wires.
I've listened to them all day now, torn between making a break

for it and their talk of the long run, the short term, of boxing clever,
fish or cut bait, make or break,
the end of the line, right down to the wire.


## RUNE

What can I tell you? Though your quarry
lies exhausted at the bottom of an exhausted quarry,

to follow that lure
will almost certainly end in failure.

While I did indeed sink
like a stone among bottles, cans, a fridge, a sink,

a slab of marble, granite
or slate I'm not. By the window of an All-Nite

Café or a 24-Hour Bank
I, too, stretched as if on a flowery bank

and admired
my shiny, former self, a self even then mired

in the idea that what you saw
was what you got.

Why would a hostage's hand hacked off with a hacksaw
weigh on me now like a blood-spattered ingot

from that 24-Hour Bank, I who once cut such a figure
in its drive-up window? Go figure.

# THIRD EPISTLE TO TIMOTHY

*You made some mistake when you intended to favor me with some of the new
valuable grass seed . . . for what you gave me . . . proves mere timothy.*
*—A letter from Benjamin Franklin to Jared Eliot, July 16, 1747*

I

Midnight. June 1923. Not a stir except for the brough and brouhaha
surrounding the taper or link
in which a louse
flares up and a shadow, my da's,
clatters against a wall of the six-by-eight-by-six-foot room
he sleeps in, eleven years old, a servant boy at Hardys of Carnteel.
There's a boot-polish lid filled with turps
or paraffin oil
under each cast-iron bed leg, a little barrier
against bedbugs under each bed foot.

II

That knocking's the knocking against their stalls of a team
of six black Clydesdales mined in Coalisland
he's only just helped to unhitch from the cumbersome
star of a hay rake. Decently and in order
he brought each whitewashed nose
to its nosebag of corn, to its galvanized bucket.
One of the six black Clydesdale mares
he helped all day to hitch and unhitch
was showing, on the near hock, what might be a bud of farcy
picked up, no doubt, while on loan to Wesley Cummins.

"Decently and in order," Cummins would proclaim, "let all
　　　Inniskillings
be done." A week ago my da helped him limber up
the team to a mowing machine as if to a gun carriage. "For no
　　　Dragoon
can function without his measure of char."
He patted his bellyband. "A measure, that is, against dysentery."
This was my da's signal to rush
into the deep shade of the hedge to fetch such little tea as might
　　　remain
in the tea urn. "Man does not live," Cummins would snort, "only by
　　　scraps
of wheaten farls and tea dregs.
You watch your step or I'll see you're shipped back to Killeter."


IV

"Killeeshill," my da says, "I'm from Killeeshill." Along the cast-iron
rainbow of his bed end
comes a line
of chafers or cheeselips that have scaled the bed legs
despite the boot-polish lids. Eleven years of age. A servant boy
on the point of falling asleep. The reek of paraffin
or the pinewoods reek
of turpentine
good against roundworm in horses. That knocking against their stalls
of six Clydesdales, each standing at sixteen hands.


V

Building hay even now, even now drawing level with the team's
　　　headbrass,
buoyed up by nothing more than the ballast
of hay—meadow cat's-tail, lucerne, the leaf upon trodden leaf

of white clover and red—
drawing level now with the taper blooms of a horse chestnut.
Already light in the head.
"Though you speak, young Muldoon . . ." Cummins calls up from
                trimming the skirt
of the haycock, "though you speak with the tongue
of an angel, I see you for what you are . . . Malevolent.
Not only a member of the church malignant but a *malevolent* spirit."


**VI**


Even now borne aloft by bearing down on lap cocks and shake cocks
from under one of which a ruddy face
suddenly twists and turns upward as if itself carried
on a pitchfork and, meeting its gaze,
he sees himself, a servant boy still, still ten or eleven,
breathing upon a Clydesdale's near hock and finding a farcy bud
like a tiny glow in a strut of charcoal.
"I see you," Cummins points at him with the pitchfork, "you little
                byblow,
I see you casting your spells, your sorceries,
I see you coming as a thief in the night to stab us in the back."


**VII**


A year since they kidnapped Anketell Moutray from his home at
                Favour Royal,
dragging him, blindfolded, the length of his own gravel path,
eighty years old, the Orange County grand master. Four A Specials
                shot on a train
in Clones. The Clogher valley
a blaze of flax mills and haysheds. Memories of the Land League.
                Davitt and Biggar.
Breaking the boycott at Lough Mask.
The Land Leaguers beaten
at the second battle of Saintfield. It shall be revealed . . .

A year since they cut out the clapper of a collabor . . . a collabor . . .
a collaborator from Maguiresbridge.


**VIII**

That knocking's the team's near-distant knocking on wood
while my da breathes upon
the blue-yellow flame on a fetlock, on a deep-feathered pastern
of one of six black Shires . . . "Because it shall be revealed by fire,"
Cummins's last pitchfork is laden
with thistles, "as the sparks fly upward
man is born into trouble. For the tongue may yet be cut
from an angel." The line of cheeselips and chafers
along the bed end. "Just wait till you come back down and I get a
        hold
of you, young Muldoon . . . We'll see what spells you'll cast."


**IX**

For an instant it seems no one else might scale
such a parapet of meadow cat's-tail, lucerne, red and white clovers,
not even the line of chafers and cheeselips
that overthrow as they undermine
when, light in the head, unsteady on his pegs as Anketell Moutray,
he squints through a blindfold of clegs
from his grass-capped, thistle-strewn vantage point,
the point where two hay ropes cross,
where Cummins and his crew have left him, in a straw hat with a
        fraying brim,
while they've moved on to mark out the next haycock.


**X**

That next haycock already summoning itself from windrow after
        wind-weary windrow

while yet another brings itself to mind in the acrid stink
of turpentine. There the image of Lizzie,
Hardy's last servant girl, reaches out from her dais
of salt hay, stretches out an unsunburned arm
half in bestowal, half beseechingly, then turns away to appeal
to all that spirit troop
of hay treaders as far as the eye can see, the coil on coil
of hay from which, in the taper's mild uproar,
they float out across the dark face of the earth, an earth without
      form, and void.

## A HALF DOOR NEAR CLUNY

```
s  t  a  b  l  e  s  t  a  b  l  e  s  t  a  b  l  e  s
t  a  b  l  e  s  t  a  b  l  e  s  t  a  b  l  e  s  t
a  b  l  e  s  t  a  b  l  e  s  t  a  b  l  e  s  t  a
b  l  e  s                             s  t  a  b
l  e  s  t                             t  a  b  l
e  s  t  a                             a  b  l  e
s  t  a  b                             b  l  e  s
t  a  b  l           b  l  é           l  e  s  t
a  b  l  e                             e  s  t  a
b  l  e  s                             s  t  a  b
l  e  s  t                             t  a  b  l
e  s  t  a                             a  b  l  e
s  t  a  b  l  e  s  t  a  b  l  e  s  t  a  b  l  e  s
t  a  b  l  e  s  t  a  b  l  e  s  t  a  b  l  e  s  t
a  b  l  e  s  t  a  b  l  e  s  t  a  b  l  e  s  t  a
b  l  e  s  t  a  b  l  e  s  t  a  b  l  e  s  t  a  b
l  e  s  t  a  b  l  e  s  t  a  b  l  e  s  t  a  b  l
e  s  t  a  b  l  e  s  t  a  b  l  e  s  t  a  b  l  e
s  t  a  b  l  e  s  t  a  b  l  e  s  t  a  b  l  e  s
```

## BURMA

*In Memory of Charles Monteith*

Thunder and lightning. The veil of the temple rent
in twain
as I glimpse through the flackering flap of the tent
the rain

flash-flooding across the shoulders and roughed-out head
of one
of sixteen elephants—putty-colored, teak-red,
blue, dun—

that now skip round the ring to flourish their blunt tusks,
their capes
of rain-dark jute or sisal or coconut husks,

to foist
themselves upon the public, one day to escape
the pavilion which, this morning, we watched them hoist.


## THE HUG

*In Memory of Joseph Brodsky*

"Of course, of course, of course," I heard you intone
in your great peaches-and-diesel tenor
as I drew up to the airport in Cologne,
"there's an Auden in every Adenauer

though politicians and poets embrace, you see,
only before a masque or after a massacre."
We sat with our daughters on our knees.
"Poets and politicians are close . . . but no Cigar."

You would break the filter tip off a Camel—
"They're infinitely better 'circumcised' "—
and pour another Absolut, *du lieber Himmel*,
eschewing absolutely the lemon zest.

You had such gusto, Joseph: for an afternoon trip
to the hallowed ground of Middagh Street;
dim sum in Soho, all those bits and bobs of tripe
and chickens' gizzards and chickens' feet

and dumplings filled with gristle
that reminded you of the labor camp
near Archangel. As I left the church of Saint Ursula
yesterday afternoon, I was already quite overcome

by the walls of *die Goldene Kammer*
swagged with human bones, already quite taken aback
by its abecedary, its Latin grammar,
of fibulas and femurs, its rack

of shanks and shoulderblades,
when a blast of air from, I guess, the Caucasus
threw its arms around me in the Ursulaplatz
with what was surely your "Kisses, kisses, kisses."

## WHITE

*In Memory of Thaddeus Wills (June 19–20, 1996)*

Your mother shows me a photograph of you got up in lace.
White crêpe-de-chine. White bonnet. White mittens.
Once, on a street in Moscow, a woman pushed snow in my face
when it seemed I might have been frostbitten.

## THE FRIDGE

An ogham stone stands foursquare as the fridge
I open yet again to forage
for a bottle of Smithwicks or Bass
when *"Beárrthóir* means 'a barber,' " O'Boyle avers,
"but *bearradóir* in Gortahork
is 'a cow that eats at other cows' tails . . .' "
and there's a faint whiff of a chemistry lab

as through the fridge door there pass
three old teachers, three philosophers
who followed the narrow track
to the highest good, followed a cattle trail
to this foursquare limestone slab
with one straight edge all notches and nicks:
Sean O'Boyle; John McCarter; Jerry Hicks.

## THE BANGLE
## (SLIGHT RETURN)

*If it is true that by death we once more become what we were before being, would it
not have been better to abide by that pure possibility, not to stir from it? What use
was this detour, when we might have remained forever in an unrealized plenitude?*
 —E. M. CIORAN, **The Trouble with Being Born** (translated by Richard Howard)

*Does the fetus dream? If so, of what? No one knows.*

 —*The New York Times*

CECILY: *Uncle Jack is sending you to Australia.*
ALGERNON: *Australia! I'd sooner die.*
CECILY: *Well, he said at dinner on Wednesday night, that you would have to choose
between this world, the next world, and Australia.*

 —OSCAR WILDE, **The Importance of Being Earnest**

## I

"The beauty of it," ventured Publius Vergilius Maro,
"is that your father and the other skinnymalinks
may yet end up a pair of jackaroos
in the canefields north of Brisbane." We heard the tink

of blade on bone, the Greeks' alalaes
as they slashed and burned, saw Aeneas daddle-dade
his father, Anchises, and his son, Iulus,
to a hidey-hole on the slopes of Mount Ida.

"The beauty of it is that I delivered them from harm;
it was I who had Aeneas steal
back to look for Creusa, I who had her spirit rub
like a flame through his flame-burnished arms,
I who might have let him find his own way through the streel
of smoke, among the cheerless dead, the dying's chirrups."

## II

Even as I felt their death throes in the thrum and throb
of a ship's engine and looked into the roil
of its wake I recognized his suitcase by the strap.
Even as a wind blew up from the Sea of Moyle

to meet a headwind from beyond Stranraer
and those two winds vied
for supremacy in the air
there was a glimmer of something from across the divide.

Even as I felt their death throes in the strim and strum
of its engine as the packet rounded a headland
there was a glimmer from across the chasm

that lit his glib all glabrous with Brylcreem,
all brilliantine-brilliant,
that glinted and glittered and gleamed as from Elysium.


### III

A restaurant off the Champs-Elysées. Ray's wing. Consommé.
The waiter about to take my dessert order
when there was a cry of *Bravo* followed by a *Bravissimo*
from the next table but one. Two men. A woman who brought back a
　　　reporter

I knew in Belfast. A moment's silence in which the men tested the
　　　nose
("We call it the 'nose' rather than the 'bouquet' ")
of their Hennessys
was broken now by the tink of ice in my ice bucket.

"A *demain*," she seemed to pout, "*à demain, mon amour . . .*"
and her bracelet would twitter and twitch
as if to stress the phrase

while, to stress it all the more,
the floor began to roll and pitch
as the headwind from beyond Stranraer reached gale force.


### IV

Now that the great engine was suddenly thrown into reverse
I studied the menu as a catechumen
might his catechism. The *gâteau au framboises et fraises*
or the *gâteau icumen*

*in, lhude sing, lhude sing,*
as the Chateauneuf du Pape
kicked in. The waiter's eyebrow ring
glittering as he drew himself up

to recommend the *Caprice des Dieux*, his *nu sculon herigean*
counterpointed by the jitter and jaunt and jar
of their harness, their own improvised *ceintures*

*de ficelle*, when my da and that other larrikin
trotted off down the road between Duchess, maybe, and Dajarra
to join the rest of the cane snedders.


## V


"The beauty of it," ventured Virgil, "is that it was I who had the
            sentries
look the other way so that Creusa might brush
like an incendiary
through your arms, I who gave strong drink to you who were ready
            to perish,

I who had Creusa pout, 'A *demain*,'
I who had you recognize his cuirass by its strap
as the packet labored against the raging main,
I who had him stand in his stirrups

as he and the other skinnymalinks rode along the track
to the slow clatter
of manganese ore, or zinc, or iron that sharpeneth iron,

I who had you look into the dark
and recognize the glitter
of stars over the mighty Wooroonooran."

## VI

The waiter drew himself up in his full-length white empyrean
when he saw me tend
toward another bottle of the Côtes du Rhône,
licked the end

of his pencil, drew a line,
and began to catalogue,
with all the little tuts and twitters and whistle-whines
that are the mark of capability and godlike

reason, the damage done by my convoy,
my caravan,
of consommé, salad, and ray's wing braked

on a bed of bok choy,
so I called out to him for a wedge of Bonderay au Foin
and he jabbed his pencil with such force it must surely break.


## VII

Even now my da and that other jolly swagman would rake
their horses over the manganese-bright stones
and into the canebrake.
That streel of smoke. That tink of blade on bone.

The Greeks' al-al-al-al-alalaes
as they fought hand-to-hand
under the shadow of Troy's smoke-blackened walls.
Until there again, as if wounded, she threw up her right hand

and I glanced the glance of one of those kookaburras
through the canebrake, the kookaburra that laughs last,
and I heard her laugh

as I continued to peruse
the dessert menu cum wine list,
every so often turning over a new coolibar leaf.


## VIII

Half a love, half a love, half a love, half a love
was better than no bride
as my da bent to unpick the clove
hitch in the twine with which his manganese-red

suitcase was bound, his tatty-natty
glib falling forward to meet that head-
wind from beyond in which she unpicked the knot
in her pocketbook, steadied herself against the bulkhead

and cupped her hands around a cigarette.
The streel of smoke. The tink and tonk
as the Greeks hastened from tent to tent

in their nightclubbers' boots and short skirts.
The waiter setting his pencil point on his tongue.
A tongue stud or some such ornament.


## IX

Now there came that sweat-and-tobacco scent
as when the spirit
rubs like a flame across the back of a spent
horse that's been spurred

on across the paddocks
to a fence it cannot but refuse.
Now shock after straw-blond shock
would fall across Creusa's face

while I continued to put the little bit of a carte
before the laughing jackass's
"*Au foin? Au foin? Au foin? Au foin?*"

at which moment she looked at me. A look of regret,
already, for what might not be. A gaze
that lasted for a count of five or six. Six or seven.


X


Even as I myself tried to keep myself on an even
keel as if I had indeed been put
drunk into the Newhaven-
Dieppe packet boat

she touched one eye, smudging her kohl,
and turned to watch the traffic flow
toward the Place Charles de Gaulle.
I had been struck no less deadly a blow

by the combination of Australian Syrah
and an intolerable deal of sack
than when, as he and the swagman rode alongside the rails,

a cassowary, heh,
stopped my da's cow pony, ho, in its tracks
and with a razor-sharp middle claw ripped out its entrails.


XI


It might have been just then as, cassawarily,
the Greeks made their way through the aftermath
of the battle, their unruly
locks all blood-brilliant from the bloodbath,

as they moved through the smoke-blackened ruins,
thatch smoldering like a black millefeuille,
that a manganese-laden train
clattered down the slopes of Mount Isa and wistfully

the waiter licked his pencil point. *"Si Monsieur l'épicure
voudrait un petit verre de Muscat*
(I noticed his pants were held up by binder twine)

*avec ses bigarreaux?"*
There was a silence more awkward than that following a miscue
on the next pool table but one.

## XII

It seems that my da might have been a little uptight, a little *boutonnée,*
even as he hurtled through the canefields
on some flea-bitten
cow pony, even as he hurtled across bogs, fens, flats,

clip joints, and clapiers—
we'll cross that bridge, we'll cross that bridge
when we come to the coolibars
that run along the ridge

of Mount Isa, the coolibars and bloodwoods—
even as she gave me that look so frank, so open,
that she herself was forced to turn

away as a frog he would, a frog he would
like to recommend a little glass of the Beaune
or maybe a little glass of the Sauternes.

## XIII

Now the packet thrummed and throbbed from stem to stern
as St. Elmo's fire
took a turn
along the deck and rigging and the cheese wire

flashed like a guillotine
from the corner of my eye. Her arm running through a terret
of cheesecloth or tarlatan.
Though I knew in my heart of hearts

I should call it quits
something made me want to persevere,
made me want to hold with the hold with the hold

with the Muscadet
de Sèvres de Sèvres de Sèvres
as the flea-bitten pony came to a sudden halt.

## XIV

As the packet tried to hold to hold to hold
its course there was a glimmer from the distant coast—
from the Mull of Kintyre or Holyhead—
though the gusts

that reached force 10 on the Beaufort scale
seemed unlikely to blow over
anytime soon and we might have to turn tail
and run for cover

since there's many a slip
twixt what one supposedly determines
and the al-al-al-al-aleatory

where a cow pony gives up on the slopes
of Mount Isa or the Hay's meanderings come to mean
nothing on the border of Queensland and the Northern Territory.


## XV

"*Si Monsieur l'épicure . . . Si Monsieur l'épicure voudrait*
*un verre de Veuve Clicquot*
*après son Bonderay*
*au Foin . . . ?*" All the little godlike clucks

and clicketings. His pants
held up by a binder-twine *crios*.
The pencil point
on his tongue. "*L'addition, s'il vous plaît.*" While across

the chasm, through the battle brume,
I could but gawk
at Creusa, could but gape at her prim,

at her prissy-prim
little mouth, while too many cooks, while too many cooks
made light work of the daughter of Priam.


## XVI

It was downhill all the way after that. The opprobrium
of the waiter of waiters. To have your cake
and eat bigarroons *and* Bonderay au Foin? His new imperium
sweeping clean through the muskeg

in which my da and your man had ridden their cock-
horses roughshod over my *crise*
*d'un certain âge*, my da trying in vain to kick-
start the cow pony, my calling out "Creusa, Creusa, Creusa"

as the packet reached the midway and turning point.
A French edition of *Chaos*. James Gleick.
I'm sure I overheard one of the Hennessy's "*Il est très . . .*

*Il a un certain . . . embonpoint.*"
Which brought a faint smile to the prim little mouth of this look-
      alike
of a reporter I used to know back in Troy.


## XVII

That thrum and throb. An engine in reverse. His involuntary
clucks and clicketings as the waiter examined
the credit card I must have set on his tray.
A train laden with manganese from the open-cast mine

where, on his first day, the foreman handed him a pink slip
which he mulled over,
I see it now: "Mul-do-on, *non? Avec trois syllabes?*"
Now I would do my best endeavors

in cutting through that force ten gale—
"Till May is out," I wanted to cry, "ne'er cast
a clout, my duck, for hold-

fast isn't the only horse that for want of a coat of mail
was lost to a hippocaust."
I watched as the cow pony watched its own entrails unfold.


## XVIII

Downhill all the way as the packet pitched and rolled
and made heavy weather
of a groundswell that seemed as likely to overturn as uphold
the established order, such order as we decipher

while we sit and play, or are played by, our toccatas,
stately at the clavichord.
As for my Creusa, as for my little coquette,
though I knew in my heart of hearts

that one night's ice is not a Neapolitan,
hey, knew that I might only aspire
to taking a turn

with her through the Latin
Quarter, ho, I nonetheless appealed to the Mull of Kintyre
for the *keee-yaah* or *kikikikik* of a common tern.

## XIX

"I make no distinction," Virgil went on, "between 'Trojan' and
        'Tyrian'
when it comes to the use of weapons
of war . . ." Now Creusa would somehow happen to turn
the world upside down just as my da would happen

to untie the not a whit
of the suitcase and shake out a pair of corduroy breeches
rolled up in which was a wad
of newspapers . . . "For it was I who had a Hennessy broach

the subject of joining their fellow nightclubbers
on the Avenue des Invalides
so that Creusa might look up . . . I make no distinction between

that and the collopers
of their own dear flesh who move through the battlefield
at the prompting of a bottle of poteen."

## XX

"*Notre ami . . .*" said the other Hennessy, "*il a une grande
        bedaine . . .*"
The rest was lost in the groundswell of Muzak
and the tough and rumble of half a dozen Bedouin
as she touched one eye, smudging her masc-

ara, a smudge that still beggars
description, the yoicks and yo-hos of half a dozen scrofulous
rag- and pocket-pickers
as a crowd of blackfellows ("*Cette carte de crédit est volée?*")

gathered around to grab at the reins
of the cow pony, my da and the other skinnymalinks both
staring into the "unreal-

ized plenitude," both looking back down the drain
of eternity on their enterprise of such great pith . . .
Heigh-ho, says Anthony Rowley.


## XXI

For "pith" read "flight path." For "Rowley" read "Orly."
When might this throwback
to my reporter from Belfast reel-to-reel
through the blazing town as Aeneas stumbled under the weight of
        Anchises on his back

like a man who's had an intolerable deal of Izarra?
Not even if a low-
flying plane with its leather-capped janissary
were to come through the window in slo-

mo, ho, would her look, so lacking in guile,
waver. "The beauty of it," Virgil was saying, "the sheer beauty
of it is not even

that would quell
the blood in her pint pot and have the storm abate
and the sea glitter as it glittered once for Xenophon."


## XXII

Even now the wind died down and the heavens
cleared as Creusa stashed away her paperback of *Chaos*.
Where the Hay gave way to the river of oblivion
my da tried to pack the suitcase-numbles back into the suitcase,

all but the newspaper sop. "A gift horse is soon curried,"
Virgil would improvise,
*"mais nous acceptons seulement MasterCard
ou Visa . . ."*

as one blackfellow drew and fired what looked like a pair of matchlocks
into the cow pony's head. A double spurt
of flame giving vent

to a double spurt of brain from the brainbox.
*"Et votre Amex est, en tout cas . . .* expired."
A twitter-twitch from the cow pony as it came and went.


## XXIII

And from the tangle of its straps and war accoutrements
all clinquant with blood and dung
nothing would seem more eloquent
than the little cow pony's snaffle-scarred tongue,

snaffle- and sawgrass-scarred,
except perhaps his forelock falling over his forehead
as my da scoured
the classifieds in *The Tyre Courier* and back by Holyhead

and the Mull of Kintyre at a rate of knots
the packet steamed as he tried to read
the small print by the Gulf

of Carpentaria and the drain of eternity and the nod
as good as sparing the rod
to a horse looked in the mouth. (See overleaf.)


**XXIV**

"For want of an ell the horse changed in midlife
was lost, as your lovely lass was lost
when she cut her coat according to the cheesecloth
or tarlatan from which there blazed

her titanium vambrace.
You can't make a bellyband
out of a silk purse.
Give them a bird in the hand

and they take not only an ell
but an ell in cretonne
or brocatelle. Your lovely lass adjusting the baldric

of her manganese-red holdall.
You can't get blood from a rolling stone.
Better late than to break."


**XXV**

A flash from the lighthouse on the southern end of Ailsa Craig
when, all of a sudden, one of the ruffians
stood a little apart from the ruffian-ruck
and, stately at the vibraphone,

began to play what sounded like "The Wild Colonial Boy"
while another held out his cap for a few spondulicks.
The sky was clearing now over Troy
as the Hennessys continued their talkee-talkee

about my waistline
and their plans for *le weekend*.
The waiter's under-his-breath "*macaron

nesoi*" as my da searched for that announcement for the Orient Line
and from blessed Ailsa Craig, again from the southern end,
the foofooraw of two alternating foghorns.


**XXVI**

"The beauty of it is that while the foofoorious pole work of Charon
made the Wooroonooran cloudier
than the Styx or Acheron
and your da scoured the claims of a pig gelder

and the schedule for the Portpatrick
passage and the price of cattle, polled and stripped,
and the proof against darnel and drawk
and this street arab

sang of the boy born and bred in Castlemaine,
Creusa, on whom you still had this adolescent crush,
passed some remark to a Hennessy about '*la senteur

des faucilles*' and, rather than 'remain
in this unrealized plenitude,' made a red rush
for the door, pausing only to air-kiss Hermia and Lysander."

## XXVII

As she twinkled there for a moment, distant-near as Alpha
      Centauri,
I recognized the opening bars
not of "Jane Shore" or "Clerk Saunders"
but "Waltzing Mathilda," played by some veteran of the Great War

on a mouth organ
and the waiter again drew himself up,
his three-fold cord broken
at last, and my da took out a plug of Erinmore and a box of Bo-
      Peeps.

"For *'demain,'*" Virgil began to sing
with a rowley-powley gammon,
"read *'de Main.'* For 'firse' read 'frise.'

For 'Diamantina' read 'Darling.'
For 'campana' read 'campagna.'
For 'phosphorescence' read 'phosphorus.' "


## XXVIII

Having looked in vain for the timetables of those P. and O. ferries
my da folded *The Tyrone Courier*, turned up the collar of the
      Abercrombie & Fitch
greatcoat that set him apart from the generality of frieze,
tossed back his glib the better to strike a match,

set the match to his pipeful of Erinmore,
and thrust his hands into his pockets.
"For 'lemur' read 'femur.'
For 'braked' read 'baked.' " The cow pony's innards packed

themselves back into the manganese-
red suitcase that would never now burst open on the border

of Queensland and wherever. "For 'samo'
read 'soma.' For *'macaron nesoi'* read *'makaron nesoi.'* "
Creusa bundling herself up in the shortest of short order,
and then some.


**XXIX**

"For 'maxims,' " Virgil again drew himself up, "read 'Maxime's.'
For 'flint' read 'skint.'
The beauty of it is that your da and that other phantasm
no more set foot in Queensland

than the cat that got the cream
might look at a king. That's the sheer beauty of it.
Ne'er cast a clout, heigh, in midstream.
No brilliant. No brilliantine, ho. No classifieds

in *The Tyrone Courier*.
No billabong. No billy-boil.
No stately at the autoharp.

No MasterCard. No mainferre. No slopes of Montparnasse. No spare
the rod and spoil
the horse lost for want, heigh ho, of enough rope."


**XXX**

A scattering to the four winds of the street arabs.
Creusa cutting me an intolerable deal
of slack as she gave me a wave of her razor-sharp
middle claw, half appalled, half in appeal,

and slipped forever from my arms.
"For 'errata,' " Virgil smiled, "read 'corrigenda.' "
He looked straight through me to Lysander and Hermia.
"For 'Mathilda' read 'Matilda.'

For 'lass' read 'less.'
Time nor tide wait for a wink
from the aura

of Ailsa Craig. For 'Menalaus' read 'Menelaus.'
For 'dinkum' read 'dink.'
For 'Wooroonooran,' my darlings, read 'Wirra Wirra.' "

# INDEX OF TITLES